OLLEGE OF HIG

JÁNOS KÁRPÁTI

Bartók's String Quartets

János Kárpáti

Bartók's String Quartets

Corvina Press

Title of the Hungarian original: Bartók vonósnégyesei
Zeneműkiadó, Budapest, 1967
First Hungarian edition © János Kárpáti, 1967
Translated by Fred Macnicol
Cover design by Erika Urai

© János Kárpáti, 1975
ISBN 963 13 3655 7
Printed in Hungary, 1975
Franklin Printing House, Budapest

Contents

INTRODUCTION

The Place of Chamber Music in the Life-work

When we devote a work to Bartók's chamber music it looks at first sight as though we were concerned with no more than genre divisions and striving for an exposition of no more than a single aspect of the whole œuvre. But in Bartók's case the chamber music is not simply a matter of grouping according to genre: it is strictly the framework for the whole life-work. And this relates principally to the string quartets, which accompany Bartók throughout his creative journey from the very earliest youthful efforts to the last—and unfulfilled—plan of his life, the 'seventh' string quartet.[1]

We shall, therefore, be chiefly concerned with the string quartets, since they occupy a central position in Bartók's œuvre. It would nevertheless be a great mistake to cut off these works from their connections with the other chamber music compositions. For these, like shrubs, stand around the towering trees of the string quartets; among them there are characteristic 'accompanying' or supplementary works, and there are also such as rise right up to the level of the string quartets themselves, and can almost be considered along with this imposing series of six works.

At the time of the development of the string quartet as a genre, in Haydn's period, it took six compositions for them to be considered a work—an opus. This unwritten law of European music's golden age bears witness to true richness: these works appearing by the dozen or by the half-dozen were not in the slightest the result of 'mass production', at least not with the great masters. The opuses of Haydn, Mozart and Beethoven consisting of groups of six string quartets are the greatest masterpieces of the literature within the genre. This creative method was a legacy from the preceding period, when it was only by being arranged into groups like this that sonatas and concertos could come to be published. Publication technique motives do, however, reveal much in connection with the contemporary practice of, and social respect (or disrespect) for, creative work in music: a single sonata, chamber work, or concerto did not carry enough weight to be regarded as a work. It is precisely in Beethoven's lifetime that a change is to be seen: string quartets and sonatas arranged into groups of six and three gradually become rarer. One sonata or one string quartet by the elderly Beethoven stands on its own: it carries as much weight as a symphony or orchestral work.

The individual nature of musical creation and this transformation of its social function, beginning in Beethoven's lifetime and having effect right up to our own times, led to the 'intensive' aspect of artistic creation—its inner weight, density of content—becoming more important than the 'extensive'. It is only in this way that the proportion shift can be explained, in which, as compared with the approximately one hundred symphonies produced by Haydn and the approximately fifty symphonies produced by Mozart, Beethoven composed only nine symphonies, and yet these nine works occupy a central position not only in his own life-work but in the music of the whole period as well.

In the same sense Bartók's string quartets are also central; through their inner weight and concentration they are characteristically representative of Bartók's art as a whole, and at the same time—by virtue of Bartók's importance—they compress within themselves the most characteristic musical achievements of the first half of the twentieth century.

The Bartók literature has been mentioning related features in the art of Beethoven and that of Bartók for a long time now. As early as 1929, for example, after the Budapest première of the Third and Fourth Quartets, Aladár Tóth drew attention to the presence in Bartók's work of a kind of periodicity also to be found in Beethoven, who generally experimented with the new in his piano works, let it mature in the symphonies, and finally sublimated it to its most refined forms in his string quartets.[2] Being familiar with the complete œuvre, and now looking back with a certain perspective, we should be inclined to modify Aladár Tóth's statement in that with Bartók the string quartets stand at the heart of individual creative periods; they do not so much contain an extract of the new as condense within themselves every element of this new message and new form. Before engaging in deeper discussion of the theme, a general critical examination of style and analysis of the works, we should attempt to form a comprehensive picture of the relationship between the life-work as a whole and the chamber works.

Among the first chamber compositions of the young Bartók it is the Piano Quintet dating from 1904 that stands out particularly. It also appeared on the programme at the 1910 première of the First String Quartet along with the Fourteen Bagatelles for piano—so that Bartók did consider it worthy of performance even *after* writing the First Quartet. And yet, strictly speaking, a sharp dividing line can be drawn between the Piano Quintet and the First String Quartet. The Piano Quintet is a significant composition only in that it summarizes on a mature level the young Bartók's romantic-national tone carrying on from Liszt. Indeed a similar role is played by the 'Kossuth' symphonic poem, the Rhapsody op. 1 and the Suite no. 1. But whereas the influence of Richard Strauss dominates through the orchestration in the 'Kossuth' symphonic poem and the First Suite, it is the Liszt inheritance that manifests itself freely in the piano chamber music.

After the Piano Quintet almost four years passed before Bartók set about writing a chamber work again. These four years constitute an important period in his life: this was the period of true maturing when the young artist pondered his aims and took stock of his possibilities with ruthless frankness. It becomes clear from his correspondence that it was precisely in these years that his personality was taking shape—under the combined influence of several failures, loss of his illusions and possibly an unrequited love. But this crisis period, as these few years are called by the biographical literature, also gathered together reserves of strength to extricate him from the crisis. After his visit to Paris in 1905, it was not only the unjust defeat suffered at the Rubinstein competition that remained behind in him but the life-influencing experience of the French capital itself. The unrequited love for Stefi Geyer likewise found its healthy artistic compensation in the Violin Concerto and particularly in the fourteenth Bagatelle (*Ma mie qui danse*). But the most important point is that, as a result of the first folk music collecting journeys, the new creative ideal was taking shape which he was to follow from then onwards throughout his whole life.

The First String Quartet, dating from 1908, is authentic evidence of the crisis, but at the same time the reservoir of all the new which was coming to life in Bartók around that time. In the slow, heavily rolling music of the polyphonically unfolding first movement we find an explanation to virtually everything. And this movement is not the only one of its kind; it has a blood-brother in the first of the *Two Portraits*, the 'Ideal', which is the first movement of the Violin Concerto written for Stefi Geyer. With its yearning and resigned character it may more or less faithfully reflect Bartók's world of thought, which was struggling with the philosophy of Nietzsche and Schopenhauer. And as József Ujfalussy points out, the 'Painful Wrestling' ('Lassú vergődés') from the Ten Easy Piano Pieces, bearing some relation to the sorrowful cor anglais solo in Wagner's *Tristan*, also belongs here.[3]

For Bartók it appears it was only in these years that the Wagner influence of his student days—then manifesting itself in mere enthusiasm—came to full realization. At all events the opening movement of the First Quartet could scarcely be imagined without the Wagner background, not only on account of the melodiousness, recapitulating on itself and resembling the 'Painful Wrestling', but because of its harmonies as well. Even the parallel thirds, which Stevens considers a Brahmsian influence, point rather to Wagner, and particularly to the Prelude to Act 3 of *Tristan*.[4] In these parallel thirds it is not the Brahms kind of strong tonality which appears but the tonal veiling characteristic of Wagner.

At the same time the movement bears evidence of other influences: the free counterpoint used for the string quartet follows the example of the late Beethoven works. And in the same movement the influence of French music, mainly Debussy and Ravel, makes its first appearance in Bartók's art. And finally, the fresh folk music experience appears here as well.

It is almost incredible that these diverse, sometimes opposite elements—Beethovenian fugue, Wagnerian harmony, the third and sixth mixtures of Ravel and Debussy, and lastly the melodiousness of folk music—meet in one single work, and indeed in one single movement, without annihilating each other.

On the basis of the most recent research results it can be supposed that the less heterogeneous, but also less inspired, second and third movements of the First String Quartet were finished before the first movement, and so the qualitative leap forward in creative development really came with the period (we do not know exactly whether it is a question of weeks or several months) when Bartók composed the first movement.[5] In any event, there is here a certain remarkable interweaving between different works dating from roughly the same time. In its tone and technique the first movement of this quartet relates to the first movement of the Stefi Geyer Violin Concerto, and at the same time—as has been noticed by Denijs Dille—its theme is akin to the theme of the Violin Concerto's second movement.[6] The Violin Concerto, however, is connected by other threads to the Fourteen

9

Bagatelles, since the final form of the *Two Portraits* came into being later by making use of the last of the bagatelles.

This inverted order of composition of the movements apparently contradicts Kodály's remark according to which the third movement is a *retour à la vie*.[7] The chronological order of the composing does not, however, unconditionally depend on the events of life. The whole creative period is also characterized by this *retour à la vie*, for the fact that Bartók added a distorted, grotesque variation to the 'Ideal' portrait likewise indicates that having succeeded in getting beyond the love crisis, he was capable of turning the idealized portrait of woman into its own antithesis, and in this way wrote it out of himself, so to speak.

The First String Quartet is much more a pioneering work, a successful experiment than a summary. Viewed from some distance, this is also indicated by its position in the creative period as a whole: the year 1908 does not finish but starts off a development which later attains consummation in 1911 in the opera *Bluebeard's Castle*; by then the folk music elements, still appearing only in an isolated way in the string quartet, have matured.

There is almost a complete decade between the composition of the First String Quartet and the completion of the Second Quartet in 1917. Of all his string quartets, it was the second which was conceived, matured, and took shape over the longest period of time in Bartók's creative imagination. He himself indicated 1915 as the date of beginning the work—that is, he worked on it, even if not continuously, over three, or at least two years. During the same period came the writing of *The Wooden Prince* and the Suite for piano, not to mention several smaller works as well.

The fertile creative work of the war years is preceded by a certain period of 'silence' in 1913. If we look for the biographical reasons for this pause, it is the increasingly far-reaching folksong collecting journeys which strike us. After the Hungarian, Slovakian and Rumanian collecting, a more distant journey was also undertaken in that year: Bartók reached North Africa and, as long as his health permitted him, he worked for two weeks in the oases of the Biskra district. Although scientific publication of the material found there came only later, traces of the creative digestion of this musical experience are to be observed as early as in the compositions dating from around 1915–17.

The appearance of the influence of Arab folk music in Bartók's art does not merely mean a new colour in the palette consisting of Hungarian, Rumanian and Slovakian elements; it also makes a certain summarizing and reinterpretation possible. In one of his later works, the 1923 Dance Suite, he shows how it is possible to combine the characteristic elements of Hungarian, Rumanian and Arab folk music. But even preceding this, the Second String Quartet, the Suite for piano, and *The Miraculous Mandarin* are examples of how this summarizing can be realized not only 'horizontally', but also 'vertically' in the Bartók style which merges the various elements into a unified idiom.

The first prerequisite for this merging into one was—and this refers back to an earlier creative phase—that the Hungarian, or, as it were, mother-tongue, elements should mature and gain their own natural supreme role. As has been said, this was still not the case in the First Quartet: it came about only later, after numerous folksong arrangements, in the opera

10

Bluebeard's Castle, the melodic world of which is pervaded in a unified and homogeneous way by the most ancient layer of pentatony in Hungarian folk music. This was, therefore, the basis which made possible the incorporation of the other folk music elements.

Between *Bluebeard* and the Second Quartet stands an individual Janus-faced work: the Four Pieces for orchestra, of which the basic conception dates from 1912, but which only came to be orchestrated once there were clear prospects for the première, in 1921. With the French-style natural poesy of its first movement, this work points back to the *Two Pictures*, and on the other hand with its painfully passionate declamation, to *Bluebeard*. At the same time, in an almost startling way, the tone of the second piece (scherzo) anticipates the cruel, inhuman tone of *The Wooden Prince* and *The Miraculous Mandarin*.

It is here, in the Four Pieces, that the structural conception of the Second String Quartet, ending with a slow movement, first appears, and—as pointed out by József Ujfalussy—it becomes the most typical formal plan of this period: we find it in the Suite for piano, the Five Songs, and strictly speaking in *The Miraculous Mandarin* as well.[8] This 'tragic dramaturgy' is the achievement of Bartók's wartime and post-war art, bearing witness to his being liberated from illusions and to his more profound and more moving vision of reality. The ascending line of the first quartet, beginning in the Wagner–Nietzsche tone, is here almost exactly reversed. The romantic voice of the then still largely personal hopelessness and death-wish is here replaced by the voice of the artist lamenting the Hungarian fate and that of humanity, a tone stemming not from individual awareness of life but from identification with the social problems of the nation and the age.

In all certainty, this is why the Second String Quartet represents an opening out towards the external world not only as regards the folk music elements: contemporary European art also makes its effect conspicuously felt for the first time here. The harsh movement, dolefully soliloquizing tone, free tonality of Schoenberg's opus 11, Three Piano Pieces, do—even though in a filtered form—unmistakably appear in Bartók's Suite for piano and the Second String Quartet, and later they demand an increasingly more important role for themselves in the op. 18 Studies, the Improvisations and the two Sonatas for violin and piano.

From the Four Pieces to the Dance Suite—that is from 1912 to 1923—we witness a unified and uninterrupted development; the works refer to each other, and although each is independent in itself, a separate world, numerous common features can be noticed in them. The most striking transformation is found in the structural conception. After *The Miraculous Mandarin* the series of slow finales falling away into a tragic gesture suddenly stops and the reverse begins to evolve: the tragic, sorrowful tone comes in the opening movements and the closing movements assume a fast, or at least faster, robust folk-dance character. Once more it is necessary to refer to József Ujfalussy's observation where he claims that, with Bartók, it is in the First and Second Violin–Piano Sonatas that the struggling tone, free tonality and harsh expressive melody indicating the Viennese style first meets the closing movements of folk music conception.[9] Among other things this is one reason for us to see in the two violin–piano sonatas a 'key composition' similar to the string quartets.

11

The Third String Quartet, written in 1927, is again separated from the second by ten years. The two violin–piano sonatas, however, form a bridge between them. Like the Second Sonata, the Third Quartet is also a two-part structure and a large part is played in it, too, by the characteristic 'micro-melodic' quality present in the violin–piano sonatas and perfected in the piano piece *The Night's Music*.

But the Third String Quartet is really the fruit of a period reflecting new aspirations. The turning point was the year 1926, which, as in 1913, was preceded by a period of 'silence'. This time, however, the productivity is quite imposing: within a single year Bartók writes the Sonata, the cycle *Out of Doors*, the Nine Little Piano Pieces, and the First Piano Concerto. And the Third String Quartet, written in 1927, is immediately followed in 1928 by the Fourth Quartet and the two Violin Rhapsodies.

The two string quartets written in such close proximity form a double central point for the works composed around them. The third is connected by strong threads not only with the two-movement Violin–Piano Sonata but to the Rhapsodies as well. The Fourth String Quartet apparently represents a great turning point, for it is here that the symmetrical five-section structure appears openly, a marked contrast to the two-part structure. Here the idiomatic–stylistic connection binding the Fourth Quartet to the Third is more important than the structure, which anticipates the Second Piano Concerto and the Fifth String Quartet. That is, in both works the thematic material can be traced back to one or two fundamental melodic germs or basic formulas.

Apart from this, the two works are also related to each other by a similar conception of tonality. In the Fourth Quartet Bartók further develops with a strict regularity and consistency the complementary twelve-note system evolved in the Third Quartet. We might also say that after the preparatory experiments of the Third Quartet, it is in the Fourth that Bartók comes closest to the Schoenberg technique without actually making it his own in its complete, original form.

In the Fourth String Quartet it is not just this formal crystallization which appears: the individual types of tone also take on a more final form. Of this the best example is offered by the second movement, the sweeping, glittering scherzo mood of which can be discovered in earlier works as well—at the end of the Second Quartet's middle movement, for example, or the second part of the Third Quartet. But what was in the earlier works merely a detail, an episode, single transitional patches in the dynamic variation or development processes, becomes here in the Fourth Quartet a complete movement, an independent unit. In a similar way the so-called night-music tone also develops. What Bartók developed into a complete work in the 1926 piano piece had already appeared earlier in an isolated way in the violin–piano sonatas; after that it appeared likewise in an isolated way in the first part of the Third Quartet, but in the Fourth Quartet it gained greater emphasis by virtue of its position: it forms the symmetry-axis of the whole work in its central third movement.

It is a curious phenomenon, but thereby demonstrating all the more clearly the complexity of Bartók's creative development, that in the Third and Fourth Quartets, which come closer to dodecaphonic technique, the folk music elements are appreciably more

12

tangible than in the First and Second Quartets. This is not a step backwards but a uniting of folk music and art music on a higher level. The two violin rhapsodies written during the same period also bear witness to this, not to mention the latest large-scale series of folksong arrangements, the Twenty Hungarian Folksongs.

Although as far as the external formal plan is concerned, the Fifth String Quartet's nearest relative is the Fourth Quartet, numerous factors do nevertheless distinguish the two compositions from each other. Between them—and at the same time between the two creative periods they represent—stands the watershed of the two great works of the years 1930 and 1931, *Cantata Profana* and the Second Piano Concerto. The latter still shows a strong bond with the 1926 piano pieces of neo-Baroque aspirations; indeed in its theme the Stravinsky influence is even more unambiguous. The *Cantata*, on the other hand, is at all events the preface to the great works of the thirties.

In the five-movement structure of the Fifth Quartet the function of the outer pillar movements has not changed in comparison with the Fourth Quartet, but the transformation in the three inner movements is all the more apparent. It is not a slow movement which comes in the centre here but a scherzo in Bulgarian rhythm, and on each side of it there is a slow movement. With an arrangement of this nature the five-movement structure is even more balanced than that of the Fourth Quartet, since, by means of their fast tempo, the first, third and fifth movements form a unified pillar arrangement into which the connecting chain of the two slow movements fits more naturally. Beyond this the Second Piano Concerto provides the direct example of this formal construction, for there the central movement contains similar slow–fast–slow periodicity. That more or less similar symmetrical organization obtains even within the individual movements also belongs to the symmetrical arrangement of the string quartet.

The Fifth String Quartet is also central within the creative period concerned. On the one hand it starts off the series of great works dating from the thirties, continuing with the *Music for String Instruments, Percussion and Celesta* and the Sonata for two pianos and percussion, but on the other hand it quite perceptibly retains some connection with the 'border compositions', the Second Piano Concerto and *Cantata Profana*. The thirties also bring a large-scale maturing and summarizing in the 44 Duos for violin, finished in 1931, and the *Mikrokosmos*, which was completed in 1937. Detailed analyses will give a real illustration of how what appears broken up into its parts in these series, forms in the Fifth Quartet a closed, complete and complex world. How curious an order is also displayed in that these three compositions represent three different structures at the peak of Bartók's creative career (1934, 1936, 1937): whereas the Fifth Quartet is built up in a five-section bridge-form structure symmetrical in its every particle, the *Music for String Instruments, Percussion and Celesta* and the Sonata for two pianos and percussion illustrate two fundamental (four-movement and three-movement) types of the classical sonata structure.

The slow–fast–slow–fast structure of the *Music* further builds a bridge in the direction of the Baroque sonata, and through this it anticipates, as it were, formal endeavours of the final creative period, showing two-section divisions. It is true that three-part and five-part structures are present here, too (Violin Concerto, the Third Piano Concerto, Contrasts, the

13

Concerto), but structurally more novelty is represented by the Baroque four-movement Sonata for solo violin, and above all by the Sixth String Quartet.

Thus we have moved over into the last creative period. Although the course of Bartók's life can be broken up into periods in a different way, it was not in the first unproductive years of emigration that the creative turning point took place, but during the last years in Europe. This curving backwards, romantic in its content, already began here in the Violin Concerto, finished in 1938, and the Divertimento, dating from 1939, its two most obvious representatives being the Sixth String Quartet and the Third Piano Concerto. Here it is absolutely not a matter of a decrease in creative power, or of diminishing demands as regards concentration of expression, as certain aestheticians have interpreted this period. The transformation is of a qualitative nature, bearing witness to a change in aims and the whole way of looking at things. Bartók is stimulated to more 'publicistic' expression by the war and the danger threatening humanity; abstractness is replaced by the demand for concreteness, the innovation attitude is replaced by the idea of preservation and protection.

At this time Bartók turns back towards his own youth: once again Beethoven, the one-time model, assumes greater importance, once again the leitmotif and the broken four-note chords reminiscent of romanticism appear. The Sixth String Quartet, composed in 1939, points back surprisingly in its cyclical monothematic quality to the First String Quartet. At the same time we are reminded of the Second Quartet by its slow ending. It would appear that with Bartók this construction consistently accompanies the 'in tempora belli' works; the earlier work was written in the very midst of the First World War, and the later work at the time of the outbreak of the Second World War. So—like its predecessors—the Sixth Quartet is also a central work, the problems of the war years are best concentrated in it, and it, too, has its hidden or open connecting threads branching out towards the other works.

To look for a direct reflection of the events of life and the world in the works would be grossly to simplify the mechanism of Bartók's creative art. Here, in the case of the Sixth String Quartet, however, it is impossible to disregard these interrelationships. Even if only because during the actual process of composing, a change came about in the conception of the work which reveals a great deal concerning Bartók's inner world. Originally he had planned a fast finale for the work, and yet in the end, in place of this, there came a sorrowful, resigned farewell. The transformation—as will be shown later in the analysis—was demanded by the inner nature of the musical material, but it is still impossible to cut it off from the external events, for at that time Bartók was urgently concerned with the dilemma of whether to emigrate or remain at home.

If the Sixth String Quartet is the work of the wartime creative period par excellence and something of a prophetical foreboding of the tragedies which did actually come to pass, the Third Piano Concerto, which really still belongs here stylistically, with its relaxing tone and its devout attitude, is the herald of a new creative period. But it has no continuation. In the last days Bartók still talked of compositional plans, mentioning among them a string quartet, but this 'seventh' quartet was not to materialize.

I have attempted to give a general survey of Bartók's life-work by way of an examination of the place occupied therein by the chamber music, and particularly the string quartets, and I have attempted to break it up into periods. Not because I consider that such division into periods is the only way towards the understanding of a genius. And not so as to create an artificial 'tidiness' out of the 'untidiness' of spontaneous development. Development—even its most spontaneous form—always has its own inner laws, especially in the case of geniuses. I have tried to divide Bartók's œuvre into periods on the basis of these inner laws, and it is precisely in the central position of the string quartets that one of these inner laws presents itself. It is very difficult to draw sharp dividing lines between the periods, and it is purely in the interests of lucidity that I have sought individual years as turning points.

The table below is yet another attempt to summarize and to make the survey clearly comprehensible. The reader should, however, consider all this as no more than greatly simplified guiding lines.

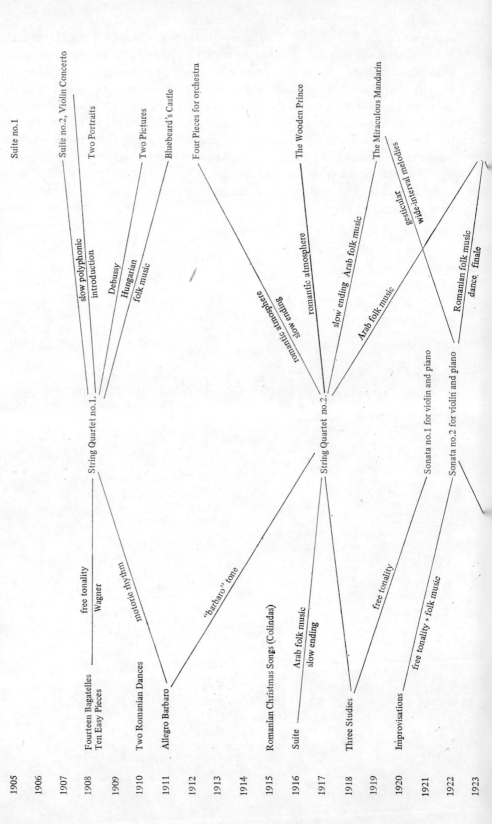

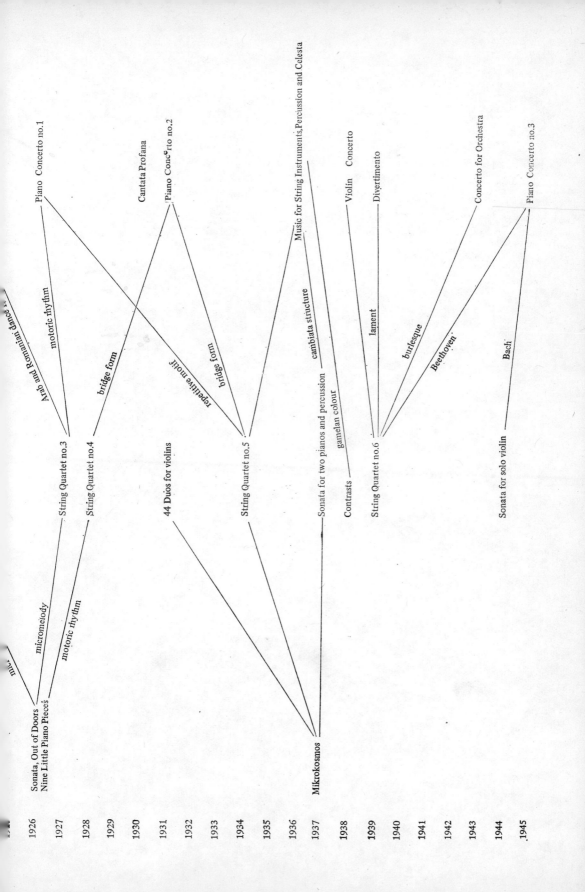

PART ONE

Musical Idiom and Style

The Legacy of Beethoven

Nineteenth century developments did not favour chamber music and particularly not the string quartet. The revolutionary branch of Romanticism was drawn rather towards new, larger and more programme-like forms. And from the so-called conservative romantics, engaged in the active continuation of classical traditions and forms, chamber music scarcely obtained any new meaning or new light to stimulate it to further development. It rather became the middle-class home genre par excellence, the indoor, small-circle art, which in this way lost its earlier perspectives not only in its externals but also in its inner conception. Thus, however faithfully the quartets of Schumann and Brahms preserve the classical form, as far as their essence is concerned they rather became estranged from the Beethoven legacy.

It was the twentieth century which brought the chamber music renaissance. This renaissance became apparent not only in terms of quantity, it was not only that interest in the genre increased, not only that the number of works was multiplied—together with this went an inner, essential rebirth, a broadening of the possibilities of the genre. The turn of the century itself still showed no such tendency: both the Debussy string quartet (1893) and the Ravel (1903) are characteristically isolated works. Their themes and their harmonic world do indeed reflect the principal features and stylistic elements of the new French school, although characteristically, they do not receive chamber music treatment. The position occupied by these works in the œuvre is very revealing: it is as if the genre were alien to the composers, and for them the two quartets appear no more than an experiment in a territory strange for them, not to be continued later. Ravel's other chamber works have even less to do with the classical tradition, representing an important step forward rather in the direction of new colour effects.

Among the great masters of the turn of the century, it is only with Reger that the quartet genre once more assumes a central position. True, with Reger this is rooted principally in his artistic attitude which still turns back towards the past. The intention to regenerate is indeed there, but behind it is concealed some convulsive attempt at resurrection. His influence, precisely in the case of Bartók, is nevertheless beneficial: in the extravagantly chromatic, verbose musical thinking of late Romanticism, loosening everything, he helped towards the recognition of the binding force in the Classical and Baroque traditions.

At first the new Viennese school which grew out of the late Romantic world also followed the paths of Romantic quartet art. This is borne out by Schoenberg's sextet (*Verklärte Nacht*), which employs the idiom of Wagner and the technique of Brahms, and also to a

21

certain extent by his first two string quartets. But at the same time it also becomes clear that with this new kind of polyphonic structural method, much more differentiated than what preceded it, Schoenberg seeks to lean more on the laws of the genre's classical period—and mainly on Beethoven.

What kinds of model can have been before Bartók when he composed his First String Quartet in 1908? The great paragons in his artistic development—Wagner, Liszt and Richard Strauss—were not able to offer him anything in this area. Brahms is the only composer who could have given a more immediate example, but in the F major String Quartet composed in 1898, the young Bartók had already moved essentially beyond this influence. In this way, he was 'obliged' to jump almost a century and go back to the classical summit of quartet music, the works of Beethoven.

In this connection a few statements by him are well known. In 1929 he wrote to Edwin von der Nüll: 'In my youth Bach and Mozart were not my ideals of the beautiful, but rather Beethoven.'[10] And in his 1939 discussion with Serge Moreux he mentions as his highest creative ideal a synthesis of the art of Bach, Beethoven and Debussy.[11] In any event, his personal attraction to Beethoven is evidenced by a very revealing quotation-like detail in the slow movement of the Third Piano Concerto. Although there can be no question of a note for note literal quotation, Bartók does unmistakably refer here to the ethereal chorale of Beethoven's A minor String Quartet op. 132, and he also builds up the whole movement in a similar manner.

This gesture of homage is to be found in another of his works as well, and this time even within the string quartet genre. In the two slow movements of the Fifth String Quartet, interconnected through a variational relationship, there also crops up a chorale-like detail in which the archaic character of the plagal chord progressions similarly reminds us of the atmosphere of the *Heiliger Dankgesang in lydischer Tonart*.

The Beethovenian features in Bartók's art, however, can scarcely be appraised by mentioning a few quotations or references. Deeper relationships than these are manifest in coincidence of creative principles and compositional methods. Straight away in the First String Quartet there is evidence of such coincidence of principles. The slow opening movement of the first movement of Beethoven's C sharp minor Quartet op. 131.

Is it simply a question of the resurrection of counterpoint here? One of the most important characteristics of twentieth-century music is the revival of counterpoint, the phenomenon preceding neo-Classicism and more deeply rooted than that, which tries not merely to bring the past to life but makes a guiding principle of a fundamental conception of musical creation which extended over a whole period. This counterpoint plays an important role in Bartók's art, particularly from the important piano pieces of 1926 and the Third String Quartet right up to the Sonata for two pianos.

A more appropriate expression than counterpoint would be 'linear structure', which can exist quite independently of certain rigid rules belonging to the old counterpoint. It is in this way that a kind of texture deriving from the combination of several structural methods evolves—and this is what Bartók learns from Beethoven. This is one of the main characteristics of the late Beethoven quartets, and at the same time it explains their peculiar significance in the history of the genre. This kind of structure secures real equality of status between the parts even where there is no question of a strictly contrapuntal texture.

It must not be forgotten that Beethoven approached Bach's technique from the direction of the music of his own period, unequivocally chordal in its principles, and in that technique—in contrast with that of his own period—it was the linear energies which attracted him. The Beethoven fugue is therefore inevitably different from the Bach fugue, and above all in this difference it becomes clear that with him a certain amount of effort was necessary for dealing with the consistency of linearity. This effort, however, is not the sign of weakness but one of the fundamental characteristics of Beethoven's creative work and his whole attitude. We should consider above all the *Great Fugue* op. 133.

But the individuality in the texture of the *Great Fugue* does not lie merely in the strict working out of the parts. The contrapuntal technique of the later sections is much more unusual than even the opening double fugue. Nor is 'free counterpoint' a fitting description of this, for the way the individual sections are fully worked out within themselves can scarcely be regarded as free. It is rather in the sense of form that there is freedom: numerous sections (for example, the Meno mosso e moderato) are not constructed in accordance with the customary fugal entrance method, but on the basis of a different freely evolved contrapuntal plan. In some parts (for example, in the Allegro molto e con brio section) contrapuntal structure becomes paired with an open, chordal structure.

Beethoven: Great Fugue op.133

This rather individual contrapuntal plan and structural combination is a virtually everyday matter in Bartók's quartets. An immediate example of this is offered by the Lento movement of the First Quartet. In Bartók's fugal exposition two pairs of parts progress as if following a double fugue pattern, but they differ from this pattern in that the two simultaneously unfolding themes are almost identical note for note, each pair operating as a canon at the fourth. But much more frequent than this—a texture generally applied by Bartók, it might be said—is the free contrapuntal structure, either in its pure form or in combination with other types of structure.

Finally, yet another very typical structural means must be remembered, the roots of which likewise lead back to the late Beethoven quartets. This is a peculiar paradox: pure homophony dressed in a polyphonic cloak. We are faced with two types of it. First, where parts playing a harmonic role take on independent life by means of rich figuration and dense, active part-movement, creating the impression of a plastically prominent contrapuntal part (e.g. op. 127, Adagio; op. 130, Andante; op. 131, Andante ma non troppo e molto cantabile; op. 132, *Heiliger Dankgesang*...). The other frequent form of this 'pseudo-polyphonic homophony' is the staggered, quasi-imitative sounding of a held chord. This technique, which often turns up in Beethoven (op. 18, C minor, Finale; op. 127, Adagio; op. 131, Allegretto; op. 132, Molto adagio, and the first movement Assai sostenuto; op. 135, Lento assai), also gains a significant role in Bartók, naturally based on different harmonic laws (Third Quartet, Prima parte; Fourth Quartet, first and third movements).

The immediate models for the inner differentiation and dynamics of Bartók's melody writing are also to be found in the late quartets of Beethoven. The variating inner forces unfolding the theme step into action straight away in the exposition and make the formal section, previously of a static nature, dynamic and development-like. Think, for example, of the first movement's principal theme in the op. 132 Quartet in A minor. Even more 'Bartókian' (the word is deliberately used since this is typical in Bartók, whereas with Beethoven it is still only an exception) is the phenomenon where a theme is so dynamic that no single one of its appearances can be regarded as a 'basic form': that is, there is no theme in comparison with which the others are variations.

The best example of this in Beethoven can be found in the *Great Fugue*. Though the introduction with the inscription 'overtura' does indeed serve as the introduction of the theme, there is not even here a so-called basic form, for the theme continuously accelerates: at the first cadence the rhythm values of the extended, slowly moving form are shortened by half, and there is further acceleration in the following bars. In a similar way, it does not become clear from what follows which of the four kinds of appearance of the theme is the essentially basic form. It is typical that after the three forms presented in the introductory section a form in yet another different rhythm appears as the theme in the first double fugue.

The first movement of Bartók's Sixth Quartet runs a similar course. Just as in the *Great Fugue*, the theme is first presented in augmented form. (József Ujfalussy points out that not only the treatment but the very theme itself bears some relationship to the Beethoven one.[12])

The increasingly dynamic themes or melodies are characterized not only by continual

24

transformation of these themes and motifs but also by the organic breaking up and putting together of the thematic units. The technique of division and disintegration set forth in the literature on Beethoven once more attains an important place in the works of Bartók. Several parts of the *Great Fugue* using this kind of structure combined with counterpoint really do have the effect of a Bartók piece (e.g. the first Allegro molto e con brio, A flat section). In the same way a very 'Bartókian' impression is made by the closing part of the second Allegro molto e con brio, interrupted by pauses, immediately before the shortened returns of the theme, or the trill motif broken up into its segments before the coda. All this, in Beethoven still exceptional treatment, becomes a familiar, everyday feature, a fundamental principle of technique in Bartók. The motive behind this is not a decompositional tendency (just as it is not so with Beethoven) but the necessity to penetrate to the essence, the almost scholarly passion to display inner interrelationships.

Bartók is the follower of Beethoven in the area of formal construction, too. It is really typical that the influential form-reformers of Romanticism, Liszt and Franck, also set out from the Beethoven sonata type, transforming this into something new in the fantasia-style, programme-style spirit. Bartók did not by any means remain untouched by the influence of the Liszt and Franck conception. Yet his own revolution in form relates more directly to Beethoven, almost conspicuously dispensing at such times with the intermediary masters.

On the other hand, Bartók resorts to sonata form not with a mind to disintegrate but with reconstructional intentions. Naturally this does not mean a revival of the classical scheme, for it was never the complete forms as such that he took over but the principles lying behind them. The key to his sonata form is therefore not the particularly determined order of themes and modulations, but the sonata principle stripped to its roots, in the free yet regular sense in which Beethoven used it.

How frequently Bartók employs development-like dynamism in the exposition can be demonstrated through virtually any sonata movement by him. For the moment I shall refer only to the Second Quartet's opening movement, which apart from this might be considered a regular sonata movement with regard to its formal elements. It is, however, not in the least 'regular' that the seven-bar principal theme forces open its original range of a seventh with three-octave leaps through the next ten bars, and then immediately switches over to imitation. After this, what more can the development bring in the way of dynamism? It is here that Bartók's genius displays its strength, nourished on Beethoven, for after this tense exposition the climax of the development radiates even more titanic straining.

The building in of the fugue form into the sonata is once more an achievement of Beethoven—from complete fugue movements (op. 106, op. 110, op. 131, and op. 133) to more isolated use of fugatos (the Third, Fifth and Seventh Symphonies). This sonata-principle application of the fugue does, incidentally, indicate that the extraction of the *Great Fugue* from the B flat major Quartet, although it may be justified from a practical point of view, is misguided as far as the original conception of the work is concerned—even if it does come from Beethoven himself.[13]

The fugue and fugato play a similar role in Bartók's life-work, too. In a few works it appears as an independent movement (First String Quartet, the *Music*) but much more frequent than this is the fugato built into a movement, used as a constructional element (third movement of the First String Quartet, Third Quartet, Fifth Quartet, *The Miraculous Mandarin* and the Concerto). Thus Bartók unequivocally follows the example of Beethoven. And it is also Beethoven, rather than Bach, who is the model in the inner structure of the complete fugue movement. Beethoven's string quartet fugue in the C sharp minor Quartet is relatively still a strictly constructed form, and yet a striving towards a new kind of articulation is quite perceptible in it, which comes into full display in the fugue of the Hammerklavier Sonata and the free recapitulatory sonata conception of the *Great Fugue*. Bartók transplanted this new kind of fugue form into his own works; with him, however, it is not so much sonata-like planning that dominates, but rather trio form.

The positioning of the fugue movement is also very characteristic: with Bach the fugue generally has a finishing function, summarizing and forcing into a strict arrangement all that was given free rein in the preceding more loosely structured movements (Prelude, Toccata, Fantasia). This completing, crowning character remains valid in Beethoven, too; only in the C sharp minor Quartet does he reverse this order. If the fugue was not so long ago a weighty completion, now let it be a prelude, a birth from nothing, the clothing of 'creation' in music! There can be no doubt that this example inspired Bartók even after the First Quartet—above all in the composing of the *Music for String Instruments, Percussion and Celesta*, where the first movement really is a structure gradually appearing out of a sort of swirling primeval mist.

But the opening fugue is not the only Beethoven movement type which rises to new life in Bartók. The innermost nocturnal monologue of the lonely man, looking both himself and the infinite secrets of nature full in the face—this kind of content connects the two men's mature slow movements. And in the same way, it is easy to find the connecting treads between Beethoven's demonic scherzos and Bartók's rustling, reverberating, glittering movements.

All this, however, finds its own counterpole. It is because of this that Beethoven is *still* classical, and it is because of this that Bartók is *again* classical. It is curious how the Romantic tendency switches over to its own antithesis: the expansion of the cycle and the almost violent transformation of the classical formal framework do not upset the balance relationships.

And here it is rather Bartók who explains Beethoven than Beethoven Bartók. The extension of the sonata cycle—now looking at it from the Bartók angle—is obviously none other than the satisfying of a specific desire for symmetry. The number of movements increases so conspicuously in the op. 130 and op. 131 Quartets not so as finally to break up the laws of classical forms, but—just the opposite—so as to create a new formal conception more closed and complete than anything preceding it. If we examine the original order of movements in the op. 130 B flat major Quartet, ending in a fugue, we will see that by means of tempo identity and thematic or character interrelationships a peculiar structure begins to take shape.

26

1. Introduction—Allegro
2. Presto
3. Andante con moto
4. Danza tedesca
5. Cavatina
6. Fugue

Thus, under the great arch of the outer movements, the inner movements are interconnected in two pairs in an overlapping way: the Presto in a popular spirit relates to the even more popular Danza tedesca, and the intimate Andante con moto to the ethereally singing Cavatina. And this is where the root of the Bartókian bridge-form is to be found. But even closer to it stands the op. 131 C sharp minor Quartet, behind the seven indicated movements of which there lie in reality five large units:

1. Fugue
2. Allegro
3. (Allegro moderato)—Andante
4. Presto
5. (Adagio)—Allegro

The most obvious interconnection is seen in the extreme movements here, too. The work's third pillar is the variation movement in the centre, on each side of which comes a quick movement scherzo-like in tone. Here we already find the symmetrically constructed bridge-form virtually in its final form, and the type which appears in the Fourth Quartet.

Thus, starting out from the purely technical aspect of the structure, and moving through the very smallest musical motifs, we have arrived at the connection between the movement, the tone, the cycle and the complete conception. At every point we have witnessed the common ground between the two great masters. But it is not merely that Bartók has approached Beethoven, not only that he has leant so heavily on the classical tradition. We have sometimes also seen that here and there Beethoven—in anticipation of his period—in reality 'ran forward to meet' Bartók, or the twentieth century, which continuously felt him to be its own.

27

Forerunners and Contemporaries

One of the principal methods of style analysis is the demonstration of conscious relationships and unconscious parallels and at the same time the making of fine distinctions between them. In an examination of Bartók's art this is especially important since it has at once a pioneering and a summarizing role in twentieth century music. Pioneering because in many respects Bartók moved invincibly in the vanguard of artistic progress, and summarizing because in his music he replaces the obsolete individuality cult by setting up the ideal of a new synthesis as an example to be followed. Thus when we investigate the inner significance of Bartók's life-work, and the logic of its development, through analysis of the various influences, borrowings and parallels, we are in no way degrading him. József Újfalussy already noticed this in connection with the 'Kossuth' symphonic poem and relating it to the complete œuvre put into words the thought which might well be the motto for this whole chapter: 'Even in these early compositions it is possible to detect the characteristic feature of Bartók's creative imagination that was to remain one of its most striking traits, the influence of contemporary music did not merely manifest itself in easily recognizable outward similarities; the music was rather a source of inspiration in the formation of his own creative work, a means to the release of his own genius so that he could make his unique contribution to music.'[14]

Demarcation of genres goes together with a certain personal demarcation, too. In the evolution of Bartók as an artist the influence of a good number of his predecessors and contemporaries has to be taken into consideration. There is, for example, Richard Strauss, who was perhaps his chief ideal in his youth, but he scarcely counts at all as far as the chamber music genres are concerned. And the influence of Liszt also makes itself felt mainly in the orchestral works, and apart from that, possibly in the piano chamber music—for example, the Piano Quintet dating from 1904. The case of Wagner is more complicated; by him Bartók was not presented with any particular genre model, but with regard to harmony and melody writing he had a strong influence on the young Bartók, especially around 1907–8. In the slowly rolling texture of the First Quartet's Lento movement, in its four-note chords, its ascents, climaxes and descents, the great German master's orchestral style unmistakably lives on in a chamber music transposition.

The curious thing is that this first 'Wagnerian' period is followed by another wave around the time of the composition of *The Wooden Prince* and the Second String Quartet. In the quartet's first movement, Wagner's technique can again be discovered in the intertwining textures of the section leading to the secondary theme, and this tone rings on in the movement's closing chord, coloured with an augmented triad.

We have also to consider another figure from the German Romantic tradition, for his influence in the First String Quartet—principally in connection with tonality—is very significant. This is Max Reger, that characteristic representative of late Romanticism, who endeavoured to build his art on the firm foundations of times long past, and above all, on the architectonics of the Baroque. Bartók knew the art of Reger well, which is proved, if by nothing else, by his buying in 1907 the following Reger works: *Aus meinem Tagebuch* op. 82; the D minor String Quartet op. 74; the C major Violin–Piano Sonata op. 72; the F major Cello–Piano Sonata op. 78; Variations and Fugue op. 81; Aeolsharp op. 75 no. 11.[15]

In Reger's works it was mainly the peculiarly floating tonality that attracted Bartók, which the German master achieved not so much through increased Wagnerian chromaticism as by an individual atomization of tonal interrelationships. That is, whereas with Wagner tonality is ambiguous all the way through long stretches, unsteady, virtually undefinable, with Reger there appear tonally unambiguous patches, yet instead of the tonality becoming stabilized, more and more new modulations sweep the musical progression still further forward.

This method is first used by Bartók in the *Two Portraits*, and then appears in the First String Quartet, and not only in the Lento movement but in the Allegretto as well. A good example is the snaking line of the frame-theme moving in parallel thirds and spanning the two movements. It is scarcely possible to determine its tonality even though individual phrases may still have tonal significance. We are faced with the process in the course of which the organically connected theme breaks up, in a tonal sense, into parts.

It is also here, in the First String Quartet, that we are first faced with the influence of the French masters. It was not during his visit to Paris in 1905 but only through Kodály in 1907 that Bartók came to know the art of Debussy and Ravel. Much later, in his study written in 1938, he himself put into words the significance of having become acquainted with this art. 'It is well known that Hungary suffered for centuries from its close proximity to Germany, both politically and culturally. The most highly educated of our citizens, however, have always rebelled against this unhealthy situation, recognizing that they had a closer spiritual link with the Latin races and especially the French than with the Germans...

* B=Bartók. The Roman numerals refer to the Bartók Quartet concerned; the Arabic numerals refer to the movement within that particular quartet.

29

It is obvious and understandable that this recognition of kinship should find an expression in music, in opposition to the German music, which until the end of the nineteenth century had dominated the musical world in Hungary. New ideas were released and the emergence of Debussy signified the replacement of German music by French music as a source of inspiration. By the turn of the century young Hungarian musicians, of whom I was one, had already been attracted for some time towards other fields of French culture. It may be readily imagined just how much significance they attached to Debussy: their discovery of his art awakened them to a knowledge of what French music had to offer.'[16]

In this study, Bartók slightly exaggerates the importance of French music as far as his own art is concerned. But there can be no doubt that the first impressions really did have an inspiring effect on him and helped him in the discarding of the 'dead weight' of post-Romanticism. In any event it is curious how well the 'battle' between the German and French influences can be observed in a single work, the first movement of the First String Quartet. While traces of Wagner and Reger can be found in the fugally structured parts, the third and sixth mixtures of the movement's trio evoke rather Debussy's G minor String Quartet or Ravel's *Ma mère l'Oye*.[17]

The pastel orchestral tone, otherwise alien to chamber music as a genre, later plays an important role with Bartók in such works as the first piece in the *Two Pictures*, 'In full flower', and the first and third of the Four Pieces for orchestra. In the chamber music nourished on the Beethoven tradition there is absolutely no room for this, and when a colour effect makes an occasional appearance here and there in Bartók's later quartets, this has by then nothing to do with the Debussy sonority ideal, but is rather the discovery of the possibilities of clusters and note-bunches.

There is, however, another point in Bartók's quartet art where the influence of Debussy is unmistakable. In the tragic tone of the Second Quartet's closing movement there appears, almost like a quotation, a detail from *Pelléas*: the heart-rending depiction of the death of Melisande.[18]

All this might be considered complete coincidence, but why should we consider it so precisely in the case of Bartók, who explicitly wished to bring about in his art a synthesis of Bach, Beethoven and Debussy. Even though comparatively few places can be found in the œuvre which refer so obviously to the French master, this does not mean the abandonment of the programme (for in retrospect Bartók himself said this to Serge Moreux in 1939)[19], but that the stimuli gained from Debussy are metastatically merged into his musical style.

In a critical stylistic examination of the First String Quartet the investigator is led to two other contemporaries whose influence, even if not lifelong, was nevertheless important for Bartók in that period. One is Ernő Dohnányi, who is basically Brahmsian, but, interweaving this feature with his Hungarian melody writing, his chamber music style was able to present Bartók with a direct, immediate example.[20] The other is Zoltán Kodály, who not only smoothed the way for Bartók to become acquainted with the French masters but with Hungarian folk music as well.[21] There are in the First Quartet a few parts where the tone resembles that of the later chamber works of Kodály, the peculiarly lyrical interpretation of Hungarian folk music melody. It is, of course, true that at this time these works of Kodály—

30

string quartets, string trio, solo sonata for cello—had still not been written and thus they could not have exercised any influence on Bartók. Here it is rather a question of Bartók striking in one or two places the peculiar lyrical note which was later to become so characteristic of Kodály's music.

After that here and there in the later compositions, too, a melody or melodic phrase similar to this crops up, for example in the Second Quartet's first movement or the Fourth Quartet's central movement. In the case of these last, we can begin to talk of direct influence, for the friendly relationship between the two musicians justifies the assertion of these kinds of artistic influence, and conscious or unconscious borrowings.

In the same way as Bartók hinted in advance at certain elements of Kodály's later style, he came across several idiomatic and expression-technique discoveries of his two greatest contemporaries, Schoenberg and Stravinsky, before he actually came to know these masters. Bartók's first mature works, the Fourteen Bagatelles and the First String Quartet, are, as regards both the time of their composition and the function they fulfil in the œuvre as a whole, parallel with Schoenberg's Three Piano Pieces op. 11, and his Second String Quartet.

31

Yet in 1908, when he composed the works in question, Bartók did not know the music of Schoenberg, as he himself states in an article which appeared in 1920.[22]

In 1911 Schoenberg knew Bartók's works—in his *Harmonielehre* he quotes a few bars from Bartók's tenth Bagatelle.[23] But he did not know Bartók's piano pieces when he composed his own in 1909.

It is mainly in their conception that the piano pieces of the two composers are related: both wrote study-like pieces of a rather free structure, as is shown to a certain extent by the titles. The works of both are equally characterized by a certain experimental harshness, a frank and eruptive tone. The peculiar and unconscious connection, however, is most manifest in the means of expression employed in the pieces: the solitarily declaiming melodies developed like a monologue, the ostinatos, and the free treatment of dissonant harmonies. Of these last it is the fourth chord which is prominent—it is a completely familiar feature with Schoenberg from the First Chamber Symphony (1906) onwards, but Bartók discovers it only in 1908. In a similar way consistently used major seventh parallels and melodies progressing in sevenths also testify to a common aspiration, and there is further a kind of loosening of tonality such as in Bartók's thirteenth Bagatelle, where the polar divergence between E flat minor and A minor triads results in tonal ambiguity.

The two string quartets are even closer to each other; almost thematic similarities are to be found in them. In the second movement of both quartets there appears a repeated-note rhythm motif in the cello, which can incidentally be traced back to a common source—the scherzo of Beethoven's F major String Quartet op. 59. Apart from that, this movement of the Schoenberg quartet uses series of melodic fourths in unisono instrumentation in a way very similar to the finale of the Bartók quartet. In the closing movement of the Schoenberg work the rolling bass ostinato before the entrance of the melodic part comes very close to Bartók's 'Painful Wrestling' in connection with which, on the other hand, the influence of Wagner has already been mentioned. So this encounter, too, takes place by way of a common inspiration. The glorious high chords of the movement's coda appear in Bartók in the Lento movement of the quartet—a similar 'post-Wagnerian' yearning tone and attitude characterize both.

It has to be emphasized that all this similarity and coincidence is not the result of direct influence. Nor can it be regarded as accidental. Schoenberg and Bartók arrived at these solutions quite independently of one another, the common root being the common tradition. We know what kind of influence was exerted on the young Bartók by Richard Strauss and Wagner. Brahms, too, was a model for him, first during his years in Pozsony, but also later during his studies in Budapest. His composition teacher was Hans Koessler, who was well known to be an admirer of Brahms. It was these same composers who were the early influences on Schoenberg, too. He also came to chamber music through the works of Brahms, and in the spheres of idiom and harmony he learned a great deal from Wagner. It was in 1899 that Schoenberg wrote the composition which stands closest of all his works to Wagner, the D minor String Sextet (*Verklärte Nacht*). As has already been said, Bartók also went through this, but with him the Wagner tone arrives in the First String Quartet in company with a host of other influences.

32

One of the most important 'common' achievements of Bartók's and Schoenberg's early, still unconscious, progress together was the breaking up of tonality. In the opening bars of the First Quartet, for example, there is an already decidedly recognizable attempt, possibly instinctive, at using all the notes of the dodecaphonic chromatic scale.

There would be no sense in trying to force the analytical method of the dodecaphonic technique onto this work as well, but from this it becomes quite clear how closely tonal floating or indefiniteness is connected in Bartók with the fullest possible use of the twelve-note range. With this, strictly speaking, Bartók moves further forward on the road leading to dodecaphony than Schoenberg, for in the Viennese master's Second Quartet, apart from a certain freedom in the tonal harmonic sphere, there is no evidence of such consistent anticipation of complementary dodecaphony. With this in mind it is scarcely surprising to find the eleven notes of the chromatic scale reeled off well within the first three bars at the opening of Bartók's Second String Quartet. And at the opening of the third movement ten chromatic notes are heard within four bars.

5

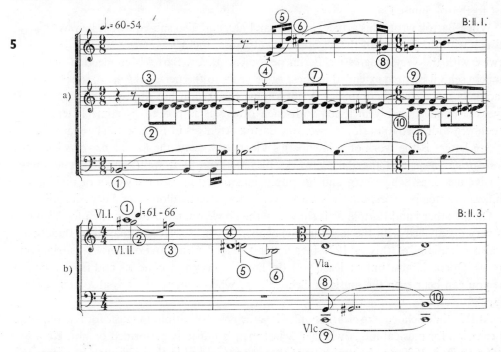

In the interval between the First and Second String Quartets, however, there was an important change of direction: becoming familiar with several of Schoenberg's works, Bartók began quite consciously to borrow elements from the Viennese master. His 1920 study which appeared in the Viennese *Musikblätter des Anbruch* is an important document concerning this change. Under the title 'Schoenberg's Music in Hungary' he writes among other things: 'In 1912 one of my pupils brought me home from Vienna a copy of Schoenberg's Three Piano Pieces op. 11, which at that time had still not been published; this was the first

33

Schoenberg music I came to know. Presumably until then, as far as I can remember, hardly anything by Schoenberg was known in Budapest, and even his name was unfamiliar to the majority of musicians. And yet from then on there were a few young musicians, scarcely out of college, who plunged themselves with great enthusiasm into the study of the Schoenberg works. It is understandable that the new possibilities of technique and expression resulting from the suspension of the principle of tonality in his works exercised a greater or lesser influence on those of our young composers (and indeed also on those more mature composers) who were already striving towards similar goals. I use the word "influence" in its best sense: in this there is no question of slavish imitation; I am thinking of a similar process to that noticeable in Stravinsky's work (from approximately 1913, i.e. in "Rossignol"): under the influence of Schoenberg he did not lose his individuality; on the contrary, in this way he unfolded, as it were, even more freely; the direction indicated by Schoenberg led him in a similar direction, but further, and on a different path...'[24] It is not difficult to read between the lines here that the phrase 'more mature composers' refers first and foremost to Bartók himself.

When Bartók wrote this article, in the year 1920, and also subsequently, he was closely in touch with the journal of the Viennese avant garde, the *Musikblätter des Anbruch*, and likewise with the very progressive Berlin periodical *Melos*. Bartók's connection with the Viennese school became extended in these same years to the personal sphere, too; whether he actually met Schoenberg or not is not known for certain but through correspondence they were unquestionably in touch with each other, as is proved by some letters from Schoenberg addressed to Bartók, now in the Bartók Archives in Budapest. The main theme of these letters is the work of Schoenberg's Viennese society, the *Verein für musikalische Privataufführungen*, and the Bartók works played there. It is well known that at these exclusive meetings Schoenberg and his pupils introduced in turn the works of their most significant contemporaries. Bartók's works were also performed on several occasions.[25]

On the other hand Bartók, as is shown by the above quoted article written for Vienna, was very dissatisfied with the fact that Schoenberg's works were not played in Budapest. He also complains of this in 1921 in a letter to Cecil Gray in London: 'It is true you have no Opera House but at least you do have some good concerts and from time to time you can hear even the music of Schoenberg, whereas here there is absolutely nothing...'[26]

At this time Schoenberg clearly symbolizes the new aspirations in music for Bartók, and the criterion for musical life is whether Schoenberg's music is performed or not. He also wrote a study in 1920 on 'the problems of the new music' and in this, although he wishes to give a general picture of the musical aspirations of the age, he above all discusses most exhaustively the tonality problem posed by the Schoenberg school.[27] It is in this study that there emerges a picture of the Bartók who searches and investigates without the slightest trace of prejudice the paths of the new music and who, with a truly scientific attitude, does not make any statement on anything in a prejudiced or apodictical way. At the same time his tone is personal and shows that he discusses these matters not as a scientist looking at them from without, but as one who has already tried all this out in his own creative work, and who has

34

his own opinion in the matter. His study is a summary of *his own opinion* and not an interpretation of the various opinions of the period.

The especially interesting point in this study is that before the definite evolution of Schoenberg's method of composing with 'twelve tones, which are related only with one another', it suggests the possibility of forming dodecaphonic composition by saying: '...the decisive change in direction towards atonality began—after the preparatory phases described—only when they began to feel that it was necessary for every single note of our twelve-note system to be of equal rank; when they attempted to arrange the twelve notes not in accordance with certain scale systems, and not to give greater or less emphasis to the individual notes on the basis of these systems, but to use the various notes in any and every combination, whether horizontal or vertical, but not determined by scales. It is true that in such treatment certain notes once again assume some sort of relatively conspicuous emphasis in the arrangement, but the basis of this difference in stress is no longer this scale-scheme or that, but the result of the arrangement currently in use. In the same way the individual parts in the groups made up attain, according to their relationship to each other, different values and different effectiveness. Through the free and equal treatment of each of the twelve notes the possibilities of expression are increased for the present to an unimaginable degree.' This is still not identical with the Schoenberg serial technique, although essentially related to it, for the dodecaphonic system aims at coherence—in relation to one work—through certain fixed distances. Bartók did not make the Schoenberg method of correlationship his own; but from as early as 1914–15 onwards he evolved for himself with increasing consistency a compositional technique in which the range of notes is presented by the dodecaphonic chromatic scale and in which the fullest possible use of this range and at the same time the forming of certain 'sonic-spatial' meeting points lead to a concept of tonality with a new significance.

It can thus be attributed to the influence of Schoenberg and the dissolution of functional tonality that from the years of the First World War onwards Bartók, without in the least moving away from folk music, increasingly definitely moved towards the chromaticism of European art music. In this a large role was played by the so-called distance phenomena—that is, the division of the octave into equal intervals. Construction based on distance principles, although it does have its own historical antecedents, is a typically twentieth century method, and it stands in a natural relationship with the break-up of diatony and functional tonality because, as a contrast to the asymmetric structure of the latter, it evolves a new kind of symmetrical scale. Strictly speaking, the chromatic system itself is a distance principle system for it is made up of equal semitones, and as a natural consequence it follows that within the possibilities of the twelve notes it produces further distance systems made up of larger intervals of two, three, four and six semitones.

Distance principle combinations appeared very early in Bartók's art, but their consistent use, and their extension to whole works, comes only in the compositions dating from the war years. The first striking example of this is the Suite for piano, the four movements of which—even if in different forms—have the distance principle as their dominant element. Simple distance methods are represented by the whole-tone scales of the first

35

movement and the augmented triads of the second. Alongside these there is a rich flow of combined distance scales, in which the octave is filled out by an alternation between a larger and a smaller distance interval. An example is the minor third and minor second scale (3+1), or the fourth and minor second scale (5+1).[28]

How this distance principle construction became naturalized in Bartók's music is still a much-debated question. Just as Bartók arrived at dodecaphonic chromaticism as an inevitable consequence of the late Romantic development, and quite independently of Schoenberg, he may have discovered the distance scales which go with it in the same way. But he may have gained some inspiration in that direction from Liszt's works, too, where virtually every distance scale appears, and from Debussy, who was one of the pioneers of the whole-tone scale. It is very probable, however, that after the first unconscious efforts, and having come to know Schoenberg's music, he took more decisive steps towards these new implements of musical language.

The fourth+minor second combination is already present in Schoenberg's Second String Quartet and can also be found here and there in the Five Orchestral Pieces. In Bartók it plays an especially important part in the Four Pieces for orchestra and in the Second String Quartet. Some characteristic examples are quoted below.

Of the minor third + minor second combination there is likewise an abundance of examples in the works of both masters. With Schoenberg this usually stems from consistent major third parallels; that is, in the case of minor third displacement of major thirds there arises a chord-change having a false relation effect which together give the 3 + 1 distance system.

7

In Bartók, too, we often meet with these kinds of phrases, but it is much more frequently a case of the minor third + minor second combination arising from simultaneous use of major and minor thirds.

8

Also to the sphere of structures based on the distance principle belong the chord types which use equal intervals piled one on top of the other. Two such types had already appeared in tonal–functional music, too—the diminished seventh chord containing minor thirds and the augmented triad containing major thirds—but both demanded resolution as a dissonance. Of these two, the diminished seventh chord is so forcefully tonal in content that it did not attract the composers heading in the direction of atonality. Much more potential lay hidden in the augmented triad, neutral as far as tonality is concerned. Liszt had a great preference for it, even lending it philosophical significance ('Faust' Symphony).

To the model of distance chords based on a structure of thirds, Schoenberg created in his work the fourth-chord and the second-pile. The appearance of the fourth-chord represented an important qualitative leap in the history of European music since it really declared war on the acoustic overtone laws of tonal music. For the heaping up of fourths emphasizes that this interval is *not* the inversion of the fifth and not insertable into the series of overtones. On the other hand it breaks the bounds of the perfect octave framework and in this way, too, weakens the foundations of tonality. It is no accident that the fourth-chords of Schoenberg's First Chamber Symphony became a symbol for the avant-garde artistic movement.

In his theoretical works Bartók stressed that he came to the fourth-chord by way of folk music examples. 'The characteristic accumulations of fourth intervals in our ancient melodies have initiated the formation of fourth-chords: horizontal succession has here... been projected into vertical simultaneity.'[29] It is extremely doubtful, however, whether Bartók's first fourth-chords in the Fourteen Bagatelles came about on the basis of this reasoning. It is more likely that the folk music example, together with the knowledge of his own art music experiences and Schoenberg's similar aspirations, gave him courage. Here are a few characteristic examples from Bartók.

38

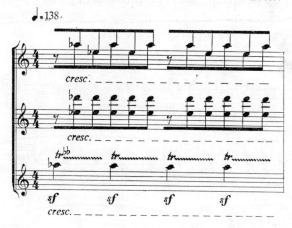

B:VI.1.

In Bartók's Second String Quartet the fourth is, so to speak, the 'parent cell'—the two fundamental possibilities of distance principle melodics built from fourths are concisely exposed in the theme: the perfect fourth-chord (conjoint fourths) and the fourth+minor second model (disjoint fourths).

The basic motif of the theme, consisting of two perfect fourths, is extended in the course of the movement's thematic work: in this way a possibly even more characteristic figure is crystallized in which the perfect fourth becomes paired with an augmented fourth.

39

This sort of formation—it may be called a heterogeneous fourth group—plays perhaps an even greater role in Bartók's style than the 'homogeneous' fourth-chord made up of perfect fourths. And Schoenberg, too, has a preference for it.

This chord almost certainly gains a place in the foreground because, in contrast with the homogeneous fourth-chord—it has a tense major seventh framework and thus its function is also more dynamic. With some degree of freedom it is possible to draw a parallel between this kind of chord with a heterogeneous make-up and the triads of the other diatonic-tonal harmonic world. Just as according to the Rameau principle whereby a major and minor third together form *harmonie parfaite*[30], that is a common chord, so the typical chord, the 'perfect harmony', of the beginning of the twentieth century arises from two intervals of different size.

The heterogeneous fourth-chord, moreover, is closely related to another distance phenomenon, the fourth+minor second model, which likewise has a major seventh framework. The heterogeneous fourth-chord can thus be regarded as an incomplete fourth model, and vice versa: the fourth model can be regarded as an augmented heterogeneous fourth-chord.

From the melodic aspect, too, there are numerous elements in Bartók's musical idiom which hint at Schoenberg—either as a consequence of direct influence or indirectly as a companion of other elements. Melody—or as a larger generalization, melodic action—has great significance in this style where linearity once more becomes a leading structural principle. At the same time the harmonic phenomena are also characterized in a certain sense by the melodic phenomena, for the handling of the vertical and the horizontal elements is in principle identical. This identity is asserted by Schoenberg in practice, too, in the technique of serial composition, and Bartók likewise builds his fundamental harmonic principles on this, as is clear from the above quotation in connection with the fourth-chord. This is why, in the course of discussing the distance phenomena, their melodic and chordal forms can be treated as equivalents.

One common feature in the melody writing of the two masters is so-called complementary melody writing. This technique, which with Schoenberg played a great role mainly in the creative period before the establishment of serial composition, is present in Bartók throughout his whole life-work. The reason for its being discontinued in Schoenberg's serial period is not hard to find: the Reihe itself ensures exhaustion of the dodecaphonic range of notes—either in melodic or chordal form. On the other hand, in pieces which are not serial but nevertheless dodecaphonic, it is precisely this complementary technique which makes full use of the tonal system possible.

Melody building based on the complementary principle can take two forms. One solution is for melody and harmony together to create a closed system; the melody is dependent on the harmony in so far as it consistently avoids the component parts of the latter. The other solution is purely linear: the melody is formed so that there will be no repetition of any note and larger leaps will be filled out by the melodic line turning back on itself. These principles of melodic creation can be traced back in music history as far as Palestrina, the difference being merely in the range of notes employed. The following are some typical examples from the works of Schoenberg, Alban Berg and Bartók.

Another important feature of melodic creation which is equally characteristic of the art of Schoenberg, Berg and Bartók is a certain geometrical construction in the melodic line. The geometric–graphic element was always of some significance in linear thinking, usually organically related to the emotional–conceptual content of the work. Albert Schweitzer elaborates on this very plastically in connection with Bach's melodic art, attributing great importance to the symbolism of these melody patterns.[31] It is virtually natural that in a musical conception which once more affords such significance to linearity as resembles that of Bach, structured melodies of this kind assume great importance. In this way are born the various kinds of straightforward melodies—horizontal, rising, and falling—expanding and contracting themes, circle-melodies in a wave line or turning back on themselves, and melodic lines which are, like a spring, stretched out tensely or pushed in close together, etc. In Bartók's first mature compositions these kinds of graphic–geometric melody formations are already present: the two-directional chromatic expansion in the second of the Fourteen Bagatelles; and the 'Painful Wrestling' of the Ten Easy Pieces is characterized by circular motion. Then later, obviously under the influence of Schoenberg—but also as the further development of his own individual experiences—these kinds of melodic patterns become condensed, especially in the compositions dating from the years after the First World War.

15

Schoenberg: String Quartet no. 3, 1st movement

With geometrically arranged, and so symmetrical–regular, melodiousness logically goes the breaking up, the decomposition of this. It has already become apparent in the case of melodic patterns opening up into great width that although the principle demands 'order', the result arising from it has the effect of being disorderly, confused and frighteningly broken up and dislocated.

Schoenberg's expressionistic ambitions found a useful implement in these confused, gesticulating melodies divested of all shape. The harshness in melodic movement, the exaggeration, the gesticulating character do, indeed, serve the purposes of increased expressiveness well, willing to give up 'beauty' for the sake of the goal—expression, impact, suggestivity, agitation.

The melody using wide intervals, however, does have another function: for one thing it loosens up in a healthy way the close, small-interval chromaticism inherited from Wagner. In one of Schoenberg's Stefan George Songs we find the following melodic unit:

Schoenberg: 15 Stefan George Songs

16

43

Here it is easy to see that wide interval melody is not used exclusively in the service of expressing a confused frame of mind: it is in a certain sense one concomitant of the chromatic,
atonal aspiration. Schoenberg might easily have formed the melody in the following way:

17

But he needed the upward transposition of the last two notes by an octave not only because
of the heightening of emotion but to avoid the monotony of chromaticism. The climbing,
swelling melodiousness of *Tristan* is replaced by intricate, sparkling melody evoking a shock
effect.

A second point is that the large intervals help to loosen up the feeling of tonality since
they extend the sonic sphere and resist the naturalness of leading-note-like attraction relationships.

With the 'vertical' break-up of the melody goes its 'horizontal' break-up, too; that is,
the occasional interruption of melodic continuity by pauses. The pause does not, however,
necessarily mean disintegratedness or bittiness; classical melody is what principally offers
good examples of this, where the pause in reality is built into the melody, giving in its inner
division and articulation. But here it is a different matter. The broken quality of the melody
springs from the same inner decompositional tendency as the vertical confusion of the melody.
This, too, is a characteristically avant-garde attitude, fitting in well with Busoni's revolutionary ideas concerning making music entirely 'free'.[32]

This tendency can be easily observed in Schoenberg as early as in the works from around
1909–10. The breaking down of melodies and the reconstruction of melodies made up of
smaller parts into a larger whole, appear perhaps most characteristically in the Five Orchestral Pieces. Many elements from this Schoenberg work are once more to be heard in Bartók's *Miraculous Mandarin*, above all in the use of melodic fragments and fragment melodies and in the ostinato technique.

Thus the broadly arching melodic ideal of romanticism turns into its own antithesis—
occasionally even in late Romantic music itself—into the differentiation and dissolution, of
melodic processes, simple to begin with but later becoming more and more extreme. This
process is very interesting even within Schoenberg's life-work: even *Verklärte Nacht*, although
it was written mainly under the influence of Wagner, betrays some tendency towards the
breaking up of the broadly arching melodies. The process was also accelerated by the
effect of Richard Strauss's characteristic short motif technique. It attains its fullest development in Schoenberg's expressionistic period, above all in *Erwartung* and the Five Orchestral
Pieces.

With Bartók this process is not so conspicuous. This is doubtless largely due to the
influence folk music had on him, preventing this extreme breaking up of melodies. That this
tendency did not, however, leave Bartók's melody untouched is a consequence of the path
of his life, and his attitude, which looked reality frankly and openly in the face. It is typical

44

that it is Bartók's most illusion-free work, *The Miraculous Mandarin*, that best shows the influence of Schoenberg in this direction. The distorted figures, alienated from humanity, of the dance-play's dramatic world, and its emotions, inevitably produced this system of expression and the linear break-up of the melodies.

In the settling down which came after *The Miraculous Mandarin*, however, there also remained something of this tendency, as is shown principally by the two violin–piano sonatas, and then it becomes transformed and a completely new form of musical–melodic expression is born from it. I have in mind those musical pictures where Bartók brings to life a completely new kind of 'micro-melodics' through the transference into music of nocturnal sounds, natural noises and movements.

It may possibly appear incorrect to apply the term 'melody' to these melodic snatches and fragments, these musical stirrings of one or two notes, but in the last analysis they do belong to the sphere of melody, for they are linear phenomena, even if they are the border-line cases of linearity.

This decomposition of melody beginning around the turn of the century and enabling the representatives of the Viennese school to formulate musically an individual view of the world, led in Bartók—and also in Webern—to the discovery of a new tonal world. Quotation of only a few examples from Bartók's works will be sufficient to prove what fundamentally important areas of expression were conquered by this conception of melody and how central it remained in Bartók's most personal articulations.

19

B: The Night's Music

B: III. Prima parte

B: Music for String Instruments, Percussion and Celesta, 3rd movement

From here it is only one step to the system of special colour effects which Bartók evolved in parallel with the Viennese school, and the expressive function of which is related to the function of the above mentioned melodic phenomena: in both, the intensification of expressiveness leads the composer to the conquest of certain 'extra-musical' territories, or at least to the extension of the 'existing boundaries' of music.

From the earliest mature piano works onwards, Bartók favours the use of grating semitone dissonance as a colouring function. Edwin von der Nüll's 1930 study contains numerous interesting statements in this connection.[33] The real terrain of these colouring pursuits, however, proves to be the string quartets, in which, from the third onwards, a completely sovereign colour-world evolves increasingly decisively, alongside the encouragement derived from the Vienna school's free use of chords and dissonances. By means of frequent use of the fourth-chord and the four-note chord with a major seventh, new tonal values become established, the major seventh loses its dissonant character demanding resolution, and it becomes possible for a new chord to come into existence by building one on top of another. The minor second, the inversion of the major seventh and equal in value to it, also begins to play a more and more sovereign role, and by accumulations of this the first 'note bundles' and 'clusters' in music history evolve, the new colour effects which were to be raised to the level of basic implements in the period following the Second World War. And Bartók was one of the first to evolve new kinds of colour effects from parts, supplementing each other in a complementary way and moving in different rhythms, another type of note bundle anticipating the means offered by aleatory, too.

20

B: IV. 2.

Bartók achieved another kind of extension of the string quartet world of colour by way of special use of the instruments. Special ways of playing string instruments which until then had been used only rarely (such as pizzicato, sul tasto, sul ponticello, etc.) are now used more frequently and richly, and apart from these new effects become naturalized—for example, the hard pizzicato obtained by slapping the string on the fingerboard, which has since become known throughout the world as the 'Bartók pizzicato'. Good examples of this kind of innovation in quartet sound are particularly in evidence in the Fourth Quartet and also partly in the Sixth.

Further common ground between the styles of Bartók and Schoenberg—and even beyond that the achievements whereby they made musical history—is to be found in the qualitative transformation of the century's harmonic world as a result of which the efficiency and significance of individual chords is determined not merely by the structure of the intervals sounded but also by the way they are distributed. The so-called distribution always played an important role in polyphonic music, determining the sonority of the texture and in many respects its function as regards meaning. In tonal-functional harmonics, however, the distribution of the notes in a chord was of secondary importance in comparison to the intervals which went to make it up. The essential nature and structure of the chord was unequivocally determined by its closest form—and possibly an abstraction of it. After the new harmonic principle became valid the analyst no longer 'had the right' to carry out any such abstraction. In the definition of a chord the closest distribution offers no help—indeed, it is rather inclined to obscure the nature of the chord. Thus here it is always necessary to consider the intervals actually sounding, taking the differences in register fully into account.

In this tonal system the colouring of the individual parts of a chord assumes great significance; the colour constitution is perhaps just as important and decisive as interval

47

structure. This first materialized in a concentrated form with Schoenberg in the third movement of the Five Orchestral Pieces. Bartók also experimented with it, though not in such an extreme form. We need only think of the central—slow—movement of the Fourth String Quartet, where different structuring and different colour distributions of a single chord essentially determine the tone of the whole movement. (Apart from this, in his 1920 *Melos* study Bartók declared himself strongly in favour of this sort of interpretation and application of harmony theoretically as well.[34])

In the sphere of the more traditional types of chord, too, there are some characteristic points of contact between the styles of Bartók and Schoenberg. Both masters use the four-note chords inherited from Romantic music, and of these preference is given above all to those in which the tense major seventh interval is present, most in accordance with the demands of tonal freedom. We are aware that this chord type very frequently appeared as a melodic leitmotif in Bartók's first mature period. It is also to be met with on numerous occasions in the works of Schoenberg dating from this time.

Alongside third structuring, however, an essentially new element was introduced in fourth-structure chords. The historical events leading to this have already been outlined in the course of discussing distance phenomena; the principal thing to be examined now is how this new means is related to the former. It has also been mentioned already that beside the chord consisting of perfect fourths, the so-called heterogeneous fourth-chord composed of perfect and augmented fourths is more frequent. When the augmented fourth is placed underneath, the chord comes very close to that type of traditional third-structure four-note chord which contains a major seventh above a diminished triad. Thus a natural summary is achieved by the heterogeneous type of fourth-chord in which the remains of traditional third-structuring, the new principle of distance structure and the seventh tension of free tonality can all assert themselves at once.

Bartók's and Schoenberg's harmonic world between 1910 and 1925 is most faithfully characterized by these two different chord types: the four-note chord composed of thirds and the fourth-chord. But the way in which the individual chords themselves are more freely structured, and the way in which they are strung together, both reflect the complete freedom of the disintegrating tonal system. In this freedom in chord progression, however, new regularities come into being, above all the law of tension in the chords. Since an important role is played in both the basic types by the major seventh, this gives the chords a common framework—more or less in the same sense as the way in which, in the functional–tonal style, the perfect fifth contained the two basic types of triad—major and minor. In chord progressions major seventh tension is an almost permanent factor without parallel sevenths actually occurring (just as parallel fifths were 'forbidden' in the earlier style). This harmonic supremacy of the major seventh does not in the least signify monotony or deterioration in the harmony. The significance and the aesthetic content of the individual chords depend on their inner structure and on their relationship to each other. Thus not even this style renounces the life-like rhythm of arsis–thesis, tension and resolution.

49

23

B: Suite, 4th movement

After digesting the direct Schoenberg influence—observable right from the Suite for piano to the First and Second Sonatas for violin and piano—Bartók turns his attention in the direction of Stravinsky's neo-Baroque style for a short time, in the year 1926. But already in the following year, chiefly in the string quartet genre, he once more returns to his own path, which comes closer to the Viennese school. Perhaps it was no accident that it was when he had the opportunity of hearing Alban Berg's *Lyric Suite* for string quartet during the concert, in which his own Piano Sonata received its first performance in Baden-Baden on 16 July 1927, that this genre made a new appearance after such a long period of neglect—for the preceding string quartet had been completed in 1917.[35] In any event it is quite striking how he began composing a string quartet as the first piece of work after this summer concert tour, and the work was already finished in September. No great significance would be attached to such external circumstances as these if the influence of Berg's work were not to be felt already in the Third String Quartet.

Without the slightest doubt, Berg's *Lyric Suite* belongs among the greatest master-pieces of this century. This six-movement composition, in which each single movement intensifies the contrast of lyric characters to a polarization level—the Presto delirando and the Largo desolato—is quite unique. It might be imagined that it was as a 'counter-piece' to this six-movement work of such enormous proportions that Bartók wrote his shortest string quartet. But shortly afterwards he once again turned to this genre, and in the following year composed his Fourth Quartet. In this he succeeded in realizing a conception related to that of Berg but which is at the same time completely different: the cycle of five movements does not travel the road of polarization expressing reality, but rather attains the harmony of classical balance. As has already been indicated in the preceding chapter, Bartók may have taken the model for his five-section structure from Beethoven. Indeed, a further possibility is that in the twenties, when he was in such close contact with the music world of Western Europe, and with the I.S.C.M., he also came to know Hindemith's Third String Quartet, dating from 1922, which likewise uses a five-movement bridge-form.

1	2	3	4	5
Fugue	Motory movement	Adagio	Toccata	Rondo

Within this the central movement itself is also in bridge-form. Thus Bartók was in a position to become acquainted with two different types in the course of his visits to Germany, but common to both is the increase in the number of movements.

Apart from this, the Alban Berg work was of inspirational influence on Schoenberg, too: in the same year as Bartók he, too, composed his Third String Quartet. And with Schoenberg an even greater lapse in time separates the Second and Third Quartets from each other—almost twenty years.

These four string quartets dating from almost the same time—the Berg *Lyric Suite*, Schoenberg's Third Quartet and Bartók's Third and Fourth Quartets—are related to each other by numerous connecting threads. The Schoenberg and Berg works are characteristic products of progressive bourgeois art, to blossom for a further decade in the Weimar Republic. A few of the larger towns in Germany were at that time the principal stage for avant-garde movements: musical life flourished in Berlin, Klemperer and Zemlinsky worked in the Kroll-Oper, and Berg's *Wozzeck* was given its première in the great Unter den Linden Opera. Until 1925, Busoni taught in the composers' master class of the Prussian Academy of Fine Arts; he was then replaced by Schoenberg, who there, too, trained several generations of young musicians. But this short period was favourable to more than music: in Weimar the Bauhaus became a great attraction, in Berlin Piscator revolutionized theatrical art, and the two outstanding writers Leonhard Frank and Robert Musil were working there, their works appearing in wide circulation through the progressive publishing house Rowohlt Verlag.

This atmosphere favoured Bartók as well. From this it seems quite understandable that his first journey after the war should lead him precisely to Berlin, where he wrote his two important articles for the periodical *Melos*. In 1923 the Melos Society organized a series of three concerts consisting entirely of his works. Among other pieces, the first two string quartets were performed and the Second Sonata for violin and piano was given its première. From this time onwards, his works had a permanent place in the I.S.C.M. festivals and concerts—in Frankfurt and Baden-Baden as well as in Berlin. At one I.S.C.M. concert Berg's *Lyric Suite* was performed together with Schoenberg's Third Quartet and Bartók's

51

Third Quartet by the Kolisch Quartet. Through this concert it was possible to notice—and indeed it was noticed by a few critics and progressive musical opinion—that although each of the three composers represents a different path in the application of atonality and dodecaphony, yet in their conception and world of expression and attitude they come close to one another.

Bartók and Berg are particularly interrelated by some novel types of tone. The *Lyric Suite*'s Allegro misterioso (third movement) and Presto delirando (fifth movement) resemble in many respects the mysteriously fleeting prestos and scherzos of Bartók (Second Quartet, second movement, Coda; Third Quartet, Seconda parte, fugato; Fourth Quartet, Prestissimo, con sordino, and Allegretto pizzicato). Bartók's and Berg's musical pictures of this nature are also related to each other in that the colour effects—in contrast with the impressionistic method—are associated with linear-polyphonic structure worked out in minute detail. These are not patches, not mood pictures, but the condensation of expressive experiences into a strict musical form.

In connection with Schoenberg's Third Quartet other kinds of relationship can be observed. This work is, in the strict sense of the term, a serial composition, in which every melodic and harmonic event is determined by the dodecaphonic note-row present in the background of the work. At the same time it represents a turning-point in the composer's creative career: since the development of the strict serial technique it is here that Schoenberg first uses the few loosening–relaxing methods which make it possible for the purely logical–speculative elements not to reign supreme, not to assume too great emphasis in the composition. So repetition of a note is not avoided, and the inner order of an occasional section of the note-row is used freely. This last assumes particular importance in the first movement of the quartet, where the basis of the musical texture is provided by an eight-note ostinato motif almost throughout.

It is indicative of the unified process of Schoenberg's creative development that the Third Quartet's note-row is composed of internally related smaller units each of which also played a part in the so-called freely atonal period. And this is the point at which kinship can be seen with Bartók's technique. In the first four-note section of the row lie concealed both the incomplete four-note chord with major seventh tension and the heterogeneous fourth-chord. The following four notes form a fourth+minor second pattern. And finally the closing section is none other than the inversion of the first four-note unit—that is, once again an incomplete seventh-chord and a heterogeneous fourth-chord.

24

Schoenberg: String Quartet no. 3,
1st movement

52

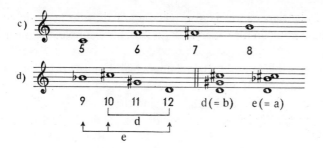

It is also worth mentioning the rhythmic relationships briefly. It is more or less common knowledge that a considerably large role is played in Bartók's work by the rhythmic influence of the folk music of various peoples. Of the different polymetric and asymmetric phenomena, the so-called Bulgarian rhythm is the most important. But the early appearance of asymmetric rhythm draws our attention to the fact that Bartók was already experimenting with these kinds of rhythm and metre even before he came to know folk music—and Bulgarian folk music in particular.[36] So it is possible to approach such asymmetrical kinds of rhythm and metre from another direction, too. Brăiloiu, the great pioneer in ethnomusicology, also made claims for the view that this rhythmic phenomenon must not be considered restricted to the peculiar metres of Bulgarian folk music, and that it is much more general and widespread than this in the folk music of the various peoples. Brăiloiu uses the term 'akzak' (which is Turkish for 'lame') and shows theoretically—that is, independently of the existing types already found—all the forms of this which are possible in principle.[37] That this rhythm is not exclusively a folk music phenomenon is proved by ancient Greek rhythm theory and prosody, which takes numerous such asymmetric formulas into account (hemiolia, paion, etc.). On the basis of all this it is by no means so surprising that even with Schoenberg, who had such an antagonistic attitude to folk music, this 'akzak' rhythm crops up, among other works, in his Third Quartet. The essence of Schoenberg's idea is to make a certain special order in the asymmetry: the $\frac{2}{8}$, $\frac{3}{8}$ and $\frac{4}{8}$ groups within the metre are placed alongside each other in an increasing or decreasing order of size.

25

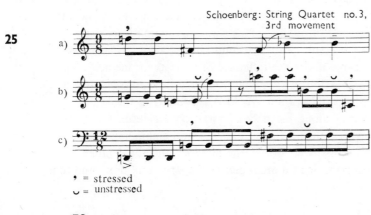

Schoenberg: String Quartet no. 3, 3rd movement

❜ = stressed
◡ = unstressed

53

One of Bartók's favourite Bulgarian metres is also made up of these same basic elements but with him the quaver groups come in the order $4+2+3$ (see, for example, the third movement of the Fifth Quartet).

But in Bartók, too, it is possible to find metric changes based on the principle of logically arranged gradual augmentation. If we take a closer look at the pizzicato scherzo movement of the Fourth Quartet, we will find hiding behind the $\frac{3}{4}$ time signature an actual metrical division in which—in logically increasing order of size—5, 6, 7, and 8 crotchets are placed beside one another.[38]

26

There is a similar phenomenon in the Burletta movement of the Sixth Quartet, too.

From all these phenomena it becomes possible to draw the conclusion that in the sphere of rhythmic innovation and refreshment Bartók and Schoenberg moved very close to each other, even if different kinds of motives were in operation in their individual efforts.

In comparing the creative paths of the two masters, it is possible to claim that in Bartók's attitude two distinct phases begin to take shape. In the first, as a consequence of the common tradition and numerous other factors, they set out, quite independently of each other, to break up tonality, and through a whole series of idiomatic–stylistic means they arrived at the same or similar results. In the second phase Bartók, in acquainting himself with Schoenberg's works, came under the influence of more than one achievement of the Viennese master, and even consciously attempted to merge these into his own works. This period extended from the years of the First World War roughly to the end of the twenties. He did not follow Schoenberg along the path of serial composition, for it was basically alien to him to force his art within the limits of a single, all-embracing compositional system. He made chromaticism his own, too, as the material and tonal range of his music, but he retained tonality in his music as a guarantee of the structural unity and tonal stability in a work.

On the other hand—and this is not taken into consideration by most studies—Bartók also remained faithful, even after his path diverged from Schoenberg's, to those achievements which he had taken over from him during the twenties, and having filtered them thoroughly built them organically into his own musical style-system. One single example which speaks for itself will suffice, and that is the twelve-note theme of the Violin Concerto which, with its many-sidedness and paradoxically tonal limitations, proves how much imagination and potential Bartók saw in the compositional principle of avoidance of note repetition.

B: Violin Concerto, 1st movement

27

Although in this study we are chiefly concerned with the Bartók side of the matter, it is nevertheless necessary to have a brief look at the other side, too. As is well known, Schoenberg, retiring within himself, proceeded through his life without paying much attention to external influences. He did, however, take notice of Bartók's music as early as 1911, and took the trouble to arrange performances within the framework of the *Privataufführung* meetings, but precisely in the period when Bartók approached him, Schoenberg was occupied with the evolution of his system. What is even more peculiar, however, is that in the thirties Schoenberg made approaches towards Bartók, at least in so far as his works showed assimilation of some typical Bartókian elements. And so in 1936, in the Fourth String Quartet, composed when he was already in the United States—in spite of the twelve-note technique, or 'consecrated' by the note-row—there appear Bartók's typical three-note motifs, his major–minor chord and his distance models.

28

Schoenberg: String Quartet no.4, 1st movement

ibid.

ibid.

55

ibid., 2nd movement

c)

The two middle parts have been omitted

B: VI.1.

d)

Schoenberg: String Quartet no.4, 2nd movement

a)

B: Violin Concerto, 3rd movement

b)

What appeared only in patches in Schoenberg's Fourth Quartet became extended to pervade a whole composition in the *Napoleon Ode* of approximately six years later. The note-row serving as the basis of the work is indeed no more than two interlocking minor third + minor second (3+1) scales, which Schoenberg uses, so to speak, in every possible form.

Schoenberg: Ode to Napoleon

29

a)

Analysis of these late Schoenberg works leads to two notions in the nature of a summary. Firstly, from the end of the twenties onwards, Schoenberg endeavoured increasingly decidedly to make the row, the preformed reference system providing the basis of the work, include those harmonic and melodic elements which, at the time of the development of the atonal idiom, came into being before the development of serial composition. From this it follows that if there are numerous points of contact between the art of Bartók and that of Schoenberg in the earlier period, then it is not possible to contrast the development of the two masters in the period following that either, at least with regard to idiomatic expression.

57

And secondly, even with his observance of the theoretical foundations of dodecaphonic composition, Schoenberg did nevertheless make a definite approach towards the 'Bartókian route'—that is, the binding of the chromatic system to distance patterns.

It is further characteristic of historical development that the younger generation following the Viennese school—Mátyás Seiber, Humphrey Searle, and others—likewise composed their serial works on the basis of the 'Bartókian' patterns.[39] This trend in the development—it would seem—is a crystallization of the most logical and most musical conception of the chromatic system.

The development of Bartók's style was further considerably influenced by his other great contemporary, Igor Stravinsky. The three stages which have been marked in connection with his relationship with Schoenberg can also be observed here. But if we take notice of the time factor in the creative development, it will become clear that the individual stages become consistently displaced, taking place later. Here it is the years 1910–11 that can be regarded as unconscious parallel progress when, roughly coinciding with the Russian ballets of Stravinsky, Bartók himself also discovered strongly rhythmic dance music of a folk character ('Village Scene' from the *Two Pictures*) and the barbaric ostinatos of primitive folk music (Allegro barbaro). Nor had he any need for the example of the Russian master in the further development of this last type of music since he studied the source itself in Rumanian and North African Arab folklore. That he found additional inspiration and encouragement in the Stravinsky music is another matter. In the most important of his theoretical writings reference to Stravinsky is virtually indispensable—whether it is a question of reconciling atonality and folk music, or the relationship between folk music and art music.

It is difficult to establish the beginning of a conscious parallel progress since we do not know exactly what Bartók became acquainted with from the Russian master's works, and when. In *The Wooden Prince* there crops up an occasional detail which can scarcely be imagined without the model of *Firebird*.[40] And the use of the trumpet in the Scherzo of the Four Orchestral Pieces also decidedly evokes the Stravinsky ballet, but it is possible that these characters only took shape in Bartók's creative imagination at the time of orchestration, that is in 1921, by which time, however, there can be no doubt that he was familiar with the Stravinsky works which had by then appeared.

In his first study to be published in the Berlin *Melos* ('Das Problem der neuen Musik') Bartók refers to the *Pribaoutki* songs composed in 1914. As far as our present investigation is concerned, this is an important document, partly because it touches on the technical problems of compositional craft, and partly because it uses the sphere of chamber music as an example and not orchestral works employing virtuosic orchestration. The effect of the Stravinsky works *Pribaoutki* and the later *Les Noces* is quite unmistakably apparent in Bartók's compositions dating from the twenties. The Slovakian folksong arrangement *Falun* (Village Scenes)—in either its solo or female chamber chorus versions—is with its hard, almost harsh tone and drily knocking instrumental accompaniment, a direct sister piece to Stravinsky's Russian wedding ceremony, *Les Noces*. On the other hand, it is chiefly in the Third String Quartet, written in 1927, that we can feel the influence of *Pribaoutki* becoming fruitful; here Bartók takes over a great deal from the idiom of the Russian master's work—the frequent metre changes, many-sided variation of small-scale motifs, the technique of roughly grating, colouring dissonances.

During these same years, neo-Baroque aspirations make themselves felt in Bartók's art: the hard concerto rhythm, the filled chord playing and the even, musical motor-movement in toccata–prelude style. This, too, can quite certainly be considered a Stravinsky influence, for of the various European composers aspiring in neo-Baroque and neo-Classical directions, it was he who gave voice to this tone in its most characteristic form. Traces of this are to be felt less in the chamber genres, but are found to be all the more active in the piano compositions: the Sonata, and the First and Second Piano Concertos. Here are a few very characteristic quotations from the works mentioned and from the Third and Fourth String Quartets, in which, even though not so general as in the orchestral works, the influence of Stravinsky does nevertheless appear.

Then in the creative period of the thirties the elements referring openly to Stravinsky disappear from Bartók's style, or at least they become so organic that their origins are untraceable. And it is peculiar that when Baroque-like phrases once more make their appearance in Bartók's last creative period, they have no longer anything in common with the Baroque tone which characterized the works of the twenties. The reason for the difference is no doubt that in the twenties it was in the same sense as Stravinsky that Bartók turned towards the Baroque masters, whereas in the period of the Third Piano Concerto and the Solo Sonata he turned directly to the source, principally to the art of J. S. Bach.

But even in this last period there is also one composition in one detail of which it is as if the grotesque Stravinsky tone were appearing for a moment: the violin's syncopated double stopping in the Burletta movement of the Sixth String Quartet reminds us of the folk violin music of *The Soldier's Tale*. This is the same sort of 'waving goodbye' to Stravinsky as the twelve-note theme of the Violin Concerto was a 'farewell' to Schoenberg.

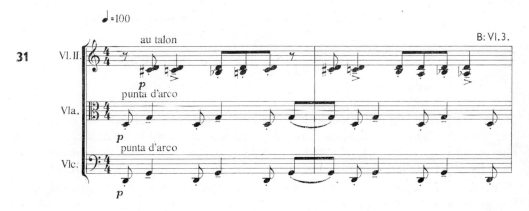

In Bartók's artistic development, in the evolution and consolidation of his style, the problem of reconciling folk music sources and modern means of expression is always present, almost like an *idée fixe*. In this, even though he had definite ideas of his own from the very

61

outset, Bartók gained effective conceptual help from the art of Stravinsky. In one of his American lectures he claimed atonality was an unnavigable route for art nurtured on folk music, but in his study written in 1920, a much more serious conceptual study, he gives quite a different opinion. 'How can this influence of folk music, tonal to its very roots, be reconciled with the atonal trend? It will suffice to make reference to one very typical example: Stravinsky's *Pribaoutki*. The vocal part of this consists of motifs which—even though they have not been borrowed directly from Russian folk music—have taken shape completely in accordance with Russian folk music motifs. The characteristically short nature of these motifs, in themselves without exception completely tonal, provides an opportunity for a kind of instrumental accompaniment consisting of a series of more or less atonal patches quite characteristic of the atmosphere of the motifs. The total effect at all events comes closer to atonality than to tonality.'[41]

In the reconciliation of the folk music influence and atonality, moreover, lies the conceptual antithesis which evolved on a larger scale in the European music of the twenties between neo-Classicism and the Schoenberg school. It is well known that Schoenberg vigorously condemned both folk music inspiration and the neo-Classical style because he saw in them avoidance of the real problems. Bartók and Stravinsky committed both 'crimes' and there is also some inevitability in this. Both aspirations were in a certain sense actually of a defensive nature: one appealed to the great impersonal community, and the other to the great tradition, after the experience of the terrifying crisis of the age. There is also, however, an essential difference between the two: whereas the influx of fresh air brought by folk music did indeed exert a beneficial influence on European art music—and this is best proved by the example of Bartók or the early works of Stravinsky—neo-Classicism brought with it the danger of an unproductive stylistic game.

Without going into a discussion of this antithesis in aesthetics and ethics, which is strictly speaking beyond the limits of this present study, we do have to consider one question. How was it possible for Bartók to take in the influences of both Schoenberg and Stravinsky at one and the same time and unite them in his own art? The stage-displacement outlined above does not really offer an explanation since some of the works of the twenties display a distinct combination of the two influences.

This question is posed even more pointedly by Theodor W. Adorno, who sees in the art of Schoenberg and Stravinsky not only two different creative attitudes but two absolutely basic and fundamentally opposed conceptions of art.[42] If we think of this as a basis, it becomes perfectly understandable that, of all his contemporaries, it is to the influence of these two that Bartók reacted most sensitively. It is scarcely possible to find a composer of any worth in that period who could have avoided the artistic pull of either one or the other. And Bartók shows his artistic greatness to be similar to theirs in that he submitted himself to the force of both of them but at the same time managed to retain his own third independent position. This was considered by René Leibowitz to be a compromise[43], and Adorno also found fault with Bartók for this 'middle' route. In his book *The Philosophy of the New Music* Adorno writes: 'Bartók strove to unite Schoenberg and Stravinsky and the best of his works—as regards density and completeness—even surpass the work of the latter.'[44]

Thus Adorno's interpretation, although his decision favours Bartók rather than Stravinsky, somewhere within itself conceals an element which in the last analysis pushes Bartók's life-work out to the periphery of the musical art of the age. It is in the conception of Schoenberg, of whom he was an absolute supporter, that he sees progress and the only possible way forwards, and the way of Stravinsky being the precise antithesis of this, is regarded as being retrogressive in tendency. And the way of Bartók—in his opinion—is not independent, sometimes following Schoenberg, and sometimes Stravinsky.

In the recognition of the polar positions of Schoenberg and Stravinsky, Adorno is unquestionably right, but the content of their positions cannot be fitted so simply into the 'progression–restoration' antinomy. And what is most important, Bartók standing between them does not vacillate between progression and regression, but takes over and filters certain elements from the art of each of them in order to merge these in a sovereign way into his own art. Bartók therefore made no compromise: he brought about a synthesis. He had no wish to make peace between the two tendencies which really were antithetic, but rather to select from them what was for him important and useful and enclose it in a dialectical unity. His success is not merely the result of his personal talent but is also due to his starting point: he wanted to take care of both the preservation of traditions and also their further development. He was able to bring about this synthesis because he found the point of contact between the legacy of the past and the revolution of the present.

The Folk Music Influence

'The melodic world of my string quartets does not essentially differ from that of folksongs; it is just that their setting is more strict', said Bartók to Denijs Dille in 1937.[45] At first sight this claim might well surprise the reader, as it did Denijs Dille at that time and stimulated him to further questions. For the concentration in the means of expression, the complicated quality of the structure, and the abstractness of the whole conception give precisely the impression in Bartók's string quartets that here it is exclusively the laws of European art music which obtain, and that this refined genre, esoteric in its function as well, is apparently irreconcilable with the simpler world and forms of folk music.

Bartók's statement, however, inspires the research worker to more profound and consistent investigations. No matter how well known the attraction of folk music for the Hungarian master is, and the relationship between folk music and his creative work, the problem is in reality multi-layered, and in spite of numerous articles and studies dealing with the topic, remains unsolved to this very day. As a starting point the study by Bence Szabolcsi which appeared in 1950 should be mentioned in particular; on account of its scope it was scarcely in a position to exhaust the 'horizontal' aspect of the question, but 'vertically' it penetrated very deeply.[46] It showed clearly in what ways this relationship changed, what kind of development it passed through from Bartók's first signs of interest in folk music right to his last period. 'This aesthetics could be introduced most authentically by a separate musicological study: in this way it would become quite clear how interest from the purely artistic point of view is replaced by the desire for scientific clarification; how he was excited from the very outset by the political attitude which became even more blatant from that moment onwards when Bartók—virtually immediately after the beginning of Hungarian folksong collecting—turning against the nationalistic slogans of Hungary in 1908, began Rumanian, Slovakian and Ruthenian collections as well; it would become clear how in the last analysis he extracts, quite beyond scientific problems, a historical, moral and social lesson from folk music: how he sees in it the problems, first, of the nation and the country, and then those of the continent, and finally of all humanity.'

In such a light the classification of Bartók as a 'national folklorist' becomes untenable: this notion does, however, crop up occasionally in a few handbooks discussing modern music now in circulation.[47] The category of folklorism, although in itself signifying no underestimation, takes only second place in the aesthetic scale of values of our age, coming after the creative artists of so-called universal significance. Thus folklorism also means a

64

certain kind of national limitation, since the driving force is generally national, and since the material itself, folk music, generally belongs to one people.

Bartók's life-path also set out in the atmosphere of national aspirations, complete with a national statement of aims: the first aim set was the creation of an independent Hungarian music culture of European rank on the social–political basis of the nation then becoming independent. In the further course of his life, however, he went considerably beyond this first, merely national goal, and it was precisely as a result of his folkloristic research journeys that he arrived at the idea of the brotherhood of men and thereafter inevitably to opposition of Hitler fascism. This broadening course along which Bartók progressed is in itself a contradiction of any classification of him as a mere folklorist.

The problem is, however, greatly complicated by the meeting of two extreme aesthetic conceptions, directly opposed to one another on theoretical grounds, on an essentially faulty platform in the judgment of Bartók's 'folkiness'. The aestheticians of the new Viennese school—above all, René Leibowitz and Theodor W. Adorno—considered Bartók's attraction to folk music a mistake, particularly in that the popular movement and the 'popular' demagogy of fascism brought great discredit to the concept and practice of popular art.[48] They therefore divided Bartók's works into two groups according to what role was played in the individual works by folk music, and all that could be recognized as a masterpiece was what came close in its idiom and technique to the aspirations of the European avant-garde. On the other hand, the Marxist criticism of the fifties confessed this more unambiguously popular branch of the life-work to be its own, and was quite prepared to hand over to the other side the very greatest masterpieces, having branded them as the products of the decadent bourgeois avant-garde.[49]

An interesting point is that both these trends later developed a more liberal, broad branch. The one side became prepared to accept—though only with some pardoning criticism—Bartók's more 'popular' works, and the other side were willing not to discard a significant section of the œuvre, but at the same time they classified it as 'deviation' and considered Bartók a great master of the age in as much as he 'was capable' of resisting the spirit of deviation and finding the 'popular' way.[50]

In recent years a more sober and scientific approach has fortunately begun to come to the surface in both Hungarian and international musicological literature, according to which Bartók's complete legacy is regarded as a unified whole, and in place of screening aesthetics the way of analytical criticism has been chosen. For if the elements of folk music influence are also to be found in those works which to all appearances follow the European tradition and also make even the newest idiomatic aspirations their own, then this means there are not two Bartóks—one keeping close to folk music, a folklorist composer using the material as a source, and another who is a great master of universal influence. There is only *one* artist here, who solved his self-posed problems on various levels and with different degrees of concentration. 'It is necessary to know the melodies of the people as we know them', he said,[51] obviously referring to the fact that the idiom used by him and comprehensible chiefly in a European context has another dimension of even more complete universality: apart from European culture, considerably closed within itself, with limitations of

65

time and space alike, the great traditions of the East, thousands of years old in their background, are also built into his art. That is, as he himself put it elsewhere, he strove for a 'synthesis of East and West'.[52]

This idea gains expression in the chamber music genre as well, and since, by means of its tradition and special texture, it is the string quartet that is related most closely to European art music, those folk music elements appearing there are of greater significance than even those to be found in other genres.

In the works of Bartók's youth, the majority of which incidentally are chamber works, the only Hungarian tone noticeable is still that which had been born as a result of the Hungarian music aspirations of the nineteenth century and which Bartók probably came to know through Liszt's *Hungarian Rhapsodies* on the one hand and Brahms's 'Hungarian'-style works on the other. It is now well known that the origins of these lay in the 'verbunkos' recruiting music and popular art songs—that is, they have nothing in common with the deeper layers of Hungarian peasant music discovered by Bartók and Kodály. It is precisely the First String Quartet which represents the turning point in Bartók's life-work: here the experiences of the first folksong collecting journeys produced their artistic fruit. The many-sidedness of the work is typical—within the framework of the late Romantic melodic and harmonic world, which forms the basic tone of the quartet, two other characteristics are perfectly recognizable: the romantically Hungarian elements pointing back towards the past and the traces of peasant music reflecting new experience and pointing decidedly forward. A good example of the 'backward pointing' Hungarian tone is the cello cadenza in the introduction preceding the third movement, behind the theme of which it is not difficult to recognize the model: Béni Egressy's setting of the *Szózat* (Appeal) or Szentirmay's well-known song beginning 'Csak egy szép lány' ('Just one lovely girl').

In both the first and third movements we can also find examples of the other, the new Hungarian tone. Pentatony is not in itself unequivocal proof of the influence of Hungarian folksongs, for Bartók might just as easily have found that in contemporary French music. Moreover in the central section of the first movement—precisely where one of the pentatonic melodies appears—the influence of Debussy and Ravel is quite conspicuous. That descending melody, however, which characterizes both details, unmistakably evokes a very characteristic type of ancient Hungarian pentatonic melody. It is shown by Bartók's later publication that he noted down one variation of this melody type in Csíkrákos in 1907, with the text 'Romlott testem a bokorba' (My rotten body into the bush).[53]

33

At this time it is characteristic how very uncertainly Bartók still used this melodic material, which contains within it so many possibilities. Indeed he does develop a beautiful arching cello melody out of it in the first movement but it remains an isolated island in this impressionistic and late-romantic environment. But in the third movement he simply does not know 'what to do' with the otherwise effectively prepared melody, and it is only its iambic cadence that he weaves on further (after **11**) or else he merely repeats it (6 bars before **35**).

The influence of folk music shows itself in a more mature way in the rhythm of the third movement. The movement's most important thematic elements can without exception be traced back to one or two typical folk line patterns. It is necessary to note that the line type of seven syllables (see *Ex. 34. b*) is frequent in the folk music of West European countries as well, and it was used even by the classical Viennese masters (for example, by Haydn in his Symphony no. 88 in G major, first movement); but in all probability it was from the freshly discovered Hungarian folksong that Bartók took his inspiration.

34

Taken together, these elements are evidence that in Bartók's First String Quartet the influence of Hungarian folk music is just as conscious and appears in just as important a form as in his later works, and it is merely a case of its not yet being built in so organically.

Several writings, lectures and studies bear witness to the consciousness and deliberateness of the use of folk music. In 'Der Einfluss der Volksmusik auf die heutige Kunstmusik'

(*Melos* no. 17, 1920, pp. 384–386), expressed in various ways, Bartók analyses with scholarly precision the three stages of the building in of folk music into art music.[54] 'The peasant melody, either with no alterations whatsoever or with no more than the slightest variation, is provided with an accompaniment, and possibly placed within the framework of an introduction and postlude.'

Thus Bartók on the first and simplest stage, to which, apart from folksong arrangements simple folksong quotations also belong. Such methods are frequently to be met with in the pre-Bartók literature as well, as witness Beethoven's Rasumovsky Quartets, so as to remain within the framework of the genre. In the string quartets Bartók avoided this method, but it is to be found on several levels in the two Violin Rhapsodies and the Duos for two violins: strictly speaking this series of forty-four duets contains folksong arrangements, absolutely in the style of the piano series *For Children*. Whereas in the piano pieces Bartók employs only Hungarian and Slovakian melodies, in the violin duos Slovakian, Rumanian, Ruthenian, Ukrainian, Serbian and Arab melodies gain a place beside the Hungarian tunes. The two Violin Rhapsodies are a special case in the 'first stage' of Bartók's folk music inspiration: all the themes of both these works stem from actual folksongs, and the majority of these are Rumanian. There are also Hungarian and Ruthenian melodies. Bartók arranged the two rhapsodies into slow and quick movements on the model of the Hungarian *verbunkos* (recruiting music) tradition and created a higher art music form from them; that is, he created a particularly high-level form of folksong arrangement which is really a borderline case between true folksong arrangements and purely art music creations. This sort of absolutely high-level folksong arrangement is not unique in Bartók's work, but whereas in the *Improvisations* the art music intervention virtually completely covers the folksongs, here in the two rhapsodies Bartók reconstructs even the folk manner of performance in the violin part.

In the string quartet genre it was the second mode of treatment that Bartók used, which he described as being 'when the composer does not use actual peasant melodies but invents instead some sort of peasant melody imitation'. In reality, the folk music phrases already quoted from the First Quartet also belong here, for there it is not the complete folksong that Bartók uses but merely a typical detail from it and even that not as a quotation but in an independently expressed form.

A whole bunch of 'folksongs' invented by Bartók himself are to be found in his dance-play, *The Wooden Prince*. In the string quartets and sonatas, however, this is rare, since a closed, folksong-like formal unit cannot be organically built into the higher-level forms. Solely in the trio of the third movement in the Fifth Quartet do we have a complete melody which is folksong-like equally in its melody, rhythm and strophic structure: it comes in a section of the structure which is able to receive this static formal unit into itself without suffering disintegration. Immediately alongside one of the bagpipe-type songs of *The Wooden Prince* (a) may be placed this song verse from the quartet (b) and a folk model for them (c):

The even crotchets of the bagpipe tunes, which change in popular practice according to the syllable values of the language, are modified by the familiar choriambic formula in the melody quoted from the Fifth Quartet, but in comparison with the simpler popular solution the rhythmic formula here is more unusual, for in place of the normal dotting in the proportion of 3 : 1, there is a Bulgarian metre using 3 : 2 dotting.

To the category of self-invented folksongs belong virtually all the themes whose structure resembles that of the strophic structure of the folksong. These themes differ from the above quoted four-line melodies in that reference to the folksongs is more free, the formal and stylistic closedness of the folksong is at some point broken. The following quotation is from the Seconda parte of the Third Quartet: the cello's pizzicato mixtures outline a three-line folksong verse in the dorian mode (a). Even though the three-line verse is fairly rare in Hungarian folk music, the theme is pervaded by a folksong character. A melody which may be placed beside it as 'model' can be found in Bartók's own collection (b).

The two melodies have several features in common: tripartite division, a dome-shaped structure in the verse, the considerable melodic emphasis of the dorian sixth degree, and the tripodic closing line with virtually identical rhythmic pattern. Whether this song or any other song did in actual fact serve as a model for Bartók is a secondary matter. What is, however, essentially important is that this kinship with the not absolutely typical Hungarian folksong is an indication of Bartók's attempts at individualization; that is, that even in his folksong-like composing he usually sought what was unique, what was special. This same endeavour is further proved by the development of the melody four bars later. Here the verse is augmented to four lines, but the means employed for this augmentation is the sequential repetition of a variation form of the second line—that is, once more a method not typical of folk music. At the same time, by retaining the modality of the melody, the tonality is relaxed and the closing cadence of the tune moves over from D to A.

In the Bulgarian-rhythm Scherzo of the Fifth Quartet we meet the following theme, likewise divided into three melodic lines. From the obvious fifth relationship of the first two lines it is not difficult to recognize that on this occasion it was the two-level melodic structure of the ancient Hungarian folksongs that served as model. Within the melodic line, there is obvious melodic relationship.

This double reference indicates the connection. But at the same time Bartók breaks right through the folksong framework, first by placing the typical first and third lines immediately adjacent to each other (as a consequence of which the verse is shortened to three lines), and also by tonal displacement of the third and closing line. In this way, therefore, a quite individual verse structure is produced which can scarcely be claimed as typical of the Hungarian folksong: a fifth-answer variation of Bar form: $A\ A_5\ B$. And beyond this, the Hungarian folk music character is further broken through by the asymmetrical rhythm of the whole melody.

An example of the further combination of fifth-answer structure and a three-line verse is offered by two interrelated melodies of the Fourth Quartet. In both, the third line comes about through the addition of yet another fifth-level. So that the third repetition of the melodic line, essentially identical in content, should not become wearisome, the melody is also enriched by rhythmic variation. Besides this, the impression of novelty is given by tonal mistuning and this also ensures the continuation of the closed verse within the form. Here, too, the principle of Bar form can be discovered, for the third line—even if it is essentially a variation of the first—has a relatively 'Abgesang' effect after the obviously identical 'Stollen' of the first two.

38

A typical example of verse structure consisting of four lines is provided by the scherzo theme in the third movement of the Fifth Quartet. The four lines are separated from each other by a definite cæsura, and the cadence of the individual lines, with the exception of the third, is reinforced by a held note. Both the position of the individual lines and the line cadences unambiguously demonstrate that here we are faced with the typical dome-shaped structure of the new-style Hungarian folksongs. Within this framework, the separate lines themselves also form a dome-like outline. Alongside the fifth-structure of the verse as a whole, each line shows a consistent third-structure, and this is likewise quite characteristic of this type of Hungarian folksong.

39

A similar dome-shaped structure in four sections is to be seen in the broad cello melody in the slow movement of the Fourth Quartet (bars 55–63). Compared to the earlier example, the structure is much more free and relaxed here, the relative positions of the lines only approximately give the outline of the dome-arch familiar from folksongs. The third and fourth lines, weaving in sequences, descend more than two octaves and in this way even the fourth-cadence of the closing line comes lower than the first line. Although the whole melody is a much more complicated construction than the folksongs serving as models, its character is nevertheless unambiguous as a result of the rhythm and the individual fourth-melody.

The above quotations have given examples of the two basic verse-types of the Hungarian folksong—the descending, two-level structure of the ancient songs, and the architectonic

71

structure of the more modern songs. In the second movement of the Fifth Quartet, however, we find a four-line melody which, as far as its structure is concerned, belongs to neither of these basic types. The lines of the melody, with the exception of the last, are of a considerably wide range and their direction consistently changes: the first line is descending, the second ascending, the third descending and the fourth, in the nature of a summary, is ascending and descending. This strophic arrangement, not at all typical of folk music, is, however, completely pervaded by typically folk music elements. In the melody the interval of a fourth plays the leading role. Moreover, the individual lines are consistently built on a fourth basis.

B: V. 2.

This fourth-structure skeleton of the melody displays three connecting methods. In the second and third lines the fourths are conjoint as in a chain, like the 'synemmenon' tetrachords of ancient Greek music theory. The first line is an example of the other kind, disjoint ('diezeugmenon') linking. And the last line is based on the fourths slipping into one another.

Behind the 'disjoint' linking of the first line, contracted into chromaticism, it is not difficult to recognize its diatonic origin, the outline of the two-level Hungarian folksongs. (The phenomenon of contraction into chromaticism will be further discussed in the chapter 'Mistuning'.) The three kinds of fourth connections are very frequently met with in both Hungarian folksongs and in the melodics of Bartók's music.

It is not only theoretically that this fourth-structure of the melody related it to the melodic world of Hungarian folk music. A verse built up in this way can scarcely be found among Hungarian folksongs, but of the individual lines it can easily be demonstrated that they are variations or condensations of certain folksong lines. The first line, for example, can be traced back to the second line of the song beginning 'Megállj, pajtás!' ('Stop, matey') from Vikár's collection (and notated by Bartók), or the first two lines of the song beginning

72

'Kérették nénémet' ('They asked my sister in marriage')—which melody was collected by Bartók in 1910.

42

The fourth-skeleton of the second line can often be discovered in a descending form in Hungarian folksongs. It does occur in this kind of ascending form, but it is rare (Bartók notated this, too, from Vikár's collection).

43

The popular character is perfectly alive in the third line as well. It is, for example, a very familiar phenomenon in Hungarian folk music that the melodic line begins from the ninth above the final note. But a descent of three fourths does not occur in a single actual folksong line, so here it is a question of the condensation of the material of two lines. For example, in the song beginning 'Mikor engem férjhez adtak' ('When they gave me away')—from Bartók's 1907 collection—this area is covered by the second and fourth lines together.

44

The folk music kinship of the last line is the most obvious: it is no more than a cadential commonplace.

45

After such relationships and agreements, it is very important to consider the phenomena which are not typical of folk music and are in direct contrast to it. Such is, above all, the already mentioned mistuning of the 'disjoint' fourth-skeleton of the first line. And, further, such are the individual lines for even if they correspond in some degree to the melodic lines in folk music, they do not come in the same place as in folksongs. The first line of the Bartók melody, for example, is such a vigorous condensation that it already includes the second line of the folksongs, descending to the keynote. The rising second line, ending on the seventh degree, is virtually absurd from the folk music aspect, since it originally has the function of a third line. The third line, as we have seen above, is the compression of the second and fourth

73

lines of a folksong, and so here it is once more a question of a deviation in function. It is only the final lines which correspond with each other in the Bartók melody and the folksong patterns.

It is now also time, in discussing structural imitation of Hungarian folk melodics, to mention the treatment used by Bartók when he takes as a basis for his melody not a complete verse but merely a single folksong line and develops it—not, however, according to the laws of folksong verse structure. In the string quartets, a typical example of this is to be found in the final movement of the Second Quartet. In this oppressive slow movement, radiating a deathly atmosphere, this melody appears with its descending line:

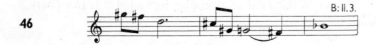

In the background it is not difficult to recognize here that type of the ancient kind of Hungarian folksong which was quoted above as analogous with the melody analysed from the Fifth Quartet (*Ex. 42*). There is, however, an example which comes even closer than this: a Transdanubian lament melody from Kodály's collection:[55]

We can feel this example to be more closely related principally from the function and tone aspects. And indeed here in the Second Quartet is born before our very eyes a type of tone to become very important in Bartók's later art: the lament. The Bartók lament is not merely an imitation of the folk lament. The folk lament melodies only supply one source for this melodic type, in which other elements are also condensed, such as the tradition of art music *lamentos*, naturalistic sobbing, other sorrowful sound effects, and the lonely monologue tone. We encountered this kind of doleful, plaintive outbreak at the end of the first movement of the First Quartet (five bars before the end of the movement), but whereas there the musical idiom of late Romanticism was the means of expression, here in the Second Quartet the mournful, resigned tone is pervaded by the melodics of folk music and the folk lament.

Even if in another sense, similar reference is made to the folk lament by the cello monologue in the slow movement of the Fourth Quartet, and within that principally by the repetitive, chromatic first part:

Relationship with folk music is here shown merely by the declamatory note repetition and the rhythm. The rhythm of Bartók's laments is generally characterized by the accented

74

iambics originating in Hungarian folk music and considerably contrasting rhythmic values. This can be readily observed in the very first bar of the example: in the iambic start there is a 1:13.5 semiquaver proportion between the values of the first and second notes. And in the next motif, in which the iambus is augmented to a fourth pæon (⌣⌣⌣—), a long note with a value of 17 demisemiquavers is connected to the three demisemiquavers. The lament in the second movement of the Sixth Quartet is likewise characterized by this kind of rhythmic contrast. Here it is the fourth-structure of the melody that indicates the relationship with folk music.

B: VI.2.

49

The application of the structural elements of folk music—or, it might be said, the undisguised imitation of folk music—is not confined in Bartók to Hungarian folk music. As a combined result of his folkloristic research work and artistic beliefs, it is possible to recognize in his works the influence of the folk music of all the peoples which came within the scope of his research. Just as in the discussion of the 'first stage', we can refer here, too, to Slovakian, Ruthenian and, above all, Rumanian examples. Among the forty-four duos, for example, we know for certain of two of them that they are not actual folksongs: the Ruthenian *kolomeika*, no. 35, and the Rumanian bagpipe tune, no. 36, were written by the composer himself. And in the First Violin–Piano Sonata and the last movement of *Contrasts* the Rumanian instrumental folk music sound is to be heard—but without using any actual folk melody.

Apart from the single Arab folksong arrangement (the forty-second violin duo) there are numerous Arab imitations in Bartók's music. These have to be discussed separately since after his becoming familiar with the music of the Hungarian and neighbouring peoples there was really only one other discovery which influenced Bartók with similar intensity: that of the folk music of the North African Arabs. The folk music of East Europe, and particularly that of Rumania, 'opened a window' for him towards the musical cultures of the East. Through this window he was able to look more profoundly into the musical world of the East than any of his western predecessors or contemporaries. He was thus given the opportunity to set himself the aim of a synthesis of 'East and West'.

Bartók's visit to the Biskra district of Algeria in 1913 remains to this day a virtually unsurpassed scientific feat. The results of his research were published in the German periodical *Zeitschrift für Musikwissenschaft*.[56] He was the first pioneer of modern ethnomusicology who collected on the spot. And he was also one of the first in so far as he strove in his investigation of Arab music to make a scientific distinction between the musical styles of town and village.[57]

The significance and the creative experience involved in his North African collecting can really be fully understood only when we reflect that Bartók composed *Allegro barbaro* as early as 1911, and thereby raised ancient rhythms of an elemental effect to the level of art music, and with it the ostinato melody composed of small units. It is thus almost symbolic that in the very year when Stravinsky introduced his *Sacre du Printemps* in Paris, the imaginary sacrificial festival of the Russian tribes of pagan times, Bartók was in Africa, getting to know *real* primitive folk music and its authentic environment.

Just as it was possible in the First String Quartet to hail the appearance of the influence of Hungarian folk music, so in the Second String Quartet we can hail the artistic reflection of the experience of collecting among the Arabs as a novelty of similar significance, which can also be found in the Suite for piano dating from roughly the same time. Bartók himself also talks of the use of Arab folk music elements but he mentions only the Suite for piano and the Dance Suite.[58] The following examples may serve as supplementary details to this, in an effort to prove that the influence of Arab music is also present in numerous other works, and especially in the string quartets. The influence can be observed equally in melodies and in instrumentation—which is the same sort of conscious association as the simultaneous use of melodic and structural elements in connection with Hungarian folk music.

The quaver accompaniment and minor third repetition in the second movement of the second quartet is none other than the stylization of the drum effects of Arab folk music. This is borne out by the accompanying part in the forty-second violin duo under the title 'Arab Song'. From this we may also conclude that we ought to seek the origin of other barbaric ostinato kinds of minor third motif by Bartók first of all in primitive folk music, and not in popular art songs by Szentirmay as Kodály attempted to assert in one of his lectures.[59] Below are quotations giving the original Arab melody (no. 15, Biskra collection), the violin duo which arose from it, and the beginning of the theme of the Second String Quartet.

50   a) Biskra Collection no. 15

b) Duo no. 42: Arabian Song

+ = 1/4 higher pitch
o = 1/4 lower pitch

The continuation of the quartet's third-motif then hints even more unmistakably at Arab folk music. In this way it becomes clear that the third-motif is really an augmented second, a typical Arab scale interval. The same can be established concerning the accompanying ostinato of the 'Arab Song'.

The scale composed of the violin duo's two parts is none other than a transposition of the two disjoint tetrachords of the augmented second scale, transforming them into conjoint tetrachords.

$$A\ B'\flat\quad C\sharp\ D\qquad E\ F\qquad G\sharp\ A$$

$$E\ F\qquad G\sharp\ A\ B'\flat\qquad C\sharp\ D$$

We are faced with this same scale in the fugato in *The Miraculous Mandarin*, the Arab character of which is determined by the scale and the melodic line winding upwards and downwards from the centre. Here is the melody and beside it the no. 48 example from Bartók's Biskra collection, which has a similar melodic outline.

B: The Miraculous Mandarin

51

Biskra Collection no. 48

On the basis of the note range, the snaking melodic line and the peculiar rhythm, we can notice Arab influence in a theme from the Fourth String Quartet, which plays an important role in both the first and last movements. Its tone in the first movement is soft and lyrical, which is not in the least alien to a certain kind of Arab folk music, and which type also appears in the Dance Suite.

52

In the last movement this same melody changes to a hard robust dance theme with a drumming accompaniment.

53

In Bartók's music the presence of Arab folk music elements is frequently accompanied by drum effects. In North African Arab and Berber folk music—vocal and instrumental alike—drum accompaniment has an important function. The percussion instruments used in these areas (bandir, tabal) have one feature in common in that the player can produce sounds at two or three different pitch levels. The metrical character of the rhythmic patterns they produce is consequently influenced by the stress (dynamic) and the pitch (colour) together. Bartók's interest was attracted not merely by the primitive, barbaric ostinato rhythm of the percussion instruments but by the frequent appearance of virtuosic polymetrics between melody and accompaniment, or even within the drum accompaniment itself.

The already mentioned second movement of the Second Quartet provides a good example of drum accompaniment imitation in a regular metre; the metrical beat of the parts imitating the drum is occasionally given emphasis by the instrumentation (pizzicato crotchets in the stressed part of the bar) and later the stressed notes are supported by melodic ornamentation (e.g. **8** and **15**). Here the deliberately naturalistic drum accompaniment in the quoted detail from *The Miraculous Mandarin* may also be mentioned.

In the 'Arab Song' violin duo the minor third repetititon is an imitation of the drum accompaniment. When the two-note accompaniment becomes three notes, a polymetric result is produced, which is similar to that found in the original Arab melody which served as model: in the drum part the stresses bring out $\frac{3}{8}$ and $\frac{5}{8}$ units which form a consistent counterpoint to the $\frac{2}{4}$ beat of the melody (see *Ex. 50*).

Similar metrical phenomena are to be found in nos. 58, 59, and 60 of Bartók's Arab publication. In the bandir accompaniment of no. 58, $\frac{2}{8}$ and $\frac{3}{8}$ units alternate in such a way that their total metrical value remains constant. That is, within the $\frac{6}{8}$ metre, a hemiola is produced: $3 \times \frac{2}{8}$ $(=\frac{3}{4})$ alternating with $2 \times \frac{3}{8}$ $(=\frac{6}{8})$. Apart from North African music, this phenomenon is very common in Spanish folk music.

A different kind of alternation of duple and triple units is the basis for the drum accompaniment of melodies 59 and 60. Here two $\frac{3}{8}$ units are followed by one $\frac{2}{8}$, giving altogether $\frac{8}{8}$, in an asymmetrical distribution.[60] A typical Bulgarian rhythm in a non-Bulgarian environ-

78

ment! But the two metric types—the earlier symmetrical hemiola and this asymmetrical metre—are not in the end all that distant from each other: rhythmic theory in ancient Greece—as Curt Sachs demonstrates—included in one category under the name of hemiola all those measures in which duple and triple units were connected.[61]

I have no wish to explain every similar metrical technique in Bartók's music by the influence of Arab music, but there can be no doubt that the drum imitation accompanying the Arab-like melody of the Fourth Quartet got its asymmetrical emphasis as a result of the influence of the Arab metre type quoted above. A better example of the pairing of characteristic Arab melody and rhythm can scarcely be found in all Bartók's works. Besides this example we can quote the two-piano version of the 'Ostinato' from *Mikrokosmos*. In this the composer gives the originally even quaver ostinato an asymmetrical stress in the second piano part, thus bringing about the same $\frac{3}{8}+\frac{3}{8}+\frac{2}{8}$ metric units as in the quartet. On the basis of its melody we feel the 'Ostinato' to be close rather to Rumanian folk music, although it does have something in common with the short motif units of the quartet as well. There are, however, no data to indicate that the metrical phenomenon already discussed occurs in Rumanian folk music too. In his published pieces of Rumanian instrumental folklore Bartók frequently makes a special point of the open fifths played by the violin accompaniment, but he does not mark any asymmetrical displacement of accents. It may be presumed that in the two-piano version of 'Ostinato' he combined the effects of two different kinds of folk music which nevertheless do come close to each other.

B: Ostinato

B: IV.5.

'And finally, the influence of peasant music can manifest itself in yet a third way in the works of the composer. That is, even when he neither arranges peasant melodies nor uses imitations of peasant melodies, the very same atmosphere flows from his music as from peasant music. In such cases one may say that the composer has learned the musical language of the peasant and can use it to such a degree of perfection as that to which the poet uses his mother tongue.' In the already quoted study this is how Bartók describes the third and even higher degree of the use of folk music. At this level we can scarcely look for concrete parallels between art music and folk music as we have done up to this point. The relationships can only be demonstrated by a method of investigation which investigates at two levels simultaneously: on the one hand, among the very smallest structural elements of the music, in the world of musical language's microstructures, and on the other hand in the area of generalized conceptual phenomena abstracted from the actual forms of music as

80

it is heard. That is, in the first case, analysis to the utmost possible degree, and in the second case abstraction in a greater measure than has been necessary so far.

Let us first consider microanalysis. A very important role is played in Bartók's melodic world by single phrases and typical melodic germs from Hungarian folk music, even quite separately from the other melodic and structural regularities of folksongs. It frequently occurs, for example, that some melody with a considerably chromatic, post-Romantic or twentieth-century harmonic background gradually—or quite suddenly—falls into a cadence of folk music simplicity. Both examples of this have been taken from the Second Quartet. The first is a clarifying moment in the first movement's development section, animated and tense from every point of view (a). And the second is the fourth-melody and fourth-harmony theme of the third movement, which in the mirror movement of its lower and upper parts comes very close to Schoenberg's style. The folksong phrase becomes heated at the end of the theme and forms a great contrast to the cold, mysterious fourth-chords. Here, too, is a justification of one of Bartók's statements in which he traces fourth-chords back to the frequent fourth-phrases of Hungarian folk music: the pentatonic system of the melodic phrase is really only the continuation of the continuous fourth-chain of the harmonies (b).

The cadence of the second example (b) is identical note for note with one of the commonest cadence types in pentatonic Hungarian folksongs. This tiny melodic germ of three notes plays a large role in Bartók's melodic world, being so to speak one of the main means of reconciling art music and folk music melodics; or, to put it another way, a means of *idiomatic* use of folk music elements.

81

This three-note melodic nucleus is the meeting point of folk music and art music traditions. As a minute cell, complete nevertheless in itself, constructed with musical logic, it fits into the musical processes. Multiplied and varied, a complete organism can develop from it. Its structure unequivocally relates it to the pentatonic system without semitones, containing as it does the two basic intervals of that system, the major second and the minor third, and through a combination of these two a fourth is produced, which is the 'proto-interval' of pentatonic systems. This three-note system may be considered, in both the historical and the logical senses, the bud, the root of pentatony. Although its use points principally to the ancient-style Hungarian folksongs, it is related by natural connecting threads to all non-semitone pentatonic folk music and is thus a real symbol of Bartók's aspirations towards universality. At the same time this melodic germ, even if only molecularly, contains within itself some important elements of the European art music tradition: the melody-formation proportion and direction laws stemming from Palestrina, and the arsis–thesis pulse relatable to even the smallest musical organism. And finally its asymmetrical structure makes it suitable for taking part in every kind of linear development process.

57

It fulfils an important, almost central, function in the Prima parte of the Third String Quartet. It often crops up elsewhere in Bartók's works, too, and everywhere—sometimes openly, sometimes more discreetly—it evokes the spirit of folk melody. It may also be pointed out that the above motif has approximately the same meaning in its inversions and rotations as well.

58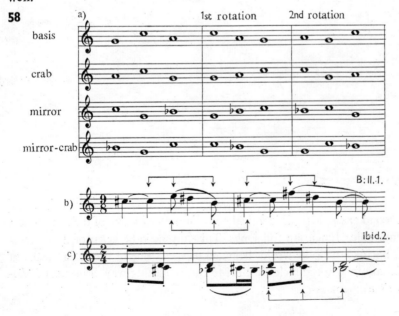

B: III. Ricapitulazione

In the first part of the Third Quartet, where this melodic cell appears as the movement's basic motif, its monothematically elaborated 'proto-motif', we also encounter a characteristic—we might say, inevitable—development of it. The three-note cell is enlarged by a fourth note. Its long chain appears in the fourth-sequences of the Fifth Quartet. The example from the Third Quartet, incidentally, draws attention to an important phenomenon: the four-note motif is really two three-note motifs fitted into one another, in which the major second–minor third structure is symmetrically enlarged by another major second.

59

B: III. Prima parte

B: V. 2.

B: V. 4.

The four-note system thus produced—we can call it tetratony[62]—exists, in the shape of two very characteristic phrases, in the older style of Hungarian folksongs: one is a cadential type, composed of two fourth-leaps, and the second is a line-starting pattern in which the notes are placed as in a scale.

60

Working right through Bartók's chamber works we can find numerous examples of different uses of this tetratonic motif. The scale-like pattern appears straight away in the First Quartet—and indeed in two places. A particularly important part is played by this motif in the first movement of the Fifth Quartet. The nearest relation of the Third Quartet's fourth-structure form is likewise contained in the Fifth Quartet. And another version of the fourth-structure method, which is identical with the folksong cadence type, occurs alike in the Fourth and Fifth Quartets.

It is from development of these three-note and four-note motifs or melodic cells that Bartók's pentatony arises. But this is the point where the examination method reaches its borderline case: minute melodic analysis meets with the abstraction of sound systems and scales. It is common, however, to find in Bartók's music that the actual musical material contains, purely and exemplarily, the abstraction.

Pentatony can also come about through simple complementing and melodic development of the tetratonic melodic nucleus. Indeed, tetratony is really incomplete pentatony, and wherever it occurs it suggests pentatony. The following example shows how Bartók develops the three-note basic motif of the Third Quartet (a, b), and the tetratonic thematic elements in the Fifth Quartet (c), into pentatony.

In the case of the Third Quartet it is very characteristic that the three-note motif is developed chromatically in the exposition and only takes on a pure pentatonic form in the calmer and more static recapitulation—that is, in the Ricapitulazione section, and even there only within a smaller range. The tetratonic theme becomes pentatonic in the development

84

section of the movement—that is, in the most dynamic part, although in a relatively static section within that, when the motif becomes firmly fixed in the area of the tonality of E (bars 104–111). Both examples indicate, therefore, that in comparison with chromaticism pure pentatony is more static, usually having some concluding, rounding off function. (It is quite another matter that in the part quoted from the Fifth Quartet the 'pure' pentatony has another pentatonic layer, displaced by a minor second, as a counterpoint. We shall return to this later.)

Every single appearance of pentatony is isolated. Thus no example can be found where one pentatonic system reigns supreme for a whole movement or even the whole of a formal section. This would obviously mean some impoverishment in the musical material, and it was precisely in the interests of enrichment that Bartók turned to folk music. And so in Bartók's musical idiom pentatony evolves a special relationship with tonal systems possessing greater and richer possibilities—for example, diatony and the chromatic scale. In numerous places pentatony is, as it were, hidden within a diatonic or chromatic texture and can only be discovered by analytic investigation. For example, in the unambiguously diatonic principal theme of the Sixth Quartet, if we disregard the various passing and changing notes, a pentatonic melody is outlined. We are faced with similar hidden pentatony in the trio of the Burletta as well: the pentatonic skeleton of the melody is reminiscent of the mysterious introductory theme in *Bluebeard*.

Another kind of treatment involving hidden pentatony appears in the Bulgarian rhythm Scherzo of the Fifth Quartet. Behind the dorian mode of the second theme in fifth-layers it is not difficult to recognize pentatonic origins, especially as the third and final melodic line does not contain one note outside the system. This third line, however, draws attention to another, no less important phenomenon: by a sudden turn the pentatonic system of the first two lines slides up to a level which is a major third higher (see *Ex. 37*). This points decidedly to Bartók's feeling the pentatonic framework limited from tonal and melodic aspects alike, and he strives after immediate broadening. In earlier examples it has been shown how he places the isolated pentatonic parts within the framework of a wider system. On the other hand this last is an example of one pentatonic system being broken up by another pentatonic system.

85

The simultaneous use of two different pentatonic systems results in a peculiar kind of bitonality. On this occasion, however, the concept has to be interpreted in a wider sense: for the pairing of systems is possible vertically and horizontally—that is, simultaneously and adjacently.

Bartók usually combines vertical pairing with imitation. Good examples can be found of even the 'pre-pentatonic' elements. In the Third Quartet, the three-note motif moves at a distance of a diminished fifth. And in the first movement of the Fifth Quartet two tetratonic levels come together separated by one semitone.

Bitonal piling up of complete pentatonic systems is to be met with in the Fourth and Fifth Quartets.

Horizontal pairing of two pentatonic systems counts as a very special technique: on such occasions the two systems meet within one part—that is, exclusively in a melodic sense. The first example of this is taken from the already quoted Scherzo of the Fifth Quartet. The mentioned three-line folksong theme already belonged to two pentatonic systems as a result of the upward displacement of the third line. But the varied recapitulation of the theme is even more characteristic. Here it is enlarged to four lines and the falling verse structure is replaced by a dome structure. The first two lines move in one related system, but in the third and fourth lines we witness displacement even within the lines. It is scarcely necessary to emphasize how essential the difference between the two methods is: in the first case tonal displacement occurs *between* lines forming a related, closed unity, and in the second case it takes place *within* each line.

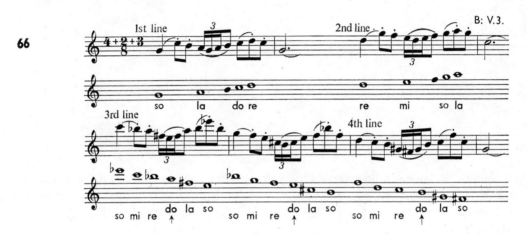

The most classic example of the horizontal pairing of two pentatonic systems is to be found in the last movement of the Fourth Quartet. (Incidentally, this will be discussed from another angle in the chapter on 'Mistuning'.) The movement's principal theme, of an Arab character, is significantly enlarged at one point in the recapitulation (bar 285): it grows to ten bars in length and its range approaches two octaves. In the melody thus developed we can observe two different pentatonic layers: a lower one from A sharp to F sharp, and an upper one from G to G.

So far we have been dealing only with the pentatonic system itself and have not taken its various modes into consideration. But since we have been looking for the characteristics of Hungarian folk music, our examples have been produced as evidence of the pentatonic quality of the ancient Hungarian melodies. With the exception, that is, of the example in which the tetratonic motif develops into pentatony; for this detail of the Fifth Quartet's first movement does not demonstrate the characteristic Hungarian pentatony. Strictly speaking this, too, is a distance scale, for the octave is divided by the regular alternation of major seconds and minor thirds.

$$\begin{array}{ccccc} 2 & 3 & 2 & 3 & 2 \\ E\ F\sharp & A\ B & D\ E \end{array}$$

87

This warns us that in examining Bartók's music we have to deal with pentatony in a wider sense and move beyond the forms of it native to Hungarian folk music. In this respect the most significant new feature is that hemitonic pentatony also finds a place in Bartók, even if it does not appear so frequently as the non-hemitonic forms. In the late works, such as the Concerto and the Viola Concerto, we can hear these kinds of phrases, absolutely free of any 'couleur locale' character.

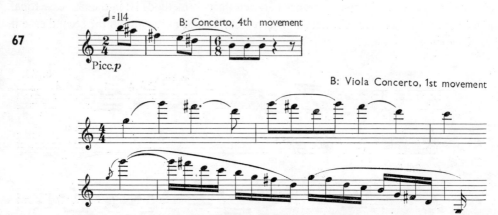

Hemitonic pentatony is, however, a very typical phenomenon in the Far East, occurring in Japan and the Balinesian Islands. Bartók was obviously quite aware of this when he used a composed fragment of the hemitonic pentatonic scale in his piano piece 'From the Island of Bali':

The minor second–major third–minor second structure of the melody is really none other than the other mode of the so called *melog* pentatonic scale of the other two examples, which shows in virtually finished form the model scale consisting of alternating minor seconds and major thirds.[63]

	1	2		4	1
Viola Concerto:	B	C	D	F♯	G

	4	1	4	1
Model scale:	D	F♯	G	B	C

With all this in mind, the principle itself stands clearly before us: using a stage of hemitonic pentatony which is periodic originally, too, we reach the same kind of model scale as the minor third–minor second or the fourth–minor second scales were in the sphere of distance phenomena. Bartók knew this very well, for in the piano piece 'From the Island of Bali' he places closely beside each other, as if they were variations of each other, the fourth–minor second and the major third–minor second forms of the theme.

69

In the course of the piece the fourth form is primary and only later does it become contracted to a major third. But in Balinesian musical practice, the *melog* major thirds are certainly typical, and the fourth form is only an art music abstraction. It is true that Heinrich Husmann, for example, introduces a Java *melog* with the following values:[64]

$$0.87 \quad 1.78 \quad 4.32 \quad 0.62 \quad 4.40$$

Here, too, there is a tendency towards 'expansion': the larger intervals spread 'at the expense' of the smaller. For the major third with the value 4.40 is almost a quarter-tone larger than the tempered form, thus approaching the fourth, while the semitones contract almost into quarter-tones (0.62).

In the *Mikrokosmos* piece in question Bartók was in no way striving after scientific precision and probably did not evolve the programme of the piece beforehand either. In all probability the fourth model supplied the fundamental idea and he connected that on a musical basis with the character of the tropical hemitonic pentatony of the Far East. In any event, this much is certain: he considered the two forms of model scale to be one identical category.

Another manifestation of the fourth model, however, is related by Bartók to Arab folk music. Of the third movement of the Suite op. 14, he himself declared that he composed it under the inspiration of Arab folk music.

B: Suite op.14, 3rd movement

70

The motory rhythm of the movement undoubtedly has much in common with the already discussed drum effects of Arab folk music, but no example of the melodic element of the movement, the fourth model, is to be found in the Biskra collection. It is to be presumed that Bartók freely associated two elements here: the motory rhythmic world of Arab folk music and the vaguely oriental fourth model.

A Far East, tropical atmosphere becomes paired in two other places with the form of the fourth model expanded to an augmented fourth: in the third movement of the *Music for String Instruments, Percussion and Celesta* and in the second movement of *Contrasts*. The instrumentation, with its imitation of gamelan colours, also makes the reference quite unambiguous.

Music for String Instruments, Percussion and Celesta, 3rd movement

71

Contrasts, 2nd movement

In this augmented fourth form the model still remains close to the perfect fourth form, and yet at the same time it is identical with the major third type as well.

72

In the quotation from *Contrasts*, incidentally, the minor third is also heard above the augmented fourth model. The minor third model, which has already been mentioned in another connection, is likewise really a typical and unmistakable stylization of the various oriental scale types. In this case it is principally Arab folk music that has to be taken into consideration, where a scale consisting of alternating minor thirds and semitones is to be found in a natural form, too, and without any stylization whatsoever (see *Ex. 51/b*). The developmental tendency of the Second Quartet also points in this direction; the melodic pattern of the second movement's Arab theme consists of a minor third and a minor second, and from this the composer develops the larger melodic lines of the coda, among which there is, indeed, no precise minor third model scale but the peculiar melody-building aspiration is nevertheless noticeable.

B: II.2.

73

If the stylization process were to be continued, the major second model could be produced from the contraction of the minor third model. But on this occasion this derivation, although permissible in theory, proves artificial in practice. That is, this new model scale does actually evolve in 'From the Island of Bali'—before the listener's very ears—from a combination of two fourth models. This eight-degree tonal system, the roots of which reach back into European art music traditions as well, is also an indirect descendant of the Far East's periodic scales.

90

B: From the Island of Bali

From all this it can be clearly seen in what a masterly and consistent way Bartók developed one or two popular and Eastern art music tonal systems (hemitonic pentatony and Arab minor third model) which served as examples. On this basis to the three models indicated by Ernő Lendvai, which are indeed the most frequent, it is necessary to add the following in both number and interpretation:

major second model (2+1):	Far East expanded melog combination
minor third model (3+1):	Arab scale or contracted melog
major third model (4+1):	Far East melog
fourth model (5+1):	expanded melog
augmented fourth model (6+1):	expanded or inverted melog

These models and the scales evolved from them have a double role in Bartók's music: on the one hand, in association with other elements, they are apt to give a particular work or part of a work its folk character, or adding colour to it; and on the other hand, changing to an idiomatic element, they secure at virtually every point the communal background to Bartók's music, its natural and popular roots. Their purpose is not in the least to produce a certain 'couleur locale': they fit rather on the idiomatic level into Bartók's music and, sometimes, his dramaturgy. To give one example: in the following detail from *The Miraculous Mandarin* the melody moves in the non-hemitonic pentatonic system. The chord mixture of two parallel diminished fifths, however, is essentially nothing but a fourth model. If we consider the latter's relationship with the hemitonic melody, we can claim that in this detail of the dance-play Bartók united the two basic types of Far East pentatony—the non-hemitonic Chinese and the hemitonic Javanese—in simultaneous horizontal and vertical movement.

B: The Miraculous Mandarin

75

And since we have already found Arab elements elsewhere in the dance-play (cf. *Ex. 51/a*), this means we have uncovered no less than three oriental interrelationships in the work.

This mixture of characters and the veiling of the purely Chinese character has a dramaturgical function: Bartók obviously did not want the character of the Mandarin to degenerate into nothing more than a stock figure of a Chinese.

All this is nevertheless of secondary importance in comparison with the idiomatic significance of the application of Eastern or popular tonal systems. For Bartók keeps neither pentatony nor the model scales for the formation of undisguisedly Eastern or popular content, moods or type depiction. As a result of his consistent forming and transforming work these models fit organically into his world of expression as a whole, leaning as it does on western art music tradition, and thus into the different diatonic and non-diatonic modes, and finally into chromaticism. This explains, among other things, why only three of the above listed five models assumed a conspicuous role continuously noticeable throughout Bartók's whole work. For the major second, minor third and fourth models fit exactly into the chromatically divided octave since their totals measured in semitones $(2+1=3, 3+1=4, 5+1=6)$ provide numbers of which 12 is an integral common multiple. As opposed to this, the value of the major third model is five semitones, which cannot be divided exactly into 12, and so it is only 60 semitones (5 octaves) higher or lower than it will reach the starting point of the scale again. And the scale of the tritone model $(6+1)$ comes back to its starting point at an even greater distance (7 octaves)—the lowest common multiple being 84.

It is not only in the melodic and harmonic sense that Bartók uses the three most important model scales: as Ernő Lendvai has demonstrated, he makes them the very pillars of his chromaticism.[65] In this way he approaches in a certain sense serial technique without completely adopting that system's organized quality, which extends to every element.

The important role and significance of these models are indicated by the fact that we have arrived at them as a conclusion in analysing the influence both of Bartók's contemporaries and of folk music. It is here that the creative method inherited from western music and that deliberately taken over from eastern music meet in Bartók's art. The question may suggest itself as to which factor—east or west, folk music or art music tradition—played the initiating role in the evolution of his compositional technique. To give an answer to this would be very difficult since it is probable that he was led thus far by a complicated network of interrelationships in creative practice. And an answer is perhaps not even necessary as in this case it is the synthesis itself which is the essential point: the fact that Bartók's model scales fit just as well into the dodecaphonic chromatic system of European music as into various characteristic scale types of eastern music. Thus when Bartók uses an expressly eastern method, the spirit of European music, matured on tonal tradition but now beyond tonality, is also present: and vice versa—the idiom of his compositions, the style of his music is at every point imbued with the influence of the tonal systems and modality of eastern music—folk music and art music alike.

For this reason it can justifiably be claimed that Bartók was the first composer in the history of European music in whose art the European principles of the West met in a true synthesis with the spirit of the East. His predecessors turned to the East to depict no more than an occasional mood, scene or atmosphere. For Bartók, however, the 'eastern experience' seeped into his whole work. And this is closely related to the maturing of his artistic world: as the sphere extended for him from the melodic world of the Hungarian and neighbouring peoples to his becoming acquainted with the music of the different peoples further away, beyond Europe, the significance of his use of folk music likewise extended and was enriched.

The movement from the more simple towards the more complicated is also expressed by the three degrees—as described by Bartók himself—of the merging of folk music into art music. And this was no mere theoretical statement: he himself carried it out. But to attempt to place these three stages into some sort of chronological order would be to misunderstand the essence of his creative development. The development of a creative artist is a much more complex phenomenon than can be depicted simply with a straight line. Return to an older method and re-composition on a higher level: it is rather thus that Bartók's development can be summarized. And this refers to the development of the creative method stemming from folk music, too. The creative period of the twenties is a good example of this: while Bartók is building folk music into his art on the very highest idiomatic level in the two Sonatas for violin and piano and the Third and Fourth String Quartets, he is composing at the same time 'simple' folksong arrangements, which differ from the first folksong arrangements of 1906 only in their maturity and exigency.

Bartók's relationship with folk music can, however, be characteristically illuminated by another category system. This category system is not completely independent of that outlined above but it perhaps shows the development on a more profound and less technical level.

Here, too, it is Bartók's own words which serve as a starting point. Replying to his critics and opponents in connection with the creative method nourished on folk music, he writes in 1931: 'The fateful error lies in that too much importance is attached to the *sujet*, the theme, which is a completely mistaken viewpoint. These people do not reflect that Shakespeare, for example, did not write a single work the story or theme of which he himself invented... The case of Molière is even more glaring! He took over not only themes but one or two things from the structure of the original texts supplying the themes as well... And what the story, or the theme, is in a literary work, corresponds to the thematic material in musical art. But in musical art, just as in literature, sculpture or painting, it is not the theme used and its origins that are important but *how* it is used.'[66]

The second quotation is taken from an American interview in 1941. 'It is rather a matter of absorbing the means of musical expression hidden in them, just as the most subtle possibilities of any language may be assimilated. It is necessary for the composer to command this musical language so completely that it becomes the natural expression of his musical ideas.'[67]

And the third quotation is from the second of Bartók's articles published in the Berlin *Melos*. '...From the point of view of its influence on higher art music we can consider pure folk music just as much a natural phenomenon as the properties of bodies perceptible to the eye in the visual arts, or the phenomena of life for the poet. This influence can have the greatest effect on the musician if he gets to know folk music not from dead collections... but purely in the form in which it exists in all its unrestrained vigour among the lower people. If he gives himself over to his impressions of folk music and of every similar circumstance, which are the prerequisites of this life, and if he reflects in his work the influence of these impressions, then it can be said of him that he has *recorded a piece of life*.'[68]

These three quotations, in connection with our analysis above and in that order, show quite clearly what folk music meant to Bartók. And the three levels are even less concerned with chronology here—at most only in connection with how the three conceptions were placed *beside one another* in parallel with his creative development and artistic growth.

The essence of the first is folk music as *theme*; the public treasury, the basic type on which the composer builds up his own individual message. When Bartók treated folk music as a theme he was not behaving differently from those of his ancestors—and here it is a question of the very greatest—who similarly evolved their music from the melodic material in general circulation during the period. Thus the profoundly variational spirit of Bartók's art manifests itself not only through the fact that it continuously plays a part in it as a musical development technique, but also through his interpretation of the whole art as variation.

Interpreted according to the second conception, folk music represents for Bartók the possibility and means of communication: *idiom*. By this there is no intention whatsoever of hinting that Bartók's musical language and the language of folk music are one and the same thing. In art, idiom is more than the mere means of communication: it has numerous relations to content, and the language of the great creative artists emerges without exception from everyday language. Bartók, too, created by himself the language of his own art, and not from one source but from several. Among these various sources, however, one of the most important was folk music. For this ensured democracy of communication for him, theoretical and practical connection with a communal tradition, powerful in space and time alike. But Bartók did not merely take over the folk music idiom: he also formed something new and universal. In his transforming intervention a large part was played by the association of the musical idioms of different peoples. It was not just a humanistic programme that lay behind this, 'the idea of the brotherhood of peoples',[69] but a sober statement of practical, musical aims towards the formation of an international musical standard language. Musical internationalism, that frequently occurring cliché, can scarcely be said to cover the whole truth; the language of music has also territorial limits, even if they cannot be defined so precisely as those of nations. This, however, does not matter. The healthy life of a language or a culture is assured by an interchange between its very separateness and its singularity. Among Bartók's greatest scientific distinctions belongs the demonstration of co-existence and mutual influence between the folk music of various peoples. In his study 'Race Purity in Music' he came to such consequential conclusions, among others as the following: '...as a result of uninterrupted reciprocal influence upon the folk music of these peoples there is an immense variety and a wealth of melodies and melodic types...

A complete separation from foreign influences means stagnation: well assimilated foreign impulses offer possibilities of enrichment.'[70] Here is a concise description of the scientific experience which inspired him to the combination of various folk music languages and idioms in his own art, always alongside the priority of the development of the Hungarian musical language and continuous observation of it.

The third conception really contains the two preceding ones and can thus be regarded as Bartók's general attitude to folk music, in the nature of his ideology. There is here no question of popularism, peasant-romanticism, but we know that in certain respects Bartók did come close to this. For him, the village and the peasantry represented closeness to nature, an unspoiled quality, that 'pure source' from which he was able to drink—not only in connection with musical material but also as regards knowledge of life. At the same time there are many documents to prove that he did not idealize this way of life in the least, including as it did so much wretchedness and ignorance.

The quotation is a pointer chiefly in that it shows that folk music meant more in Bartók's thinking than merely a theme or an idiom; in a certain sense it was to assure his immediate relationship with reality itself. This is an attitude of an ideological nature, a true, realistic *ars poetica*, which sets 'the recording of a piece of life' as the task of art.

The realism of Bartók's art is, of course, not determined by this statement, but it is nevertheless characteristic and revealing that this statement of his aesthetics is also related to folk music. For in this connection this means that the humanistic nature of his art lies in his communal and man-centred attitude related to folk music.

But how are these two category systems related—the three levels described by Bartók and the other kind of tripartite division deduced from the life-work? I consider the second to be merely a broader projection of the first and at the same time a kind of summary. This can be clearly seen if the two are placed beside each other:

I Folksong arrangement

II Folksong imitation

}

I Folk music as theme

III Idiomatic assimilation of folk music

II Folk music as idiom

III Folk music as ideology

Thus the first two levels of the first system are merged into one in the second category arrangement, since as far as an individual work is concerned, it is an absolutely subsidiary matter whether its basis is formed by an original melody or an imitation. Folk music's becoming an idiom is striking in both, but whereas in the first system it is the 'final' degree, in the second it is in the middle, a transition. And perhaps precisely because of this the second is more complete, more characteristic: the large role of folk music on the ideological, conceptual level—on the basis of a summary and synthesis of the categories mentioned—is the key to the aesthetic appreciation of Bartók. For this is how it happens that an essential qualitative difference separates his art from the work of other musicians of his time who were similarly inspired by folk music.

95

It was this interpretation on the conceptual level of folk music and the great communal tradition that enabled Bartók to carry out the great synthesis of his period. It was this that gave a broad and secure basis for a revival of the values of the European art music legacy, the worthy continuation of the great tradition, and at the same time for the authentic application of the newest aspirations and technical revolutions. It was this that enabled him to assume the Schoenberg ethical attitude and ruthless facing up to a crisis without the tragic consequences of it influencing his faith in the future of man. Schoenberg's humanism tried to protect no more than the bourgeois culture of Europe, but from the same standpoint Bartók cried out for the whole world.

Monothematicism and Variation

Monothematic structure is to be found in virtually every one of Bartók's composite musical constructions. The monothematicism of the stage works further demonstrates that it is also of dramaturgical significance: not only the structural unity of the composition is secured—the logic of the interrelationships in content is also revealed thereby.[71]

'You have probably noticed that I lay great emphasis on the work of technical development, that I do not like to repeat a musical thought identically, and that I never bring back a single detail exactly as it was the first time. This treatment stems from my inclination towards variation and transformation of themes.'

This is how Bartók describes in one of his statements, already quoted above, his attitude in connection with structure based on variation.[72] Here there is already an indication that variation in the art of Bartók is not a strictly observed formal category but that it permanently goes along with the various musical processes. And for this reason in this chapter the concept referring to development—that is, variation—is examined in relation to the structural concept of monothematicism.

Variation is really one of the very oldest forms of existence in music, being present throughout its whole development from the most primitive folk music to the highest consummation of European musical culture. In comparison with this, the phenomenon of monothematicism moves within much narrower limits: within the framework of sonata form it is *one* formal principle of the so-called Viennese classics, the period of thematic principles. It first comes to light in the works of Haydn and blossoms forth more fully in Beethoven's late period. It is, however, characteristic of its significance that this so-called monothematic, single-theme sonata form also proved the most long-lived classical achievement in the following stage of music history: it was further developed by the nineteenth-century masters and has played a large part in the music of the twentieth century, too.

As a result of the most recent research of form history it is generally accepted today that the sonata based on the monothematic principle is not really a special separate branch of the form but an inevitable consequence of its development, a fuller and more consistent realization of the form principle.

Rudolph Réti has very convincingly shown that the so-called 'inner unity' of the works by the classical masters using a sonata construction is the result of thematic-motivic relationship between the apparently different or even contrasting themes.[73] Thus Beethoven's monothematicism and the romantics' development of it, the cyclic sonata, differ only from the 'normal' sonatas of the classical masters in so far as the monothematicism is more frank and emphasized.

In the development of the monothematic conception after Beethoven, two different tendencies become apparent. The first is romantic and typical of the nineteenth century; to counterbalance the enlargement of the dimensions and the weakening of the formal contours, the central theme demands open, easy perceptibility. The most characteristic type here is the Franck kind of cyclic sonata, in which the work's monothematic system of interrelationships is secured by one or two basic motifs. Strictly speaking, Liszt's B minor Sonata belongs here, too, together with all his symphonic poems based on a single theme.

The other tendency in monothematic structure seems more conservative for, leaning on Beethoven and the other classical masters, it uses a method of thematic interrelationships which is more subtle and possibly only discoverable through close analysis (Schumann, for example).

This is the point where the formal conception of monothematicism and the systematic conception of variation begin to approach each other. It can scarcely be mere coincidence that the greatest master of this monothematic principle—Beethoven—was at the same time the greatest master of variation form: the dynamism of the variational process, continuous change, the dialectic spirit of identity and difference of thought permeated his monothematicism.

So when Bartók made construction formed in the variational spirit and structure based on the monothematic principle the very centre of his art he was committing himself to the two greatest and most fundamental traditions in music: folk music, and the greatest products of European art music. The double variational conception represents two widely different levels of the artistic creative method; folk music is *still* variational in spirit since it does not know any means of recording or fixing a musical idea, or the possibility of a single form. Here variation is truly the form of existence of the music, for every folksong is a single way of performing a melody based on an outline everywhere identical, a unique realization of an imaginary general form. As opposed to this, the classical tradition is *already* variational, inasmuch as it regards continuous and conscious transformation of the material to be the essence of musical creation. Here variation finds an explanation in conscious creative aspiration: to show some thought or other as richly as possible, from within and without, from every side and every angle, in every dynamic form. It is precisely this dynamism that is one of the greatest achievements of Classicism: the shaping of the musical form in such a way that the material should not cohere arbitrarily but that as a result of organic development all new material should be interrelated with what has preceded it.

In the twentieth-century development of form we can see a definite tendency to revive monothematicism in the classical sense. This process is characteristically visible in, for example, the art of Schoenberg; starting out from the cyclic method of Romanticism, the Viennese master arrived at his own less perceptible, but inwardly more organized monothematicism. His first and second quartets are good examples of the exaggerated organicism typical of late Romantic music, where virtually every detail of the musical process is 'bound up' with the complex system of thematic-motivic interrelationships. In Schoenberg's later style thematic relationships are replaced by the serial relationships. But it must never be forgotten that the twelve-note technique itself is the ultimate product of continued development of thematic-organic interrelationships.

The art of Bartók also sets out under largely similar circumstances. Like Schoenberg, he, too, inherited the direct tradition of Romanticism and followed its cyclical pattern in his early works. As early as in the 1904 Piano Quintet there crops up a melody which returns several times, and which bridges over the more important formal sections. The subtle thematic interconnections in the early two–movement Violin Concerto then change to an open, unambiguous monothematic conception in the later variation under the title *Two Portraits*; the two human portraits, developed from exactly the same material, follow a high-level, Lisztian method of monothematic structure.

The First String Quartet offers a beautiful example of cyclic, organic monothematicism. In the form of a four-note motif the work's central idea traces its way throughout the whole composition. In its complete form it first appears in the framework theme of the second movement (a), and then immediately afterwards the principal theme's ostinato accompaniment (b) is formed from its mirror-inversion. Corresponding with this last are the finale's sharp principal theme (c) and its scherzando-like transitional theme—that is, the fugato theme (d).

76

The melodic root common to all these themes is to be found in a four-note figure in which a 'clinging' melodic step is followed by a leap over a larger interval and the motif is completed by another close step, in the opposite direction. In this it is not difficult to recognize the so-called 'cambiata' figure of the Palestrina style, which became crystallized from the disjunctive changing note and its melodic resolution. It must be emphasized, however, that the Palestrina cambiata can be compared with the string quartet's four-note formula exclusively in a melodic sense and quite independently of the harmonic content concealed within it.

77

In the course of later development, and particularly in the functional-tonal style, the changing note ornament, mainly harmonic in content in the modal style, became independent: since it was built up from conjunctive and disjunctive melodic details it was especially suitable for the leading-note support of tonal nuclei. Its outline changed, too: along with its original form, as a result of the laws of linear style, its mirror, crab, and mirror-crab forms also appeared. It is in Bach that the best examples are to be found.

From the structure of the cambiata motif it follows that not only its inversion but also its permutational variations give similar motifs. If the outer notes change places, the line of the melody does indeed change, but its symmetrical structure remains intact. The B-A-C-H theme also belongs here.

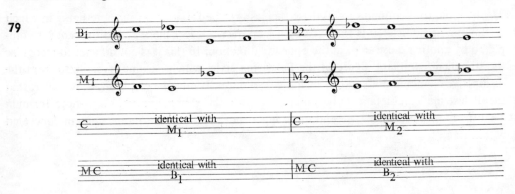

With the tonal application of the motif it went almost inevitably that the two outer 'cling-ing' intervals, depending on the position of the melodic formula, might equally be a minor or a major second. Thus, for example, the version of it to be found in the 'Jupiter' Symphony (the so-called Mozart call-card) contains an upward major second and a downward minor second.

It is to be met with on numerous occasions in Beethoven, too: for example, the F major String Quartet op. 59, and the Adagio of the A flat major Piano Sonata op. 110, or the orchestral Præludium before the Benedictus in the *Missa Solemnis*. But it finds its most significant role in the last string quartets: this is what forms the common thematic root of the B flat major, op. 130, the C sharp minor, op. 131, and the A minor, op. 132, Quartets and the *Great Fugue* op. 133.

80

It becomes quite obvious from the examples that in the majority of cases the cambiata motif comes on particular degrees of the scale—usually on the VII–I and VI–V degrees of the minor scale. Thus the 'clinging' part of the cambiata coincides where possible with the leading note attractions given at the outset by the scale, and the 'leaping' part is formed according to where the motif is positioned in the octave. The interchangeability of the two positions is also demonstrated by the C sharp minor and the A minor Quartets. This type from among the various cambiata motifs enriches with tension–resolution content the dense, balanced musical event offered by the melody. The fundamental idea common to the last Beethoven quartets is, therefore, not merely one melodic idea among many but one of the tersest basic types of melody with a functional content.

However, the tonal–functional content of the cambiata motif began to disintegrate even within Beethoven's own life-work. In the introduction in the B flat major Quartet, for example, the clinging interval does not come about through the system but by way of alteration. An even better example of this is the theme of the *Great Fugue,* obviously connected with the preceding example, the double cambiata of which, with the exception of the cadence, contains altered leading-notes not in the scale.

The theme of the *Great Fugue* is therefore a purely melodic form of the cambiata motif, quite similar to the Bartókian cambiata. In this case the purpose of the chromatic changing notes is not to reinforce the tonal centres but the very opposite—to veil the tonality. This tendency can of course be found even in Bach's chromatic works, for example in the *Kleines harmonisches Labyrinth* or the A minor Prelude from Book Two of the *Wohltemperiertes Klavier.*

It is characteristic of Bartók's endeavours that in the cambiata motifs of the First String Quartet the 'clinging' parts do not reinforce the fifth basis of tonality but move around a diminished or augmented fifth—that is, a mistuned basis.

This brief survey of the harmonic and melodic content of the cambiata motif and its role in history paves the way for a more profound illumination of the monothematic construction of Bartók's First String Quartet. For in the above example only those occurrences of the cambiata motif were quoted in which it played a strikingly emphatic thematic or motivic role. The various versions of the cambiata motif can also be found, however, in the contrapuntal texture of the first movement, although here the figuration does not stand out motivically, remaining hidden within the parts.

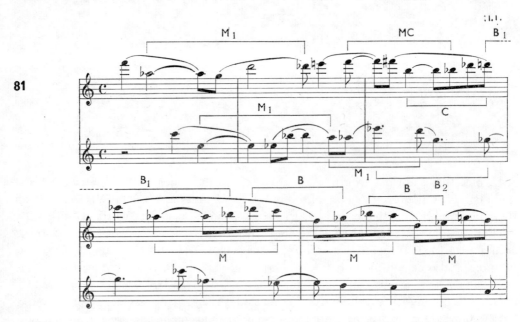

81

This last way of using the cambiata figure really represents a return to its original meaning as it was with Palestrina: the four-note melody formula is a melodic structural element of harmonic function and without any motivic–thematic significance. This explains the peculiar intertwining character of the fugal parts of the movement; for the kind of melody which uses cambiatas so frequently creates the impression of a dense, complicated texture returning back on itself. Between the small intervals, tense larger intervals naturally make the complementary weaving of two pairs of parts possible: the melodic leaps of one part are consistently filled out by the other part.

Thus the monothematic construction of Bartók's First Quartet is a unique example of the central thought being used in two fundamentally different conceptions within a single work: in one part it is an organic, but not emphasized, structural element in the melodic processes; and elsewhere it is a motif of thematic significance—that is, the theme itself.

At the same time this also represents a historical synthesis: the former method is characteristic of polyphonic music, and the latter of homophonic-thematic music.

The cambiata motif also appears in several other compositions by Bartók—and indeed in both its functions: sometimes as a melodic structural element and sometimes within the closed framework of a theme or motif.

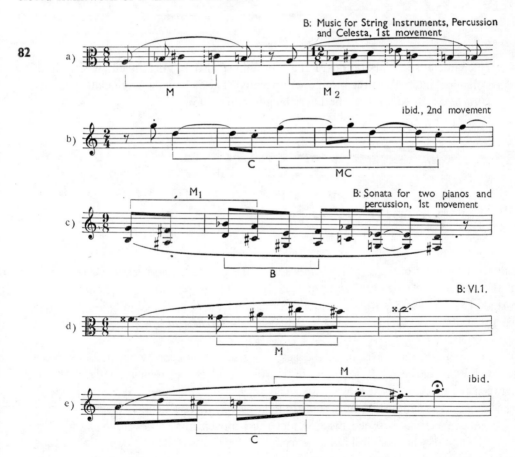

82

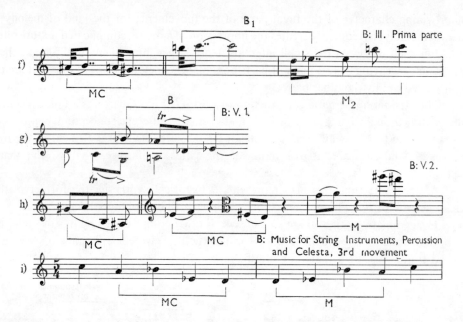

A very characteristic elaboration of the motif must also be mentioned: where the two outer 'clinging' intervals of the motif are duplicated. This is how the gesticulatory motifs of *The Miraculous Mandarin* and the Divertimento come about.

83

Naturally it is not only in Bartók's music that the cambiata motif assumed importance: it was used as a classical principle of melody writing by several other composers of the period. Thus the famous B-A-C-H motif, for example, is to be found in two representative works of the new Viennese school: Schoenberg's *Orchestral Variations* and Webern's String Quartet.

The monothematic system of the Second String Quartet is partly more simple and partly more complicated. It is simpler in that there are obvious thematic interrelationships between the first and third movements. And yet at the same time it is more complicated since other interrelationships only come to light by way of very detailed analysis.

The connections between the first and third movements can be followed along two lines, the first of which is kinship in the melodic line. The two themes, one rising in fourths and the other a descending fourth, are so close to each other that one can scarcely accept the story produced by John Vinton according to which Bartók was not even aware of the thematic connection.[74]

The other connecting thread relates this same first movement theme to the lament theme of the last movement. Outwardly the two themes have a considerably different effect, the first being an arch-shaped melody, whereas the second follows the characteristic descending line of the Hungarian folksong. And yet the inner parts agree note for note, reminding one of César Franck's cyclic method.

84

The monothematic relationship between the two outer movements is therefore doubly founded, and this—also taking the tempo into consideration—indicates that on this occasion the monothematicism is of importance mainly in the structure of the form: it rounds the work into a finished whole. But monothematicism also has another function in the quartet. By means of the common melodic arch all the first movement themes are organically related to each other. Thus the secondary theme is born from the principal theme and its development, and the development of the secondary theme prepares the way for the closing theme.

85

105

This gradual building up of the material, in which relatively remote forms are connected with the help of organic structure, is a typically late Romantic phenomenon and again we are reminded of Franck's cyclic sonata and the Schoenberg method likewise coming close to it (First and Second Quartets). It is also part of this closed organism that the motif of the development section, which strikes us as being something new at first hearing, is strongly related to the cadential part of the main theme.

In the variational system resting on identity of melodic line it is mainly the consistently diminishing amplitude of the arch that appears regular: the line of the principal theme consists of fourths, and accordingly its amplitude reaches a minor seventh; the secondary theme is made up of major thirds and so reaches only an augmented fifth. (A detail from the last movement 'rhymes' with this major third version, where the arch-motif is compressed into a diminished fifth made up of two minor thirds.) And the closing theme, as compared with the seventh of the main theme, is squeezed within the framework of a minor third.

This second system of motivic interrelationships shows that the central movement of the work takes part—even though only indirectly—in the process outlined above. In its first form the theme of the Allegro appears to have nothing in common with the arch-motif just analysed. In later versions, and especially in the melodic figures of the Coda, the arching quality is not so concealed. Here, too, the expansion and contraction of the arch-motif, originally extending to a third, is carried through in a consistent way. Virtually the whole movement is enclosed within the framework of the arch motif: the D-F-F sharp opening gesture at the beginning of the movement is completed at the end of the movement by an

F sharp-F-D motif. The string quartet's system of cyclic interrelationships is therefore consistently complemented by this other system of relationships based on the dome-shaped melodic outline of the arch-motif.

In the Third Quartet there is only one single sign of cyclic monothematicism: in the development section of the Prima parte, as if in anticipation, one of the themes from the Seconda parte appears. And this makes it all the more conspicuous that each of the two parts—and especially the second—forms in itself a very closed monothematic system. The relationship in the Seconda parte thematic material is so obvious that it even leads the analyst astray in his judgment of the form; the sonata-like construction is almost obliterated by the conception of free variational development. The truth is that the three themes of this movement, which is built on the sonata principle, are evolved from the same melodic idea. Here, too, as in the second quartet, the dome-like melodic arch dominates, the essential difference being, however, that here the arch is of much larger proportions and both branches display scale-like straightforwardness in outline.

The variational character lying behind the movement is also reinforced by the fact that of the themes which may be regarded as variations of each other, two (b, c) are varied even within their own scope in the development section and in accordance with the norms of that section. So in this way there are really two variational processes of different dimensions progressing in close relationship with each other: first, ordinary theme-variation based on identity of melodic line, and on the other hand development-like variation of themes, following the thematic–motivic development technique of the classical sonata tradition.

These two do not contradict each other—indeed in certain cases they rather reinforce each other. So, for example, the fugato version of the second theme (b) makes the dome-shaped structure of the theme even more obvious. And the completely chromaticized basis

107

of the third theme (c) (at **40**) proves the principle of 'straight-lined' melody. At the end of the developmental process the themes—now stripped to their bare essentials, to their very skeleton as it were—appear in the glissandos which extend the stepwise quality of the scale to the very limits of absolute continuity.

The abstract melodic outline of the movement, the maqam, is therefore not just the dome arch but, in an even more emphasized form, the *straightly* rising and falling line. What is brought to the surface by the analytical process of the development section has really already been heard *in nucleo* in the movement's introduction. For at the beginning of the Seconda parte, against the background of the horizontal trill organ point, small melodic fragments anticipate the rising and falling straight lines.

The monothematic conception of the Prima parte is not so obvious and for this reason I have left discussion of it until later. It is constructed on the sonata principle, but the thematic material is provided exclusively by motifs of small proportions. The interrelationships between these motifs are only to be found through penetrating analysis. The opening gesture of the main theme serves as a starting point, a small musical idea of three notes. Profound folk music connections were shown in this respect in the preceding chapter.

B: III. Prima parte

90

This three-note melodic germ is given its 'proto-motif' character not only by its having the nature of a 'pre-pentatonic root' as analysed in the preceding chapter, but also by the role it has played in European music. Just as with the cambiata motif, this, too, has two interrelated, but essentially different musical aspects. The first is melodic: the feature characteristic of melody writing in polyphonic styles of linear structure, where a larger intervallic leap is followed and filled in by a smaller interval turning back in the opposite direction. This is perhaps the most classical example of the most concise melodic events of molecular proportions. As a thematic basis it is often to be found in Bach but it is quite at home in Beethoven's thematics as well. Here are a few typical examples.

91

Piano Sonata op. 90

E flat major String Quartet op. 127

Piano Sonata op. 110

Piano Sonata op. 111

B flat major String Quartet op. 130

Thus this small motif from the first part of the Third Quartet, on which strictly speaking the material of the whole movement is based, is firmly rooted not only in folk music but in the European art music tradition, too. But now let us look at how the motif is used. Just as with the cambiata motif, this is likewise equal in value with its inversions.

92

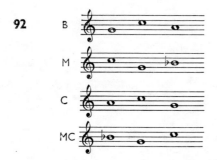

And apart from the inversions, the rotations of the motif have also to be taken into consideration. The first rotation produces a fairly open form, but it is also used less frequently. The second rotation, however, is a very important and frequent version of the original pattern, the only difference being that it is not a third that stands opposed to the leap of a fourth, but a second. If we disregard the actual proportions of the intervals and depict the motif in abstract line form, the latter does not differ at all from the original form.

109

93

This theoretical generalization of the motif has to be supplemented by another generalization: retaining the outline, the three-note pattern has the same significance in wider and narrower forms. The metamorphosis of the motif can easily be observed in the movement: its framework consistently expands from the narrowest form of the introduction, through the 'normal' form of the main theme, to the wide form in the closing theme. In each of its appearances it is the abstraction of the melodic event expressed in a line that is common: one larger and one smaller interval turning into each other combine to make a complete, closed unit.

94

It has already been mentioned in connection with the cambiata motif that its use as a melodic structural element produces the intertwining musical texture of the First Quartet's Lento movement. A similar result is also occasioned by applying the three-note motif in this way, for here, too, the curling back of the melodic line creates a rolling musical texture which revolves round itself.

Now it is possible to see the monothematic structure of the Third Quartet as a complete whole. There is no question of a single musical idea weaving its way through the whole composition: it is a case of two basic principles of melody writing which, in correlation with one another, create a unit. The monothematic axis of the Prima parte is the melodic *circular movement* produced by the texture of the three-note motif, and that of the Seconda parte is *straight movement*[75] realized in the scale theme. Contrasting the two different movement conceptions with each other, their conditionality and complementary function here replace the monothematicism evident in the string quartets which precede this one.

The key to the Fourth Quartet's monothematic system is given by the small emblem-like motif of the first movement. It is functional on a considerable number of levels. After its first appearance in bar 7 it is given canonic treatment in a closed mass and is repeated in this way in the course of the movement, as if filling out the segments of the various formal sections. Its final appearance forms at the same time the end of the movement, and this returns almost note for note at the end of the fifth movement. This identity in the ends of the framing movements is quite a simple solution from the monothematic aspect; it fulfils fundamentally and exclusively a form-building function. When we take all the occurrences of the motif together, we can find the following forms of it: chromatic basic form (a), a larger chromatic form (b), and a quasi-diatonic closing form (c).

The way in which the second main theme of the first movement (which Bartók calls a transitional theme) assumes the leading role in the final movement and is transformed is typical cyclic principle monothematic treatment: the almost rocking theme, at first lyrical and relaxed in rhythm, changes later into a hard, virtually barbaric dance theme, notwithstanding the note for note retention of its melodic structure. This is the same sort of contrasting monothematicism as that in the *Two Portraits*, where the same melodic outline, through use of different rhythms and being performed in different tempos, portrays two contrasting characters (see *Exs. 52 and 53*).

This free and richly imaginative renewed use of unchanging and slightly changing elements secures the relationship between the two outer movements and through this the foundation of the work's architectonic structure. This same architecture is served by the variational relationship between the two inner movements—that is, the second and the fourth.

In the examples which follow almost all the themes of these four movements of the work (1, 2, 4 and 5) are placed beside one another, and from this it becomes unequivocally clear that on this occasion it is once again—similarly to the second part of the Third Quartet—a straight line arch-motif which provides the key to the monothematic structure. It is quite easy to see that the arch-shaped themes or theme-forming motifs, disregarding their rhythmic profile, differ from each other only in their spaciousness and—connected with this—in the basic unit of their scale progressions. (Mirror inversion, in this connection, cannot be considered as a separate variation, since from the point of view of the arch-motif principle rising and descending are of identical significance.) The basic motif is the most compressed form, and every other version is therefore produced by an expansion of it. The most immediate variants have already been shown. The closing theme of the first movement is similarly a close variation of the fundamental motif (b). In the Arab-like theme the chromatic arch expands into a mistuned tetratonic arch (c). In the first movement's group of secondary themes the tight chromaticism of the basic motif is transformed into a whole-tone scale with a very spacious effect (d, e). And finally the theme of the two scherzo-like movements (f, g.) is a chromatic and 'quasi-diatonic' variation of the arch-motif, increasing it to fifth and octave amplitude respectively.

112

If along with all this we also consider that in the dynamic process of the composition these themes and motifs form further variations even within themselves, retaining the rising–descending or descending–rising line throughout, then it becomes obvious that the arch-motif condenses within itself the most basic melodic regularities of the whole composition.

The slow central movement is almost conspicuous by its absence from this closed and tightly constructed monothematic system of relationships. From the aspect of the symmet-rical structure this is perfectly understandable, since this movement is an axis which almost inevitably differs in quality from the structure developed around and about it. But in spite of this the movement is part of—indeed the key to—a system of relationships extending throughout the whole work, one which is much more general than the monothematic struc-ture hitherto discussed, and becomes manifest in an essentially different sphere.

Here it is a matter of a new conception of monothematic relationships which is rooted not in concrete melodic interconnections but in permanence of certain intervals and inter-val-complexes. It is Colin Mason that we have to thank for the working out of this peculiar system, and since it is the intention of this book to give the reader an indication of the most important research results as well, his thought sequence is given briefly below.[76]

Incidentally other interrelationships akin to this had already appeared in earlier works. Thus, for example, in the Second Quartet, fourth-structure formations and those built on the fourth model and the minor third model dominated, in the melodic and harmonic sense alike. All this, however, did not determine the whole work in such a unified way as in the present case.

According to Colin Mason's analysis, all the melodic and harmonic formations of the Fourth Quartet can be traced back to a *row* which is actually heard at the beginning of the central movement, and which radiating outwards from there as it were, fundamentally influ-ences the structure of the whole work. Its upper and lower sections contain a three-note and a four-note whole-tone scale respectively (A, B). It is from this that the work's vertical major second piles also come about. The part produced by the meeting of the two half-rows gives a four-note chromatic row, from which scale chromaticism and complementary chromaticism can equally be deduced (C, CC). And finally the outer notes of the two half-rows explain the origin of the tritone and fourth model (D, DD).

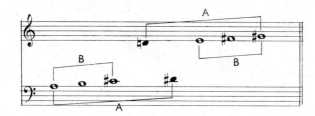

This Bartók method comes very close to the serial technique, at least in so far as the inter-relationship between all the themes or motifs of a work—in the linear and vertical senses alike—is provided by the relationship system existing between certain intervals. There is, however, one essential difference in that with Bartók this 'row', although it is applicable to almost every particle of the work, makes a more free order possible, and does not in addition serve the absolute application of the twelve-tone range.

As a result of its similarly symmetrical construction, the Fifth Quartet offers us numerous monothematic methods which we have already encountered in the Fourth Quartet. Here, however, the first and last movements are not connected by such obvious theme identity as in the former case. Only one single quotation-like element is to be found: in the central section of the final movement—in a way closely resembling the corresponding part of the Fourth Quartet—a variant of the first movement's principal theme appears. Another characteristic similarity is the 'rhyming' between the two outer movements. Here there is indeed no literal identity as there is in the Fourth Quartet, but the tetrachords and opening in mirror movement refer to one another directly enough.

Before making further analysis of the other, and more profound, interrelationships between the two outer movements, it would be wise to examine the interrelationships which exist within the movements. It is possible to discover various kinds of relationship even within the first movement's thematic material, on so very many levels as regards character. The movement's 'leaping' secondary theme (B) is connected to the rising central part of the principal theme by a cyclic principle relationship; the secondary theme, leaping over and over again back to the same support note, makes the same chromatic journey tensing outwards from a minor third to a tritone.

B: V.1.

98

And in the lyrical closing theme entering at C we can recognize the inversion of the principal theme's rising melodic line.

The thematic relationships in the final movement are even more obvious. The two themes making up the first large formal unit are really a variation–inversion of each other. The composer makes immediate use of this ambiguity when he places adjacently to one another the literal note for note inversion (b) and the variated, free inversion (c).

B: V.5.

99   a)

116

ibid.

Further, a very strict motivic connection can also be found between these two interrelated themes and the scale theme which has a rounding off function; this last is no more than a special concentration of the two former.

100

B: V. 5.

This thematic interrelationship, on the other hand, draws attention to the tetrachord motifs which frequently appear in the work. In the final movement this is again quite obvious; apart from the themes already mentioned, they are to be found in the continuation of the contrast theme beginning in bar 202 and strictly speaking the framework motif itself also stems from them. Varied use of the tetrachord motif is also aided by rhythmic elements. Two basic types can be distinguished: one with an unstressed beginning and one with a stressed beginning. That with the unstressed beginning has a metrically rising character, its ending is stressed, and that in itself makes it have a finishing function. That with the stressed beginning, on the other hand, has an unstressed end, and its role has thus rather the nature of an opening. An interesting combination of the two tetrachords is to be found in the last line of the second principal theme where the opening and closing tetrachords appear telescoped into one another (f).

101

117

After this the relationship between the two movements is even more obvious. The rising and descending melodic outline of the first movement's principal and closing themes is related to the melodic outline of the fifth movement's two principal themes. (All the themes appear in inversion as well and so the matter of direction is of subsidiary importance.) The first movement's closing theme, consisting of tetrachords built upon one another, comes very close to the fifth movement's scale motif which has a closing function. And finally tetrachord filling out of the fourths can be observed in all the themes.

102

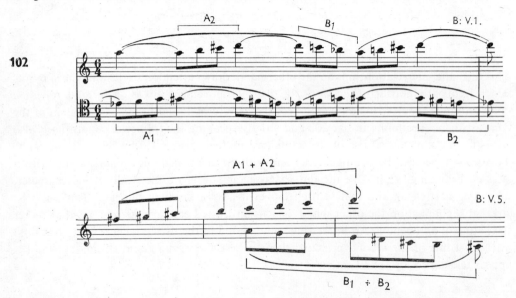

The close variational connection between the two slow movements will be discussed in detail in the course of the formal analyses. For the moment we have to concern ourselves only with the question as to whether their relationship is valid merely with reference to each other or whether they form a part of the monothematic system of the whole work. Now, on this occasion the relationship is not completely self-evident. It is, however, clear that the tetrachord motif has a determining character in these movements, too. We have only to think of the scale theme, surrounded by static chord masses, after the introduction (second movement, from bar 10; fourth movement, from bar 31). Apart from this the accompanying melodic figures of the central folksong theme in the second movement also usually consist of small tetrachord motifs.

118

The most important relationships, however, are to be discovered in the folksong theme in the centre of each movement. Concerning this theme it has already been demonstrated, in connection with its relationship to folk music, that it is based in its every detail on a fourth framework, using separate and interlinking fourth chains. The most important themes of the outer movements are also constructed on these fourth outlines, and so it becomes quite clear that this is where the inner thematic cohesion lies in the four movements of the work.

This system of interrelationships is considerably complex; it cannot be traced back to any single melodic basic pattern or fundamental motif. Here, too, we have to deal with the same sort of thing as in the Fourth Quartet: there is a surface system of relationships which more or less openly connects the material of the movements which can be put in pairs (1–5, 2–4). But behind this there is a deeper system of relationships which essentially reduces all the formations of the four movements to a single interval complex. Encouraged by the example of Colin Mason's 'serial key', we have looked for the 'row' which contains everything in the Fifth Quartet. In this case it is the fifth movement's scale motif, which has a closing function, that gives a 'key' to the outlined thematic phenomena. It has been mentioned above that this theme has been produced by means of a combination of the tetrachord elements of the two principal themes. If, however, we interpret this scale in the sense of an abstract 'seria', then it offers even more complex summations: virtually every melodic detail in the four movements of the work can be extracted from it.

103

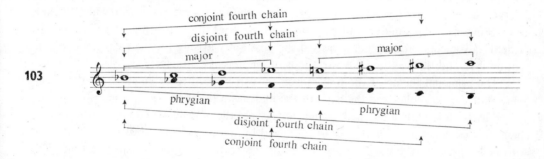

The 'row' consists of two 'disjoint' fourths built one on top of the other, filled out in an alternating way with tetrachords: if the movement is in an upward direction then they have a major nature, and if the movement is in a downward direction, they are phrygian in character. In this way, incidentally, it becomes clear that in a system which has not a bottom keynote but a *central* note, major and phrygian have really exactly the same meaning as each is the mirror of the other. The codas of the first and last movements also provide good examples in this connection. It should also be noted that the major and phrygian are not just one of several possibilities but the solitary possibility within the diatonic tetrachord system, since the other possible diatonic tetrachord structures are identical in mirror inversion (either symmetrical: 2–1–2; or distance: 2–2–2). At the same time the 'row' contains the upward phrygian tetrachord as well (an exceptional case), which in its mirror in-

119

version naturally presents the major. Placing the major and phrygian tetrachords on top of one another produces the complete chromatic range. Apart from this the 'row' also contains the fourth framework of the themes mentioned from the work—that is, both the disjoint and the conjoint fourth chains.

On this occasion the third movement really does remain outside the work's monothematic network. It rises above the rest as a centrepiece, as an element of architectural completion, as a neutral foreign body. Its themes, as opposed to the fourth structure and scale-like melodics (seconds) of the outer movements, are characterized by third and fifth (= two thirds) structure, together with third melodics.

In comparison with the monothematicism of the preceding quartets, the sixth brings a new method. The ritornello melody heard at the beginning of the first three movements and eventually growing into the final movement of the whole work, is not stronger than the earlier methods as regards its unifying effect, but from the 'dramaturgical' point of view it is more open. The evolution of the ritornello theme, the course it travels, will be discussed in detail in the formal analysis.

It is perfectly characteristic of Bartók's creative method, however, that this open monothematicism has another more complicated and more subtle system of relationships weaving its way behind it: the material of the individual movements is connected to the various elements of the ritornello theme by motivic threads. It is well known that Bartók worked on the ritornello theme for a long time, chiselling and polishing it, almost in parallel with the composition of the other movements.[77] All this is no contradiction to the assertions made above—indeed, it rather bears them out. For we are not to take the ritornello which 'includes everything' as being some sort of prefabricated material. It evolves together with the individual movements—it is rather a case of the possibility arising for the elements concealed within it to find the way towards variations of a different character.

The principal theme of the first movement can be said to originate from the closing phrase of the ritornello—on the basis of the indication made by the gradual process composed by Bartók. Only a detailed motivic analysis of the movement would show in its complete fullness what an important part is played by the three-note motif at the end of the ritornello theme in the whole course of the movement. Here, too, it is a question of the three-note motif which played such a large role in the first part of the Third Quartet. The principal theme of the Sixth Quartet's first movement is no more than the building into each other of three versions of this three-note motif.

104

B: VI.1.

This motivic interrelationship is reinforced by another kind of connection: in the rising melodic line with the octave framework it is possible to recognize the second line of the ritornello which has an augmented octave framework. That is, from the chromatic mistuned

120

melodics of the ritornello is born the pure diatonic melodics of the Allegro. (The ritornello extract is transposed here so that the relationship may become easier to see.)

105

Similar motivic and melodic outline connections can be found in the other movements, too. The characteristic opening motif of the Marcia stems from a motif from the second line of the ritornello just quoted. On this occasion it is as if the composer wished to 'unmask' the relationship: at the end of the ritornello he inserts an intermediate chain link in anticipation of the opening motif.

106

The Burletta's 'bear-dance' theme, coloured by quarter-tones, has some connection with the third line of the ritornello—likewise with the aid of interval expansion. Here, too, Bartók constructs the intermediate chain link when he forms the ritornello's descending sequence motif so that it comes closer to the 'bear-dance' theme.

107

When we consider that the Sixth Quartet's first movement was formed from the fourth and second lines of the ritornello, the second movement from the second line of the ritornello and the third movement from its third line, being, as it were, their fuller development over a large area, then it would be logical and inevitable to expect the fourth movement to make use primarily of the ritornello's first line. In this way the individual balance of the piece is set up: in the last analysis the four movement composition is none other than a many-sided unfolding of the principal idea embodied in the ritornello.

121

The various monothematic methods in the string quartets have given a complete and graded picture of Bartók's compositional technique from this angle, from the aspect of consistency and variety of monothematic structures and variational methods. In their survey the outlines of certain new methods and individual creative endeavours have been displayed before us. Bartók's romantic start was influenced by a Lisztian and Brahmsian heritage. But all that did not prevent him from going even further back to draw—as early as in the First String Quartet—inspiration and methods from Beethoven's monothematic technique. From then on, as we have seen, there are in all the string quartets—in parallel with each other or in close relationship, and sometimes exercising organic mutual influence—three or four different monothematic concepts lying behind the system of interrelationships unifying the work. We must now attempt to sort these out from each other and view them systematically.

In the art of Bartók, monothematicism based on *cyclic* principles is characterized by variation of one complete theme. The fundamental melodic structure of the theme remains unchanged or undergoes no more than the slightest alteration. It is, therefore, chiefly its character, its intonational nature or its presentation that changes. To this same type belong thematic interrelationships where some part of the theme appears in an unaltered form but is placed in a different setting, and in this way the meaning of the whole theme is transformed (a technique typical of César Franck). Fine examples of themes which change only in character are offered by the second and third movements of the First Quartet, the first and last movements of the Fourth Quartet (Arab theme), and the Sixth Quartet. And a good example of an unaltered section of melody placed in a different setting can be found in the first and third movements of the Second Quartet.

Bartók frequently uses this cyclic principle monothematicism for the expression of basic contrasts—combined almost without exception with dramaturgical significance. The best examples of this are supplied not by the string quartets but by such works as the *Two Portraits* or *The Wooden Prince*. Both of these compositions are an extension of the principle of Lisztian duality of the Faust–Mephisto variety, showing two contrasting sides of the same phenomenon. The 'dramaturgy' of the string quartets is naturally more abstract; such concrete conflicts or elemental duality can scarcely be found in them, but a generalized aspiration in that direction can. In the thematic relations in the First Quartet, based on the cambiata motif, there also lies the same sort of ideal–grotesque, serious–ironic confrontation as in the *Two Portraits* or in the dance-play. In comparison with the romantic brightness and almost pathetic radiance of the second movement's framework theme, the first theme in the final movement is considerably wry and grotesque. And in the Fourth Quartet the fine, subdued, almost lyrical theme of the first movement returns in the last with a hard dance-like intonation. And finally, the contrast-dramaturgy of the Sixth Quartet's monothematicism scarcely needs explanation: from different details of the lonely, contemplative, resigned melody are born surprisingly a wry march and a mocking burlesque, as alternating contrasts to the central idea.

It is formally characteristic of cyclic principle monothematicism that themes confront themes, and for this reason, although dynamism is not at the outset excluded, this kind of

122

monothematicism is relatively static. We might even say that the melody itself is virtually untouched by variation; setting and character may be altered but the *framework is permanent*.

A relatively more dynamic monothematic principle is in evidence in the first movement of the First Quartet. For here the cambiata motif, which forms the thematic basis of the second and third movements, is contracted into a melodic structural element. In this method, which afterwards assumes even greater significance in the later string quartets, we recognize one of the most important elements of Bartók's compositional technique: *motivic* monothematicism. Here it is no longer a case of whole themes standing in relation to one another, but merely small motifs consisting of three or four notes.

This motivic monothematicism is not by any means an absolute contrast to the cyclic method—it is rather partly a means within it or is complementary to it. In connection with the First Quartet this has already been referred to. In Bartók's creative development, however, this motivic technique frequently becomes independent: the composition or certain parts of the composition are completely pervaded by motif development; that is what directs, as it were, the whole musical process. Good examples of this are the first movement of the Second Quartet, the Prima parte of the Third Quartet, the very varied development of the Fourth Quartet's basic motif in the first and last movements, and the whole of the first movement in the Sixth Quartet.

The technical means of motivic monothematicism are supplied by those of contrapuntal variation–inversions and augmentation and diminution. At the same time there is another means of variation which had been used earlier but which became permanent only with Bartók: 'spatial' expansion and contraction of the motif—with retention of the original interval proportions. This spatial augmentation and diminution might also be called 'projection variation', since the proportional enlargement or contraction of the interval structure can be thought of as being parallel to the phenomenon of projection.

Motivic monothematicism makes use of the most dynamic forms and possibilities of variation. The large role it plays in Bartók is also explained by the fact that development-like motivic-thematic work—as with the masters of the contemporary Viennese school—overflows into the other parts of the composition as well. Instead of the order of closed, complete themes and thematic units, free and non-thematic writing dominates in which cohesive strength is secured by the varied basic motif being built in many different ways. For this reason it can be said that in this conception of monothematic structure everything is dynamic and changeable; it is solely the motif that is *permanent*, as a *melodic structural element*.

Extension of the framework or motivic monothematicism, of which the Second Quartet is an example, leads to so-called *maqam-principle* monothematicism. Taking the basic melodic patterns and melodic outlines of Arab music as a basis, it was Bence Szabolcsi who first used this term to describe certain melodic variations in European music.[78] In the music of Bartók the maqam principle is found in the outline which can be abstracted from the melodic line and in the permanence of this outline. In analysing the Seconda parte of the Third Quartet we demonstrated that behind all the melodic movement lay the rising or descending straight line: this is the movement's melodic maqam. A similar system of inter-relationships is used by the maqam of the Fourth and Fifth Quartets: in the former, from the proportional enlargement of a small arch-motif is born the dome maqam which stretches over the whole work; and in the latter it is the straight-line scale melodies, fourth-framework maqam structures that ensure the structural and conceptual unity of the work.

Maqam-principle monothematicism, like the motivic method, is a purely melodic phenomenon. The large part it plays in Bartók's music is at the same time one indication of his being a comprehensive master as regards melodic traditions; in spite of all tendencies to break things down to small units, he retains the original meaning of the melody, its kinaesthetic significance. Maqam principle monothematicism secures the greatest rhythmic and melodic freedom for the composer; the quantitative relationships between the intervals forming the melody become of secondary importance, and the *only fixed* thing is the abstract *melodic line*, which may also be depicted graphically.

Finally we can see a fourth monothematic principle in Bartók's art in the shape of interval consistency, which is akin to certain simpler forms of *serial* technique. As we saw with the Fourth and Fifth Quartets, there is no question of serialism in the original sense. It is clearly apparent, however, that in these works of Bartók certain fixed interval relations have a differentiated role, providing as it were a key to the work's monothematic system of relationships. Thus the 'seria' does not exist in Bartók as prefabricated compositional basic material, but as a monothematic principle which may be valid in a melodic and a harmonic sense—in other words, in a linear and a vertical sense. In this conception everything changes freely but the *relationship between certain intervals is fixed.*

These four different conceptions of monothematicism are characteristically present throughout Bartók's chamber music, and in this way virtually throughout his whole life-work. The various monothematic ideas and methods appeared and developed largely in the order outlined above. That is, the cyclic method presented itself as a natural starting point, but that he should go beyond that was demanded by the very use of the classical heritage; it was for this reason that Bartók immediately turned to motivic monothematicism. From this, an abstraction of it as it were, was born maqam principle monothematicism, and finally, the last stage in the development, appeared 'serial' principle monothematicism.

This gradual appearance of more and more new monothematic methods, however—and here we can once more grasp one of the important features of Bartók's art—never signified that Bartók gave up earlier principles and methods and moved over absolutely to using the new results. It becomes clear from the analysis that the various new methods bring with them an enrichment of means, and they are organically built in alongside the earlier ones. This is the explanation for Bartók's monothematic richness, too: not one single work is to be met with in which the monothematicism is limited by one kind of method, one kind of conception. In the First Quartet cyclic and motivic monothematicism appear together, and in the Second Quartet the maqam principle also appears in the company of cyclic and motivic monothematicism. The Third Quartet puts the cyclic principle in the background but there is rich development of motivic and maqam monothematicism. And in the Fourth and Fifth Quartets all four are present, and appear closely interrelated with one another.

124

In comparison, the Sixth Quartet is a 'step backwards', for here only three monothematic methods are used together; the cyclic principle comes once again into the foreground accompanied by motivic and maqam phenomena.

This use of several monothematic methods alongside each other not only displays the ever present striving towards synthesis lying concealed in Bartók's work; it indicates at the same time one of the most essential differences between the compositional methods of Bartók and the new Viennese school. It was by approaching from the angle of monothematic aspirations that Bartók came to an individual technique for the serial creative method, and this bears witness to a certain historical developmental inevitability in this creative method. Bartók, however, in possession of this new serial technique, did not, therefore, sacrifice everything else: on the contrary, he brought in the older elements to the service of the new. That he also used the maqam principle along with serial elements, for example, proves that in his music the intervals did not become absolute but retained their original melody-forming significance. Movement 'up' and 'down' primarily possesses melodic content with him, too—which nevertheless does not in the least mean that these directions are not interchangeable, for in Bartók's musical thinking based on the central principle it is precisely mirror inversions that assume importance. His art is, however, characterized by preservation and new interpretation of the real, melody-forming content of intervals.

'Polymodal Chromaticism'

As a natural and direct consequence, the folk music basis of Bartók's art brings modality along with it. Numerous examples have been mentioned—and more will be mentioned in the course of analysis—in connection with how an individual modal melody leaves its stamp on the whole of a movement or formal section. This is, however, only one side of the manifestation of modality. For the phenomenon of modality must not be restricted to the melodic use of church modes. It was modality, as a 'pre-tonal' conception, that character-ized a significant period in the development of European music, and it is virtually inseparably bound up with purely melodic kinds of music—from the folk music of different peoples to Gregorian chant and the art music traditions of the East. It is not possible here to go into a discussion of modality in full historical and theoretical depth, and only its most typical features will be brought out—in support of the thought process which follows.

Modality in the wider sense is not to be thought of as limited to use of the diatonic modes known under the name of 'church modes', for strictly speaking it includes every divi-sion possibility of the octave.[79] In European art music practice, it is chiefly the modes of the diatonic system we encounter, and this is why we—summarily—connect the concept of modality with these.

In Bartók's music modality was the means of avoiding, expanding, or developing major–minor tonality. Bartók's modal attitude would demand a separate study in itself; for the present we shall restrict ourselves to the few aspects which are the premise of the question posed. In this wider conception of modality all notes of the tonal system are equal—this, too, is a step towards free atonality—and the mode is chiefly determined by the inter-val structure between the lowest and highest notes of the melody, and the relationship be-tween the repercussions and final notes standing out from the melody.

A phenomenon connected with the modal conception in Bartók is the diminishing of the role or importance of the keynote of tonal significance and closely related to the tonality system. The note determining tonality, the centre or 'framework' note does not absolutely have to be positioned at the lowest point in the musical texture—it often comes in the middle or uppermost part. This indicates not only that Bartók broke with functional tonality in this respect as well, but also that in its place—even though not exclusively—he set a method which is modal in spirit. For it is one of the fundamental features of modality that it recog-nizes no basic keynote and related to this is the fact that in this kind of musical thinking 'below' and 'above' do not have a decisive role as they do in the functional–tonal system built on overtones. The scales are recorded in a descending form by ancient Greek music theory and numerous eastern music theories.[80]

That in Bartók modality transcends the limits of the diatonic modes is best shown precisely by his 'ultra-diatonic' modes. Otherwise why should he have sought those special scales which sound foreign to the ear of the European musician, which appear to be combinations of different diatonic modes, in which special intervals—augmented second, diminished fifths and augmented fifths—make them different from accustomed tonal associations? In this way he arrived, among other things, at the scale of Máramaros Rumanian folk music which has 'borrowed' its lower tetrachord from the Lydian mode and its upper tetrachord from the Mixolydian mode. He showed such a preference for this scale that for a while the analytical literature called it the 'Bartók scale'.[81] Ernő Lendvai, on the other hand, calls it the 'acoustic scale' on the basis of the emphasis placed on the characteristic degrees of the overtone series.[82] And the latest research by Lajos Bárdos has resulted in showing that this scale is none other than one mode of the tonal system called 'second diatony' (heptatonia secunda).[83] That Bartók did indeed reach this 'second diatony'—even if not on a theoretical basis—is proved by his numerous 'ultra-diatonic' modes—for example the opening line of the *Cantata Profana*, which is not only the mirror of the closing Lydian–Mixolydian scale, as interpreted by Lendvai, but another 'offcut' of heptatonia secunda, another of its modes, as has been revealed by József Ujfalussy.[84]

Similar interrelationships can be observed—though not within one work, but certainly at the level of obviously related works—in the final movements of the First and Second Sonatas for violin and piano. The two dome-structure themes, both of a folk character, are two different—hexachord—sections from heptatonia secunda.

Because of their structure, these scales, although they are from a seven-degree system, contrast even better with major–minor tonality than the diatonic modes do (with the exception of the rarely used Locrian), since they consistently avoid the perfect fifth. A similar result is produced by manipulation of the seven-degree scales in a way which, avoiding not only the perfect fifth but the perfect octave as well, expands the limits of modality in the direction of twelve-degree chromaticism.

Another kind of expansion of the seven-degree systems is represented in Bartók by the oscillation of the degrees within a single melody. To take a typical example, in the principal theme of the Violin Concerto's first movement, the third and sixth degrees of the melody, which is unmistakably in the tonality of *B*, are not fixed: minor and major third and minor and major sixth appear equally. This wavering results in the latent presence of four different modes: namely minor third + minor sixth—the *Aeolian*; minor third + major sixth—the *Dorian*; major third + minor sixth—*one of the heptatonia secunda modes;* and finally major third + major sixth—the *Mixolydian*.

Another very characteristic example is to be found in the *Music*'s last movement, where, in the closing phrase's melody, also static on account of its function, the lower, unambiguously Lydian octave section (y) is answered in the upper octave by a diminished fifth, minor third mode (x).

Before we draw any theoretical conclusions from this phenomenon, it is worth noticing that examples of this kind of degree-wavering are to be found in folk music as well. And here it is not chiefly the well known third-fluctuation in Transdanubian folksongs I am referring to, but to Máramaros Rumanian instrumental folk music. The example quotes melody no. 42 of Bartók's publication.[85]

The great Rumanian folklorist, Constantin Brăiloiu, draws attention to a similar phenomenon in his essay 'Un problème de tonalité'.[86] That Bartók on his own account was consciously aware of this phenomenon from the composer's point of view becomes clear from one of his American lectures—unpublished to this very day. He writes: 'It is very interesting to note that we can observe the simultaneous use of major and minor third even in the instrumental folk music. Folk music is generally music in unison; however, there are areas where two violins are used to perform dance music; one violin plays the melody, the other plays accompanying chords. And rather queer chords may appear in these pieces.'[87]

This wavering of certain degrees is not, either in folk music or in Bartók's music, to be regarded as alteration, in the functional–tonal sense of the word, since here there is no question of some given primary scale, the individual notes of which become altered for this reason or that. The phenomenon is much rather to be explained by the latent presence of several different modes. The mechanical placing of the notes of such melodies alongside each other leads to partial chromaticism, to systems of eight, nine or ten degrees, and the inner structure of Bartók methods shows that this partial chromaticism comes about through the insertion of different modes into each other.

Starting off with modality in the wider sense, we have therefore arrived at the phenomenon of simultaneity of various modes—that is, 'polymodality', as it is called. This is no new observation and no new term in literature connected with Bartók. As early as 1930 the pioneer analyst of Bartók's compositional technique, Edwin von der Nüll, pointed to the so-called 'tonal neutrality' (*Geschlechtslosigkeit*) formed from simultaneous use of the major and minor third, and to the theoretical result of simultaneous use of the church modes, called 'tonal mixing' (*Tongeschlechtervermischung*).[88] This trend in analysis was then somewhat pushed into the background and it was only in 1957 that this same thread was again taken up by Colin Mason in connection with the analysis of the Fourth String Quartet.[89]

Although it does not belong to the Bartók literature, an important contribution to the theme is offered by the Rumanian Gheorghe Firca's work *The Modal Foundations of Diatonic Chromaticism*.[90] With an imposing critical apparatus Firca analyses the works of the East European composers—Bartók, Stravinsky, Enescu, Janáček—and on this basis arrives at the conclusion that the chromaticism produced by them rests on foundations which are quite different from the chromaticism of the Romantic and post-Romantic music of West Europe. Firca's research broadly bears out the view expounded by Bartók in 1921, namely that '... The genuine folk music of eastern Europe is almost completely diatonic and in some parts, such as Hungary, even pentatonic. Curiously enough (in view of this fact)... a tendency (appeared in our art music) towards the emancipation of the twelve tones comprising our octave... (This has nothing to do with the ultra-chromaticism of the Wagner–Strauss period)... for there chromatic notes are only chromatic in so far as they are based upon the underlying diatonic scale. The diatonic element in eastern European folk music does not in any way conflict with the tendency to equalize the value of semitones. This tendency can be realized in melody as well as in harmony; whether the foundation of the folk melodies is diatonic or even pentatonic, there is still plenty of room in the harmonization for equalizing the value of the semitones.'[91]

The decisive word in the polymodality question was, however, pronounced by Bartók himself, although it is well known that it was always very laconically that he spoke of his own work as a composer. It was in the already mentioned study by John Vinton that some later statements by Bartók came to light, for the time being only fragmentarily: one lecture in English written in 1941, and one in 1942–3, together with the foreword to a piano anthology which was never carried through.[92] Of these it is *The New Hungarian Art Music*, dating from 1942–3, that contains the statements which are of greatest value to us. It becomes perfectly clear from this that Bartók used the technique of polymodality quite consciously. Here is one detail from it. 'As the result of superimposing a Lydian and a Phrygian pentachord with a common fundamental tone, we get a diatonic pentachord filled out with all the possible flattened and sharpened degrees. These seemingly chromatic flat and sharp degrees, however, are totally different in their function from the altered chord degrees of the chromatic styles of the previous periods... In our polymodal chromaticism, however, the flat and sharp tones are not altered degrees at all; they are diatonic ingredients of a diatonic modal scale.'[93] Elsewhere, but in the same lecture, Bartók returns to this same theme. 'I must state again to what results the superimposing of the various modes led us. First

129

result: a kind of restricted bimodality or polymodality. Bimodality again led towards the use of diatonic scales or scale-portions (that were) filled out with chromaticized degrees... This modal chromaticism, as we will call this phenomenon henceforward... is a main characteristic of the new Hungarian art music.'[94]

As an illustration of Bartók's words, here are three quotations: an extract from the baritone solo from *Cantata Profana*, an extract from the first movement of the Sixth Quartet, and an extract from the second movement of the Third Piano Concerto. It is common to all three that the fifth or the octave is filled out by superimposition of the Lydian and Phrygian modes upon each other.[95]

To make the true meaning of polymodality quite clear, it is necessary to show counter-examples of the phenomenon. It is not possible to interpret every single one of Bartók's chromatic themes or twelve-degree structures as polymodality. In the rising melody of *Cantata Profana*, formed in a Bachian way, it is the spirit of functional leading-note attraction that obtains and here the chromatic degrees are indeed the products of alteration.

In Bartók's life-work it is also possible—indeed, frequently—to find examples of the musical fabric arriving at chromatic dodecaphony not by means of polymodal treatment of diatonic cells, but—as with the representatives of the Viennese school—the musical fabric

130

makes use of the already given tonal range of the twelve-tone chromatic system. The fugue theme of the *Music*, or the introduction of the Sonata for two pianos for example, can scarcely be analysed on the basis of polymodality.

Although his endeavours are undoubtedly fine, Colin Mason follows an erroneous path in his analysis of the opening bars of the Fourth String Quartet, because he attributes a modal significance to individual isolated notes of the chromatic scale.[96] The phenomenon of polymodality, however, in my opinion, is justified only when connected melodies or at least melodic cells or closed structures separately represent the individual modes.

In the lecture already quoted a statement was made by Bartók himself against another mistaken interpretation of polymodality. 'You can't expect to find a work among ours in which the upper part continuously uses a certain mode and the lower part another mode. So if we say that our art music is polymodal, this only means that modality or bimodality appears in longer or shorter portions of our works, sometimes only in single bars.'[97]

Then there is yet a third misguided interpretation, which crops up with Edwin von der Null and Colin Mason: the theory of simultaneous presence of all the diatonic modes. The outstanding English musicologist demonstrates each diatonic mode to be represented by at least one degree in the first four bars of the Fourth Quartet, and from Bartók's careful segregation of the use of the major third and the minor sixth he draws the following, considerably adventurous conclusion: 'There is no traditional mode with major third and minor sixth, and this suggests that Bartók wished to make it clear that he was not inventing new modes of his own but was simultaneously using all the existing ones.'[98]

Perhaps it is not even necessary to stress the indefensibility of this argument. We should note nevertheless that the major third–minor sixth scale, 'non-existent' according to Colin Mason, is referred to by Bartók himself in one place and this is none other than one mode of heptatonia secunda (see, for example, the principal theme of the Violin Concerto mentioned before).

Simultaneous use of three or four different modes is naturally still a realistic possibility as Erich Kapst has shown of the Bagatelles and the Fifth String Quartet.[99] But it is no accident that Bartók uses the term 'bimodality' so often. For practice does indeed prove that even two appropriately chosen modes are sufficient to break up and develop further the old functional-tonal phenomena, and, in the last analysis, to form the complete twelve-note scale on natural foundations. Of the fair number of aspects involved in the complex of questions posed here I should like for the moment to deal with no more than two—superimposition of major and minor, and bimodality arising from mirror symmetry.

Bartók's creative development was accompanied from an early stage by simultaneous, sometimes even tonally ambiguous use of major and minor. This is present in the First String Quartet as ambiguity between relative keys. This same confrontation of relative keys is also to be found later in a considerably emphasized form in the Marcia movement of the Sixth Quartet. In the case of two pieces from *Mikrokosmos* even the title betrays the composer's intention: in no. 59 the F Lydian and F minor pentachords are used together, and in no. 103 the A minor and B major pentachords. In the latter bimodality is apparently supplemented by bitonality, but in actual fact the B major pentachord does not represent an

131

independent key level—it is reproduced on the A minor level, and as opposed to the minor, the major is in the end represented here, too, by the Lydian mode. Simultaneity of major and minor often appears in the melody and harmony relationship as well. Think of the closing theme in the first movement of the Second Quartet, or the principal theme of the Violin Concerto.

Modal confrontation of major and minor in the chord named the alpha chord by Ernő Lendvai is one of the most frequently occurring phenomena in Bartók's music.[100] Edwin von der Nüll was right when he described this chord with two thirds as being 'tonally neutral' since the major and minor characters mutually extinguish or neutralize each other. But he was not right when he claimed that this neutrality of character deprives the chord of its expressive value.[101] The chord has—on account of its actual structure—the special tension of the diminished octave, and depending on the different ways the notes may be distributed, it has a large expressive range.

Major–minor bimodality, however, became a permanent element in Bartók's musical language not only through one chord but also through an individual scale. What I have in mind is the scale consisting of periodic alternation of minor thirds and minor seconds, referred to by Lendvai as the 1:3 model. Without the slightest desire to refute Lendvai's theory in connection with the distance principle origin of this series, I should like to put forward the possibility of a different origin. In the centre of the first movement of the First Quartet (the end of the trio) a detail can be found in which an adjacent chromatic note is attached to each degree of the B flat major triad. Thus the minor third model comes about not on an inter-key basis but with a definite B flat basis. After this it can justifiably be concluded that the adjacent notes colouring the major degrees have also a minorizing function. And indeed the 3+1 model scale may be the most complete combination of the major and minor modes, since apart from the pillar notes (base–fifth–octave) the scale contains none other than two of the most typical degrees from both major and minor—or more precisely, the Ionic and Aeolian: the major third and major seventh of the Ionic, and the minor third and minor sixth of the Aeolian.

113

In this brief summary of polymodal phenomena, our last theme is the modal significance of mirror symmetry. As has been mentioned already, the structuring in tonal thinking which takes place exclusively from below in an upward direction is joined in Bartók by the freedom of modal thinking. Indeed, musicality based on mirror inversions and centre notes in one sense stands opposed to the tonal conception, since the functional content of a given interval movement depends on whether it is directed upwards or downwards. Bartók's music, therefore, reflects a modal attitude in this respect as well.

132

This kind of thinking based on the symmetry principle, however, already includes polymodality concealed within it, too, for the exact mirror inversion of any melody produces in the majority of cases a change of mode as well. The diagram below shows clearly that, with the exception of the Dorian, the structure of which is identical upwards and downwards, all the diatonic modes are also mirror inversions of each other.

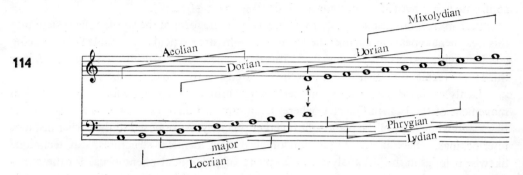

Since this change of mode arises from the non-distance structure of the scales, we can arrive at the same result through the mirror 'reflection' of the heptatonia secunda modes. (A good example of this is the two already mentioned scales from *Cantata Profana*.)

Bartók was very much aware of this phenomenon, for the two pentachords put forward by him are also mirror inversions of each other. And he makes use of this possibility in numerous works: the best example is nevertheless to be found in the Fifth String Quartet, where the whole of the final movement, and partly the first movement, are based on virtuosic motivic development of major and Phrygian tetrachords corresponding to each other in a mirror-like way. In the closing episode of the first movement, in the nature of a summary —and on two occasions, as appropriate to the sonata form—two superimposed layers of major and Phrygian tetrachords produce complete chromaticism. In the last movement there is a scale motif which corresponds to this same detail, where the major-Phrygian complementary filling out points similarly in the direction of chromaticism (see *Ex. 102*). This same phenomenon, related to a common centre, is found in the closing parts of the two movements.

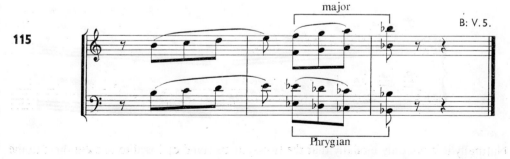

In the style of the modes fitting in this way into each other like cog-wheels, Bartók liked to bring together other complexes as well in the interests of bringing about chromaticism

133

naturally. Traces of this can be discovered as early as in the whole-tone scale theme of the second movement of the First Quartet (after **9**): the six-degree whole-tone scale is accompanied by a chord which is taken from the other whole-tone scale. The result is not yet twelve-degree, only nine-degree, but complementary aspirations are clearly evident in this. Then later Bartók draws the final conclusion when he makes complete six-degree units confront each other (*Mikrokosmos* no. 136: 'Whole-tone Scales').

Perhaps it is not accidental that it is precisely in the form of the whole-tone system that this treatment appears in Bartók; the distance systems are particularly suitable for producing complete chromaticism by being fitted together. The other six-degree system, the minor third model scale, is also such that two can be fitted exactly into each other.

Lastly, a classic example of complementary chromaticism can be found in the central movement of the Fourth Quartet, where pentatony and diatony—in the same way as the black and white keys of the piano—fit together precisely. As opposed to the earlier distance interlockings, where it was a question of absolutely identical structures, this technique likewise belongs in the last analysis to the sphere of polymodal phenomena, for the structures here confronted, pentatony and diatony, meet as 'different modes' in the chromatic system.

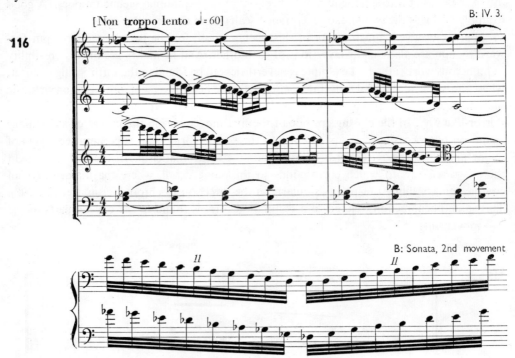

Naturally it is not only modally that the two systems stand opposed to one another; to the notes of a diatony without key signature symbols is linked the pentatony of a system of six sharps (say, F sharp major) or a system of six flats (say, G flat major). Modal superimposition is therefore supplemented by tonal superimposition. In a similar way the major-Phrygian bimodality of the Fifth Quartet only exhausts all twelve degrees because the two tetrachords are linked to each other by one semitone and in this way the unity of the tonality disintegrates. That is, both examples show that the phenomenon of polymodality does not give an answer to every question without being accompanied by a consideration of tonality.

Tonality

The question of tonality in Bartók, although the literature has dealt at relative length with it, has so far received an answer only in part. The reason for the matter being so complicated is that on the one hand Bartók did not make such a radical break with tonal idiom as Schoenberg—to take an example from among his contemporaries; but on the other hand he did not retain such a firm relationship with it as, for example, the neo-Classical French composers. In his harmonic language the elements of the old world of harmony appear in abundance, while from the tonal point of view almost consistent identity of opening and closing notes is present virtually throughout the whole life-work of Bartók. Both phenomena create the impression of harmony and tonality in the older sense, although their real significance only develops fully within the framework of a new system of relationships. Bartók himself also referred to them in his already mentioned study. '...Well thought-out (but not too frequent) use in atonal music of chords from the old tonal phraseology does not conflict with the style. An isolated triad from the diatonic scale, a third, a perfect fifth or octave among atonal chords—in any event only in quite special places suitable for this—still does not rouse a feeling of tonality... Indeed even a whole series of such triads and intervals can be taken as perfectly in style if they are not in themselves tonal. To leave these earlier chords out completely would mean renouncing a not insignificant part of the implements of our art...'[102] And in connection with the other phenomenon, he writes: 'The last step leading to atonality is indicated by those works—disregarding their tonal start and their ending which likewise returns to tonality (in this way, going according to an ancient pattern, they strive towards a unified effect, and try to create a firm framework)—which are atonal in their effect.'[103]

Both quotations definitely indicate that Bartók took into consideration all stages of the development of musical language, and he did not sever the contemporary phenomena at all from his own creative aspirations. Thus when he wrote a study on the problem of tonality and atonality, he not only described the objective phenomena but also—and this can be felt in the study—his own subjective attitude. Even the very first sentence betrays a great deal. 'The music of our time is striving decidedly in the direction of atonality. Nevertheless it does not appear correct to interpret the tonal principle as being the absolute opposite of the atonal principle...'[104]

Thus in the course of examining tonality in Bartók's works it would appear expedient to start out from some ideas which make it possible for us to approach the problem in all

136

its many aspects. The first such idea is that Bartók never considered atonality to be musical anarchy—he rather emphasized that it was precisely the inevitable result of historic development. Secondly, we must regard as a starting point that Bartók was not in the least reluctant to use the atonal way of expression. At the time when he wrote the study for *Melos*, a broader interpretation of the term atonal music was generally accepted: to this category belonged all expressive means which were based on equal use of the twelve chromatic degrees. From his first mature works onwards Bartók used this system augmented to twelve degrees, and—as was demonstrated in the comparison made between him and his contemporaries—in certain periods he did indeed come very close to using this chromatic system in a way which was free from all restrictions—so-called free atonality. And finally the third thought concerns the fact that, once he was able to make free use of the twelve-degree system, Bartók strove to re-establish the role of tonality, but the tonality which he brought about is essentially different from functional tonality in the old sense.

Here, too, it is necessary to emphasize, as in the other analyses so far, that Bartók's art cannot be contained conveniently by one single compositional technique system. An early and surprisingly good explanation in this respect can be read in Edwin von der Nüll's book which appeared in 1930; that he cannot, however, give an answer to everything is due chiefly to his effort to force the phenomena of Bartók's musical language, even though with praiseworthy freedom, into the Procrustean bed of earlier functional music.[105] He accepts the new but explains it from the point of view of the old. I sense the danger of a likewise exaggeratedly unifying system in the works of Ernő Lendvai. The harmony system and axis-tonality theory discovered by Lendvai are undoubtedly one of the most significant products of Bartók research, and a scientific approach to the problem without taking this into consideration would be unimaginable today.[106] The limitations of this theory, however, stimulate more recent investigators not to be satisfied with it. The approach is no longer exclusively analytical, precisely because it is not the recording of individual phenomena that is the expressed aim. There is rather an endeavour to seek out the lines of development and a striving in this respect towards synthesis and the demonstration of the interrelationships between different phenomena discoverable at various points. The main aim, therefore, is to give a more graded and authentic picture—by means of the genetics and dialectics of these phenomena—of this great, comprehensive genius of our own century.

There are a considerable number of aspects to the question of tonality. For this reason, before entering upon a discussion of tonality in the strict sense, we must touch on some phenomena which are indispensable for any investigation of the whole complex, and of which the lessons—directly or indirectly—contribute to a more profound clarification of the problem.

The Phenomenon of Mistuning

The term 'mistuning' was first used in connection with Bartók's music by Bence Szabolcsi in his study on *The Miraculous Mandarin*.[107] This excellent observation supplied a new starting point for the deeper analysis of Bartók's compositional technique. It provided inspiration to examine this phenomenon methodically throughout the whole life-work, taking into consideration and—if possible—forming into a system the various ways in which it manifests itself and the inner relationships in its expressive function.

The phenomenon of mistuning can be traced back to string instrument practice. This is also indicated by the internationally known Italian term *scordatura*. While in the seventeenth and eighteenth century it was used primarily to extend the possibilities of the instrument (Biber, Strungk, J. S. Bach), in the nineteenth century one or two composers resorted to it to obtain special effects. For example, in his *Dance of Death* Saint-Saëns tunes the solo violin's E string to E flat, thereby attaining a formidable, ghostly sound.

Bartók also used *scordatura* in its original sense. In *Contrasts*, the trio for violin, clarinet and piano, dating from 1938, he prescribes G sharp–D–A–E flat tuning for the violinist in the first thirty bars of the last movement. Bartók uses the sound of diminished fifths heard on open strings as an introduction, presumably on the basis of folk music examples.[108]

The original conception of the phenomenon makes the possibility of the expansion of the phenomenon, its wider interpretation, very clear; since *scordatura* generally refers to one or two strings, it is only the pitch of notes played on these that is changed, thus it usually breaks the otherwise 'level' plane of the tonal structure. Continuing the optical comparison, we come to the conclusion that we can regard as mistuning every phenomenon in which a certain distortion is produced as a result of partial alteration of some real or imaginary 'musical picture' or tonal structure.

The word 'distortion' draws our attention to the other root of the phenomenon, no longer practical, but having a figurative aesthetic meaning. In the music of the nineteenth century—chiefly in Liszt—one can observe the variational process, the essence of which is the expansion or contraction of the 'spatial' range—the interval structure—of a theme or motif. This is a natural and logical extension of the augmentation and diminution of the temporal relations—the rhythmic values. In certain cases the expansion or contraction of the interval structure creates the impression that the structure is being distorted, especially if the alteration is partial—that is, if it only affects a part of the structure. Bartók's life-work starts off straight away with a Romantic character-variation—or, rather, caricature, when he quotes the melody of *Gott erhalte*, the imperial anthem, in the 'Kossuth' symphonic poem, first of all in a minor form and then later further distorting this minor form.

Use of mistuning for distorting purposes of this kind in the works of Bartók's youth is still an expressly Romantic legacy which is bound up with a programme. But another trend also appears: displacing one or two notes of the melody presents a possibility to relax the framework of tonality. For example, when at the opening of the first of the *Two Pictures* the note G sharp appears in the oboe melody, this is quite noticeably no more than the mistuning of one degree of the pentatonic melody which opens like a folksong. The G sharp appearing in place of G suddenly tips the melody out of the expected pentatonic framework and fits it into the tonal system of the accompaniment, which moves in the whole-tone scale.

In the introduction in the last movement of the First Quartet the cello solo begins with the fourth motif characteristic of Szentirmai's 'Csak egy szép lány' or Egressy's 'Appeal'. To move out of this folk atmosphere, the composer mistunes the second half of the melody and stretches out the expected octave framework to an augmented octave. Then when it is heard for the second time, the opening fourth is also mistuned into an augmented fourth so as to lead even more decisively into the tonally wavering cadence which follows.

This mistuning technique also appears later in Bartók's art—in the course of an occasional folksong quotation or development of a theme with an obviously folk character. In the *Improvisations* the line-end of the folksong beginning 'Kályha vállán az ice...' suddenly slides upwards. And in no. 116 of *Mikrokosmos* ('Melody') the cadences at the ends of the lines sometimes slide upwards and sometimes downwards.

In the last movement of the Fourth String Quartet we are presented with a classic example of the splitting in two of an imagined pure pentatonic system, of semitone mistuning. The lower section of the melody, developed from a four-note motif, is a pentatonic row extending from A sharp to F sharp, but the upper section is not the natural continuation of this but a mistuned variation extending from G to G.

This treatment of pentatonic systems points to Bartók's endeavours to make folk music elements fit into the higher order art music form not 'in the raw' but as the result of some transformation. Examples can also be found where it is precisely folk music that inspires Bartók to mistune the accustomed tonal structures.

It is one of the chief characteristics of the age of tonality that the foundations of its melody and theme formation—and indeed its tonal system, too—are provided by the fifth-octave relations. Use of the diatonic modes did not represent any essential change in this area, since they, too—with the single exception of the Locrian—have this perfect fifth and octave structure. In Rumanian and Arab folk music, however, Bartók discovered numerous scales in which the melody is virtually completely independent of these acoustic–tonal limitations, and in which it may happen that the basic note has no perfect fifth or octave. Among the small-range Arab melodies the diminished or augmented fifth is almost an every-day phenomenon, and among the Máramaros Rumanian melodies there are some—Bartók himself refers to this in the foreword—in which, as a result of placing two pentachords one above the other, one finds within a single melody F below and F sharp above (no. 42).

Since Bartók draws special attention to both these phenomena, this obviously means that he, too, was particularly sensitive to such irregular elements. He used the lessons to be learned from this in his own melody writing and evolved numerous new scales. Here are a few examples. In the last movement of the First Sonata for violin and piano the theme has a diminished fifth instead of a perfect fifth. In the Second Sonata for violin and piano we find an augmented fifth scale. Diminished and augmented fifth scales appear together in the exciting string crescendo of the finale of the Concerto. Likewise in the Second Sonata we find the sort of thematic development in which the scale-like melody avoids the perfect fifth and perfect octave alike.

B: Sonata no. 2, 1st movement

122

This is also to be observed in one of the important scale themes in the First Piano Concerto.

The 'revolving theme', centred on E flat, in the Seconda parte of the Third String Quartet—which is, incidentally, the most important material in the movement—at first avoids the fifth altogether and then in the fugato variation it touches the diminished fifth.

Regarded from the tonal music point of view, all these instances appear as mistuning for in that kind of musical thinking, no matter how much the melody may be enriched by alteration, the perfect fifth-octave framework is permanent and virtually impassable. Bartók also approaches the problem from this angle—as is shown by the fact that perfect octave-fifth relations were by no means excluded from his theme writing, thus creating the specific meaning for the mistuned form.

As melodic outline and structural factor the fifth-octave framework plays an important part in Bartók's art, particularly in two respects: (1) in folksong structures and (2) in contrapuntal structures. Let us therefore examine these two problems from the angle of the technique of mistuning.

It is more or less general knowledge that Bartók took over not only scales and typical melodic phrases from different kinds of folk music but also structural elements: the line and verse structures of folksongs. Hungarian folk music differs from the melodies of West Europe in more than one respect, but they are identical in so far as the octave-fifth structure plays a similarly large role in both. So when Bartók built on the structural factors of Hungarian folk melody, he inevitably took over line formation with a fifth and fourth framework and the further development of this in an octave framework.

It is a more special but not at all unique phenomenon when Bartók constructs the melody on a mistuned fifth-octave framework—even though the folk origin may be perceptible behind it. Behind the plaintive lament melody in the slow final movement of the Second Quartet, for example, it is not difficult to recognize the line structure of a Transdanubian lament melody from Kodály's collection.[109] Similarly it is possible to compare the first line of the Sixth Quartet's motto melody and the melody of no. 119 of 'The Hungarian Folksong'.[110] In the first example, instead of the perfect octave structure consisting of two fourths there is an augmented octave structure. And in the second example, the perfect fifth framework of the folk melody line is retuned to a diminished fifth.

In these two examples we naturally only imagine or suppose the perfect structure source behind the mistuned melody. In numerous cases, however, the perfect structure form and the mistuned version appear alongside one another in the same composition. A good example of this is also to be found in the Sixth Quartet. The principal theme of the first movement is immediately mistuned in the course of thematic development, and this mistuned form remains in the inversion of the theme as well.

142

A good example of the mistuning of the fourth structure in folksongs is offered by the central melody of the two slow movements in the Fifth Quartet. In the four-line melody, ending on G, the downward displacement of the upper G–D fourth by a semitone is readily noticeable. This theme from the second movement returns in a varied form in the fourth movement. Here the theory of the mistuning of the perfect octave framework is proved: the perfect and the mistuned forms appear alongside one another.

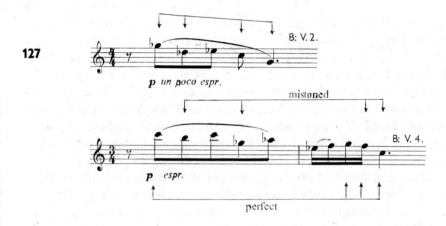

127

To follow the descending fourth structure, here is a fourth structure with a rising line taken from the last movement of the First Sonata for violin and piano. The gradual unfolding of the melody demonstrates very clearly that the composer first of all securely lays the foundations of the lower fourth of the melodic structure and after that builds the upper layer upon this—sliding it down a semitone lower than the diatonic.

128

Mistuning of the division of the octave is to be discovered in the principal theme in the first movement of the Fifth Quartet. One could imagine the melody, unfolding step by step and then ending with a pentatonic phrase, in a closed pentatonic system as well:

129

143

This perfect fifth-octave structure, however, would obviously have been flat and uninteresting for Bartók and so he transformed the melody so that the upper layer slides down a semitone and in this way the augmented fourth–major seventh became the framework of the melody.

130

Bartók uses a similar method to transform—to mistune—the tetrachord structure of the diatonic modes, too. For the double fourth structure of the folksong lines—if the melody is not pentatonic—contains two tetrachords, namely so-called disjoint tetrachords. Now Bartók, without laying a finger on the inner structure of the tetrachords, replaces the whole tone which separates them with a semitone—that is, he tunes either the upper tetrachord lower or the lower tetrachord higher. A classic example of this phenomenon is offered by the last movement of the Fifth Quartet where major and Phrygian tetrachords appear in this way within a diminished octave framework (a). And similar mistuning of major tetrachords occurs in the finale of *Contrasts* (b). It is as a result of this same kind of development that the version of the E flat centred revolving theme of the Seconda parte of the Third Quartet's Coda is produced, where it becomes straightened out into a scale (c). Here we are faced with the mistuning of tetrachords of a minor structure. It is to be noticed that in all three examples the 'dramaturgical' function of the phenomenon is very similar: towards the end of a movement, as a result of some development work, like a summary, the parts become arranged into a scale and in a stretto canon move in parallel or in mirror inversion.

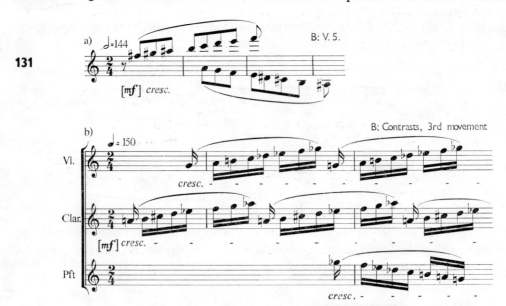

131

As regards structure, the three mistuned scales fit exactly into Bartók's favourite fourth-model.

132

Since two minor tetrachords of identical structure produce, within the framework of a perfect octave, a Dorian scale, we may consider their mistuned form to be a descendant of the Dorian. This mistuned Dorian scale, incidentally, is none other than the periodic scale consisting of alternating whole tones and semitones (according to Lendvai, the 1:2 model). It is not to be claimed that this scale can only have come into being by means of mistuning, for roots can be discovered for it elsewhere, too, but here in the Third Quartet, where the Dorian mode plays such a large part, it is certainly this that provides the best explanation for the genesis of the phenomenon. And beside this can be listed two further examples—no. 33 of the Violin Duos and no. 101 from *Mikrokosmos*. Each is a two-part contrapuntal texture, and apparently bitonal, for as opposed to one part moving within a tetrachord framework the other moves in a tonal plane which is displaced by a diminished fifth. To the *Mikrokosmos* piece Bartók himself gave the title 'Diminished Fifth'. But it is precisely the mistuning which creates the impression of bitonality. Let us try to prove it by a counter-effort! If, for example, we transpose the lower part of the duo a semitone down, the two parts move within a perfect octave framework; hearing this, no one would think of calling this perfect fifth bitonality since in a contrapuntal texture it is a perfectly normal occurrence that one part is imitated or 'countered' by the other at a distance of a fifth.

133

145

For Bartók what is special is naturally that he replaces the perfect fifth counterpart with a diminished fifth counterpart, but this does not mean that here there really are two tonal planes confronting each other at a distance of a diminished fifth: the perfect octave framework has been contracted as a result of the mistuning of one tetrachord or the other.

Besides these two examples unequivocal proof of the phenomenon is provided in the first movement of the Fifth Quartet. Two tetrachord layers move in a similar contrapuntal fabric, but that it is not a matter of diminished fifth bitonality is proved by Bartók's fitting the diminished octave movement in a D–A–D perfect octave framework.

The true contrapuntal forms, however, do indeed pose the problem of the perfect and mistuned fifths. And with this we have arrived at our second large group of questions.

One important permanent factor in invention, fugue and fugato structure with J. S. Bach is the tonal reconciliation of the *dux* and *comes* entering at a distance of a fifth. As a natural consequence of the octave it followed that, for example, if a theme with a fifth framework was transposed a fifth upwards it moved outside the framework of the octave, and as a result outside that of tonality, and so in the interests of preserving the tonality the composer often transformed it into a fourth framework in the plane of the dominant. How strongly Bartók preserved this Bach technique is clearly shown in the 'hunter's fugue' in *Cantata Profana* where the B flat–F incipit of the first and third voices *(dux)* is answered by the F–B flat thematic motif of the second and fourth parts *(comes)*. Bartók, however, not only preserved the tradition: he also transformed it. This sort of effort becomes manifest in his introducing the technique of mistuning into counterpoint as well, when he replaces the perfect fifth answer in many of his fugally structured works by a mistuned fifth answer. As early as in the First Quartet's opening movement he works the imitation so that the major sixth leap of the thematic motif is answered by a minor sixth—that is, after starting perfectly regularly a fourth lower he puts the whole lower part at a distance of a diminished fourth (augmented fifth). He later uses this same diminished fourth canon technique in the first part of the Third Quartet.

136

B: III. Prima parte

In his later works it is another form of fifth mistuning that steps into the foreground. It will be enough to refer to no more than no. 145 of *Mikrokosmos* ('Chromatic Invention'), the 'Chase' from *The Miraculous Mandarin*, the centre of the Fifth Quartet's final movement, or the slow introduction in the Sonata for two pianos and percussion.

Of these two kinds of mistuning the latter is obviously more refined, more classical, because it *solves* the problem of uneven (fifth–fourth) division of the octave by means of the distance principle, the diminished fifth–augmented fourth way of halving the octave, and —although it is built on the twelve-note chromatic system—it removes the danger of toppling tonality over.

The problem posed by contrapuntal forms leads back once again in one respect to folksong structures: namely, the two-layer structure of Hungarian folksongs. The most ancient pentatonic type of Hungarian folksongs, which displays close relationship with the folksongs of other Asian related peoples, has an individual verse structure in which the material of the first two melodic lines is repeated a fifth lower. This fifth layering is naturally not a characteristic which is exclusively found in the folk music of these particular people; obviously it appears in the music of other peoples as well—as a result of the acoustic phenomenon of fifth relationship. In Bartók's melodic writing and also in his structuring of form it is possible to observe this peculiar fifth layering of folksong structures. For our present purposes it is those occasions when the basis of the structure is provided by the mistuned fifth instead of the perfect fifth that are interesting. A very characteristic example of this is the first theme in the last movement of the Fifth Quartet: it is constructed on descending levels in the style of the old Hungarian folksongs, but the material of the first two lines is repeated not a perfect fourth or fifth lower but a diminished fifth lower—that is, on a mistuned level.

Taking all these examples into consideration, therefore, it can be said that in Bartók's compositional technique there is a definite tendency towards the mistuning of perfect octave and fifth intervals, frameworks, structures—either by contraction or expansion. In the compositions of his youth mistuning was still chiefly a means in character variation for producing distorted, grotesque, ironic moods. In the course of further creative development, however, mistuning assumes increasingly great importance, making a break with the distorted-ironic character and becoming one of the chief means of personal expression. This process strictly speaking begins in the First Quartet and reaches its full development in the works of the twenties; by then it is by no means only an occasional episode in the musical fabric, but one of the fundamental components of Bartók's individual musical language.

Behind such a dominating role played by the phenomenon of mistuning lie two tendencies—each closely related to the other: one concerned with technique and one concerned with expression.

The technical trend is closely bound up with the development of the musical idiom: with the breaking down of the framework of tonality and the expansion of the twelve-note chromatic system. In the first decade of this century there appears in the music of both Bartók and Schoenberg, in parallel with each other but quite independently of each other, a denial of perfect fifth-octave structures. In this respect Schoenberg was more consistent than Bartók, for the Hungarian master was held back by the folksong from drawing the complete range of conclusions. But that he, too, progressed in this direction has already been proved by numerous examples. Bartók was inspired towards a twofold method by his close relationship with folk music: first he sought out those places where *the various kinds of folk music themselves step outside the perfect fifth-octave limits*, and secondly he increasingly consistently sought a way in which to fit folk music elements with a perfect fifth-octave structure into the framework of the twelve-tone chromatic system by means of *mistuning*.

There follows just one example as evidence of this latter trend, but this is typical in every respect. In the preceding chapter it was discussed how Bartók's chromaticism was formed chiefly by means of superimposition of different modes—that is, by bimodality or polymodality. One classic example of this bimodality is offered by the Fifth Quartet where two scales which mirror each other exactly—the major and the Phrygian—are superimposed. These two diatonic scales, however, add up to no more than eleven degrees. On the other hand the mistuned form used by Bartók—already referred to above—gives the full range of twelve degrees. Thus in certain cases it is precisely mistuning which makes polymodality a suitable means for achieving complete chromaticism.

So far we have considered the phenomenon of mistuning on the level of scales, melodies and complete structures. There is, however, a manifestation of this phenomenon which affects matters of harmony. An early example of chords which have been put 'out of tune' in Bartók's art is the 'Grotesque' portrait (the fourteenth Bagatelle). The interval structure of the melody does not in itself change in comparison with the 'ideal' form; thus the composer has achieved the transformation into the distorted form by altering the rhythm and the harmony. The melody, transformed into a waltz rhythm, is accompanied by the stereotype two-function chord alternation of waltzes—but in place of the dominant we get an 'out of tune' chord: the most important components of the V^7 chord are mistuned; they are replaced by adjacent chromatic notes.

137

Starting out on this track we find the phenomenon of mistuning in Bartók's harmonic world, too. And as we saw to be the case with melodies and structures, the word 'mistuning' loses its pejorative sense here, too, and the phenomenon, stepping outside the distorted intonation circle shown in the above example, directs attention to important, and indeed fundamental, regularities in the harmonic sphere. Before entering upon deeper discussion of the question, we must touch on Bartók's technique of using 'adjacent chromatic notes', which became so characteristic in his style.

Edwin von der Null was the first to draw attention to this characteristic quality in Bartók's chords.[111] Even in the world of chromatic harmony there appear chords in which some notes are sounded which are foreign to the theoretical structure of the given chord. One of the earliest types is the so-called *sixte ajoutée* which colours the triad in a characteristic way.

In Bartók's chords the adjacent notes also have this kind of colouring function. At the same time Null's analysis demonstrates that the friction of minor seconds, possibly minor second piles, is in many cases a substitute for noise or percussion instrument effects, above all in the piano works. Although this is simultaneous sound if we consider external appearances, it is still not a harmonic phenomenon. In a similar way colouring notes also have significance which is beyond, or just on the border of, harmony: this extension of colouring notes over a larger area is strictly an early form of cluster which is likewise not to be classified as a chord but as an effect.

It is, however, of essential importance that in Bartók's compositional technique adjacent notes have yet a third function, and this is a characteristically individual phenomenon in Bartók's musical idiom: the colouring note which becomes a chord note.

In the central part of the opening movement of the First Quartet we have the following considerably impressionistic sound:

B: I.1.

138

149

Each component of the B flat major triad is coloured by one adjacent note—the root and the third by the lower adjacent chromatic note and the fifth by its upper chromatic neighbour. Here there can be no question of doubting the colouring function of the adjacent notes, although the fact that the structure which is thus produced is none other than a minor third model cannot be considered to be of merely secondary importance either.

Later there is another example, incidentally in the same tonality, where the colouring function of the adjacent notes is considerably diminished. In the closing chord of the Suite for piano—taking the whole work into account—the tonality of B flat can scarcely be doubted. But here the notes are not arranged unambiguously round the major triad as they were in the example taken from the string quartet, since the B flat–C sharp–G flat–A chord (in Lendvai's terms, the G flat alpha chord) is heard equally with the B flat–D major third. Of these notes, the C sharp is the chromatic neighbour of the major third and the A is the chromatic neighbour of the root; and the G flat *would be* the chromatic neighbour of the fifth if the fifth of the chord were heard at all. From this, too, it can be seen that it is not in the least colouring notes that this second level of the chord contains but degrees which are equal in rank with the basic level, their function being to make the harmony complementary. Thus the C sharp really means D flat and is none other than the minor third placed alongside the major and equal in value to it; the A is complementary to the root and the G flat to the imaginary fifth. Then these two basic levels of the chords are joined by two more notes forming a third level—F flat and C flat. The third level has an unambiguously colouring function but this follows rather from their positioning, since, by their note values, these are also neighbouring notes of the root and the missing fifth.

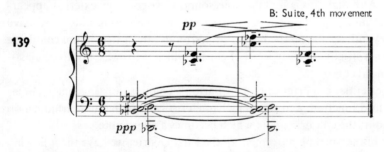

B: Suite, 4th movement

139

The closing chord of the Suite for piano encourages one to draw a further conclusion. We have now for a long time been interpreting the alpha chord as a double third chord in which the major third is underneath and the minor third up above. But in the closing chord we have just been considering, where there can be no doubt as to the B flat tonality, the notes B flat and A cannot be the thirds of some chord with a G flat (F sharp) root. Is it thus possible for an alpha-type chord to be a root position and not a first inversion? It would appear so, particularly if we take into consideration the substitution technique just discussed. On this occasion, therefore, in the chord B flat–C sharp–G flat–A, the B flat is the root, the C sharp (D flat) is the minor third substitute for the major third, the G flat (F sharp) is the minor sixth (mistuned fifth) substitute for the fifth, and the A is the chromatic note adjacent to the root, or its complementary note (a mistuned octave).

150

In the example taken from the Suite for piano, substitution was present only in the case of the missing fifth, and apart from that the adjacent chromatic notes appeared together with their real main-note partners. But other examples can be found where the double third chord can be interpreted as having double roots. The following chord occurs in the First Sonata for violin and piano:

140

The chord's being supported by the held D shows unequivocally that the A flat–D flat–E level is a substitute for the A–D–F level: that is, it has been slipped down (mistuned) by a semitone.

In a similar way in 'The Chase' from *Out of Doors* the ostinato figure contains the tonality of F and not C sharp: the notes G sharp–B–C sharp are the adjacent chromatic notes (substitute or mistuned degrees) of the imaginary major third (A) and the perfect fifth (C); and the E is the complementary note of the root, or a mistuned octave.

141

Seen in this light it becomes clear that two important and characteristic structures in Bartók's compositional technique, the minor third model and the alpha chord, are not just a 'distance scale' and a chord reflecting golden-section proportions (Lendvai), but on the one hand, the complementing of the major triad by adjacent chromatic notes of equal rank, and on the other hand, substitution or mistuning of the triad. In one case the adjacent notes stand beside each other (minor third model), and in the other the new adjacent notes replace the old 'main notes', or we might also say that they mistune the perfect octave-fifth (and major third) structure. And finally the minor third model scale can be broken up into a major triad and its mistuned 'minor' variation, which fits in with the spirit of polymodality just as with that of bitonality (for example, C major–A flat minor).

142

151

With this we have come to one of the basic problems in Bartók's chordal world. Although chords which deviate from third-structure have an important role to play in his work—various kinds of minor and major second piles, fourth-chords and fifth-chords—third-structure does not lose its significance and is not pushed into the background. This is a typical Bartók attitude in the area of compositional technique; by introducing new means he does not exclude the earlier means—for then the range of these means would not be enriched. In his treatment of third-structure chords an entirely new way of using the earlier methods manifests itself very characteristically.

Bartók's third-structure chords can really be traced back to two basic types, one being the four-note chord with a major third and the tension of a major seventh ('hyper-major', to use Lendvai's term), and the other being the Lendvai alpha chord ('golden section chord', according to Lendvai himself).[112] The first of these is not in the least a new harmonic phenomenon, being a seventh-chord on the first degree, which had already won complete acceptance in Romantic and post-Romantic music, and which, typically, appears particularly frequently in the works of Bartók's youth—an unambiguous reflection in Bartók's art of his affiliation with the Romantic harmonic world—especially the harmonic language of Wagner and Richard Strauss.

Although within the framework of the major seventh there may be some wavering as regards the third—and sometimes the fifth—this chord type is chiefly characterized by its major third and perfect fifth. Indeed in its own inner structure both of these occur twice, because the seventh is the perfect fifth of the third and also the major third of the perfect fifth.

The other chord type has chiefly been interpreted as a double third-chord by Bartók research, and there can be no desire to doubt the correctness of this interpretation—indeed this origin of the phenomenon has been even further emphasized in connection with the phenomenon of polymodality. The question is, however, whether the simultaneous presence of the two tonal types is so dominating in the case of the already *evolved* chord type. Whether the inversion into a diminished octave (major seventh) of the major and minor third clash (semitone interval) does not decrease the contrast between the tonal types.

In the course of the analysis given above, as a result of Bartók's adjacent chromatic note technique and the substitution or mistuning technique related to it, we have reached a position where we also interpret this chord in a different way. Some help is also offered towards this new interpretation by the correlation of the major seventh major chord. For if an important role is played in Bartók's musical language by a chord which is major in its every particle (justifiably named 'hyper-major' by Lendvai), the other basic type, which in a certain sense provides a contrast to the first, is not a chord 'without tone species' (to use Null's expression) which mixes major and minor, but a chord which is minor in its every particle—we might say 'hyper-minor'.[113]

We can repeat the claim—with the insertion of a new viewpoint—that in the chord in question the major third is replaced by the minor third and the perfect fifth by the augmented fifth (and together with this, the diminished fifth). The diminished octave may be interpreted in two ways: it may signify the mistuning of the perfect octave, but taken from the

152

major seventh major chord angle it may be the same kind of permanent framework in Bartók chords as the perfect fifth was in the earlier period. That is, within this interval framework of eleven semitones (major seventh or diminished octave), chord structures of varied meaning appear: there is one which has an emphatically acoustic, major character dominated by the major third and perfect fifth, and another which has an emphatically minor character dominated by those intervals which differ from the acoustic and indeed stand directly opposed to it—the minor third and the diminished and augmented fifths. And we have already noticed that Bartók formed fourth-chords so that an augmented fourth should if possible be connected to a perfect fourth and so that in this way this chord, too, should fit within the major seventh framework.

143

What comes into the foreground even better in the course of investigating these chord types is the function and meaning of individual intervals. Naturally it is not a matter of examining isolated intervals on their own; it is merely that it is necessary to devote some attention to those intervals, and their use, which have a distinctly differentiated significance in the various melodic and harmonic structures.

In the structures which have been examined so far it has become evident that there are perfect, acoustic intervals which are in a certain sense static, and opposed to these there are tense, dynamic intervals. The relationship between these two groups can be assessed according to the natural phenomenon of the overtone series: the tense dynamic intervals come about through the *mistuning by plus or minus one semitone* of the acoustic 'perfect' intervals which come at the beginning of the overtone series. The intervals of the first part of the overtone series (discounting octave identity) and the mistuned intervals clearly demonstrate this peculiar relationship if they are placed alongside one another. (On this occasion, too, the value of the intervals is expressed through the well-tried scale of values where one semitone=1.)

Overtone number	Acoustic interval		Mistuned interval (± 1)
2	octave	12	13 minor ninth
			11 diminished octave
3	fifth	7	8 augmented fifth
			6 diminished fifth
4	octave of no. 2		
5	major third	4	5 fourth
			3 minor third
6	octave of no. 3		
7	minor seventh	10	11 major seventh
			9 major sixth
8	octave of no. 4		
9	major second	2	3 minor third
			1 minor second
10	octave of no. 5		
11	augmented fourth	6	7 fifth
			5 fourth

The upper section of the table is perfectly clear and only the fourth as a mistuned interval, with the value 5, requires explanation. Now it is easy to observe in the music of the twentieth century that the fourth is far from identical in value to the fifth; it cannot be regarded as simply the inversion of the fifth. We reach the same result if we examine this from the acoustic side as well, for we only meet with the perfect fourth of the fundamental note in a distant and virtually indistinguishable section of the overtone series.

The lower part of the table, beginning from the sixth overtone, displays some secondary interrelationships. The higher the individual overtones come in the series, the more their purely acoustic content decreases. In numerous cases intervals which were produced earlier are produced once more (11, 3, 1); and the double role of the interval with the value 6 is very characteristic. This is the meeting point of acoustic and mistuned structures, but only in theory for in practice in Bartók's music its acoustic use (cf. *The Wooden Prince*, Lydian-type scales) is well differentiated from the form produced by means of mistuning (cf. fugue structure, etc.)

It must be stressed that it is not as consonance and dissonance that these two kinds of interval types contrast with one another. This would lead in a mistaken direction, for consonance–dissonance is dependent upon convention determined by the period. Here, on the other hand, it is categories of an objective physical nature that confront one another; they naturally can—and do—appear in the form of a contrast between consonance and dissonance, but their classification is relative. The minor third, for example, which is the mistuned form of the acoustic major third, has now been present for a long time in European music as a consonant interval. But think of Bartók's characteristic minor third motifs (the Second String Quartet, the Dance Suite, the Second Piano Concerto, etc.). Pregnant with tension, their function, expressing barbaric primeval strength, is very far from creating an impression of consonance.

The phenomenon of mistuning the major third is extended in Bartók's music; alongside the natural acoustic intervals come their 'artificially' mistuned partners. Thus it becomes evident from yet another angle that the fourth, as soon as it becomes independent and suitable for forming chords, is not merely the inversion of the fifth but an individual antiacoustic interval loaded with tension. In the same way the minor sixth is, in this connection no longer the inversion of the major third, but an independent and tense interval, really an augmented fifth (or 'diminished' major sixth). There is no need to offer explanations for the other primary mistuned intervals, their 'anti-acoustic' nature being self-evident.

If we now examine the basic chord types anew in the light of all this, the lesson to be learned is clear: the structure of the major seventh chord is 4–7–11 semitones, that of the alpha chord 3–6–8–11 semitones, and that of the chord composed of two different fourths 5–11 or 6–11 semitones. If we disregard the framework which has a fixed nature and consists of 11 semitones, the structure of the first type is characterized by acoustic intervals, and that of the second and third types by mistuned intervals.

Yet another brilliant proof of Bartók's comprehensive genius. He does not throw away tradition but retains it, and, transforming it, builds the new upon it. Unlike the dodecaphonic doctrine he does not exclude from his system the acoustic intervals offered by earlier music, but brings about new relations through them. Thus he continues and reinterprets the major–minor duality of the tonal age. After the analysis given above it will scarcely seem exaggerated or contrived to draw an analogy between major–minor duality and Bartók's acoustic–anti-acoustic duality. Bartók developed major–minor duality by taking all the acoustic intervals to be major and then placing their mistuned versions alongside them as their minor counterparts. On this basis we can indeed speak of a 'Bartók major' and a 'Bartók minor'.

Ernő Lendvai also arrived at a kind of duality theory when he contrasted Bartók's diatony and chromaticism, or the corresponding 'acoustic types' and the 'golden section types'.[114] One may, however, argue with this contrast in several respects. In the course of the analyses made so far, it has been proved by an abundance of examples—particularly in connection with polymodal technique—that in Bartók diatony and chromaticism do not oppose one another. Moreover, the so-called acoustic scale, although it consists of diatonic tetrachords, is not diatony but 'heptatonia secunda', and so it cannot, even in a figurative sense, be the representative *par excellence* of diatony.

A further question presents itself as to why pentatony becomes excluded by Lendvai from the order of the acoustic musical world and why it fits unambiguously into the 'chromatic or golden section system'. If we examine not only an arbitrarily selected section of the pentatonic scales, as Lendvai does, it becomes clear that a major third is also present, and a perfect fifth, and a major sixth and a minor seventh. It is obvious that in the case of pentatony, too—as with almost every means—its character depends on the way it is used, and so also on which side of the duality it is placed. Bartók rarely uses pentatony in its original form; usually—as we have seen—he mistunes it in some way or other. For this reason Lendvai is partly right; in Bartók, pentatony belongs rather to the 'chromatic world' but not because of its original nature but because Bartók has *transformed* it in a particular way.

Similarly the golden section system does not provide an explanation in the case of alpha-type chords, for the structure of these is actually not shown by the series of golden section proportions 3–5–8–13, but by the following interval structures: 3–6–8–11, 3–5–8–11 and 3–6–9–11. Of these it is only the lower part of the second that can really be fitted into Lendvai's golden section proportions.

Thus Bartók's major–minor duality cannot be expressed by the contrasting sides of the diatonic–chromatic system or the acoustic–golden section system. The real duality behind Bartók's music is the dialectics of the acceptance and denial of the acoustic world.

This duality includes the preservation and mistuning of the perfect octave-fifth structure of scales, melodies and form, and also the preservation and mistuning of third-structure chords inherited from European art music. This extension and reinterpretation of major–minor duality has more than technical–idiomatic significance; it provides possibilities for double development of processes, for tension and resolution undulation, and for lifelike breathing in the organism of the music. And the analogy of the major–minor system of meaning presents itself as an aesthetic component. On the other hand the problem cannot be simplified to contain no more than this contrast. By their being constructed on natural, extra-human phenomena, acoustic elements and modes of expression are identified with the objective, the natural in their aesthetic significance as well. And as a contrast to this, more human and more subjective content is given to the musical system of symbols which transforms what is given by nature, what is acoustically satisfying, and artificially reshapes it into something else.

What is characteristic of the very greatest masters is precisely that the two activities involved in accepting and transforming, or the two conceptions behind the natural and the artificial, are in classical balance with each other. Here is yet another point where the difference between Bartók and the majority of his contemporaries becomes apparent and with the aid of which it becomes possible to demonstrate Bartók's place in the list of great men of music history. There have been and are trends in which imitation of the given natural world and striving in the direction of acoustic euphony reigned. Such was the discovery of the major third and its virtually immoderate use during the Renaissance and later in the so-called Gallant period (Johann Christian Bach). Or another example was the discovery

156

of the euphony of pentatony at the turn of the century, primarily with Debussy. On the other hand there have been and are trends which are dominated by rebellion against the natural and dominated by artificial, logical elements. One example of this was the polyphony of the Dutch masters, refined to a complex game at the end of the fifteenth century, and another is the trend represented by 'orthodox' dodecaphony in the first third of the twentieth century which wanted to exclude every natural, acoustic element from the sphere of musical expression. It is typical of both these one-sided aspirations that each places in the foreground one or the other part of the process of artistic recognition and expression. This major–minor duality in Bartók's music, however, which grows beyond the technical framework of mere tonality and manifests itself on an aesthetic level as well, bears witness to the kind of dialectical relationship and classical balance between those elements naturally given and those transformed by man which are characteristic of the work of only the greatest artists.

Thus for Bartók, when he got beyond the first Romantic period, mistuning did not stand for distortion and the ironic but signified rather rebellion, pain, suffering, the deeply personal. This is once again a point of contact with the expressionism of Schoenberg; the denial of perfect fifth and octave structures was the denial of the customary, banal, petty bourgeois melodics. Structures which mistuned the perfect fifth-octave—that is exclusive use of the most crudely dissonant intervals—meant intransigency for Schoenberg and in Bartók dialectical rebellion, and a parallel can obviously be drawn between this and the visual art of the period, not yet abstract but tending towards abstraction, in which the misdrawing of forms for purposes of expression represents more or less the same artistic attitude as the mistuning of perfect interval structures in music.

In this rebellious period in the arts—and, it might be added, at the time of the evolution of abstraction—the distorted and the amorphous lost their nineteenth-century meaning. What was alien then now became the innermost subject of the artist; forms and chords offered by nature could no longer be put to canvas or paper in their own original, unaltered form; these raw, natural forms and harmonies were made suitable for artistic expression by the activity of transformation—misdrawing and mistuning.

And so followed the great change around, the great change in meaning: the misdrawn and mistuned form became normal, personal and fine, while natural drawing or pure, banal consonance signified what was unacceptable, to be ridiculed, what was alien to man. Just as the little naturalistic landscape set up on the easel in one of Magritte's fiery landscapes seems laughable, the banal little melody which appears before the Coda in Bartók's Fifth Quartet is also odious and to be dismissed.

This enigmatic, quotation-like episode in Bartók's quartet can indeed be explained only by the mistuning phenomenon. The banal major melody is not a variation of the movement's second principal theme but its *non-mistuned* form. If we compare the two melodies we can see that the downward displacement—mistuning—by a semitone of the upper tetrachord of the major scale was enough for the banal theme to become Bartók's personal, demonic theme. This episode before the end is therefore the same sort of gesture on the composer's part as when the magician reveals the secret of his trick to the public at the end

157

of his display. And at the same time it is a quotation, a reminder, the suggestion of a tone which the composer immediately thrusts angrily away.

Does this mean that everything which is not mistuned or everything which belongs to the sphere of perfect fifth-octave structure is inimical and odious for Bartók? Not in the least. And this is where Bartók's path moves away from Schoenberg's. The art of the mature Bartók does not on principle refute perfect fifth-octave structures and does not replace them exclusively with mistuned forms: he uses the two together towards the enrichment of his artistic universe.

Polytonality

The Allegretto con indifferenza episode provides what amounts to a spectral analysis of the theme just discussed and, at the same time, of the mistuned tonality of the whole movement. For what was built into the theme in an organic way here becomes separated into an unambiguous A major melody, and onto the A major as a separate key the composer sets the same melody in B flat major. But the end of the A major melody and the beginning of the B flat major melody are connected to each other precisely like the real theme and its scale-motif, which has a closing function.

This also proves that these kinds of structural mistuning usually have bitonality concealed somewhere within them. A melody clearly of tetrachord structure which—to return to its original position—starts off in G flat major and ends in F major is in the last analysis bitonal, in a special, linear-projection kind of bitonality. In the same way the mistuned pentatony of the Fourth Quartet also contains a linear manifestation of bitonality. Even these few examples indicate that at certain points Bartók's bitonality comes into contact with the phenomenon of mistuning.

It is almost symbolic that even at the beginning of Bartók's career, in the first of the Fourteen Bagatelles, bitonality is present; the right hand part moves in a tonal system of four sharps and the left hand in four flats. Here, too, there is immediate evidence of poly-modal thinking since it becomes clear that the system of four flats is not A flat major or F minor but C Phrygian, which, progressing together with the other part in C sharp minor, represents an individual colour.

From this relatively early starting point the development of the various key relationships and key associations can be followed quite clearly. For the present only a few typical examples will be given. Not long after the bagatelle mentioned above came the second of the *Three Burlesques*, the wry, ironic tone of which is secured by chromatic adjacent note relations. To the triads which give the melodic line are attached unstressed *Vorschlag* chords, and so each chord note is provided with its own chromatic neighbour.

If we examine the connections between the chords in more detail, however, our attention is drawn to something important: the *Vorschlag* chord before the E minor triad is an incomplete D sharp minor third inversion which is enharmonically identical with an A flat major triad. The position is the same with the other chords, too. As a result the notes of the minor triad are preceded not only by lower adjacent chromatic notes but by a chord of a different structure which reaches the root from below and the third and fifth from above. The effect created by these chromatic adjacent note connections is refreshed to a great extent by the fact that it is a major triad that is attached to a minor triad and the parts do not move mechanically.

146

In the quickly flitting chord connections in the second burlesque, another method appears which was later to become of great significance in Bartók's compositional technique: use of an extreme case of third-relationship triad connections, where every chord note moves on chromatically (for example, D major–A flat minor). In this relationship the essential point is that in place of simple chromatic connection—that is B major or D flat major related to C major (in other words chromatic approach of the root)—it is the chromatic neighbour of the

159

triad's *fifth* that becomes the root of the triad. It should be noted that the minor third model is produced by this chord relationship, too—that is, in the last analysis the minor third model contains two tonalities, namely a major and the minor of its augmented (mistuned) fifth.

Thus if we were able to regard the minor third model as a bimodal phenomenon—a compression of major and minor—based on a common root, in this new light we can see that bitonality also lies concealed within it, for it is scarcely possible to imagine simultaneous presence of these distant triads within one single tonality.

Although we are concerned with a third-relationship connection here, it must be emphasized that the essential point in the phenomenon—at least with Bartók—is the chromatic displacement of the fifth and the adjacent-note tension of the triad built upon it. Thus the major third distance appears as a diminished fourth (or augmented fifth). And this brings to light still further interrelationships.

It is really to this type of tonality pairing that the fugue technique of the Lento movement in the First String Quartet belongs. The first violin part is imitated by the second violin a fourth lower, which fits in perfectly with contrapuntal tradition, but from the second note onwards the imitation proceeds at a distance of a diminished fourth (major third). The same applies to the canon-like texture of the first part of the Third Quartet. From this parallel movement a minor third model is clearly outlined (see *Ex. 168a*).

These examples were mentioned when the phenomena involved in mistuning were being discussed in connection with the fact that we do not usually speak of bitonality when we are concerned with a fifth or fourth canon. Yet here it is precisely as a result of mistuning that we get the impression that the two parts in the contrapuntal fabric move in two different tonalities.

A good example of tonal levels separated by a diminished fourth (augmented fifth) being placed together can be found in the first movement of the Fourth Quartet where the canon of the 'Arab theme' is accompanied by C major and G sharp minor ostinatos. The minor sixth canon between two parts in the fifth quartet has a similarly bitonal character.

160

The other technique very characteristic of Bartók is the use of tonal levels separated by a diminished fifth. It has already been pointed out in connection with mistuning that this occurs most frequently in contrapuntal structures because it solves the problem of the asymmetrical fifth–fourth division of the octave. The literature refers to this relationship as a polar relationship since the two keys are placed at opposite points of the fifth circle, that is polar points, and for this reason it also leads to the disintegration of tonality. But it is these contrapuntal examples—and they are in the majority—which prove that the diminished fifth answer replaces the perfect answer of polyphonic structure (which Bartók did not renounce in other cases), and the *dux–comes* relationship also demonstrates that it is not a question of two equally important tonalities but a parallel between one dominating tonality and a secondary tonality which is complementary to the first, colouring it and veiling it over.

It also happens sometimes that the two tonal levels separated by a diminished fifth form an ostinato, either as a 'background'—as, for example, in the Prima parte of the Third Quartet—or as a 'non-thematic' transition section, as in the first movement of the Sixth Quartet.

148

In the second movement of the First Sonata for violin and piano, a violin melody which is unambiguously in the tonality of C unfolds above the deep F sharp organ point of the piano. Coming very close to this detail even in intonation is an already mentioned part of the central movement of the Fourth Quartet, where the melodic material is likewise heard in the tonality of C above a G flat pentatonic ostinato. This latter example, which

161

was referred to earlier as being one of the finest examples of complementary chromaticism, is also unequivocal proof of the complementary tendency of diminished fifth bitonality.

Finally, the third typical combination of tonalities in Bartók's music is semitone bitonality. The roots of this phenomenon go back as far as the consistent major seventh parallels of the 1908 Bagatelles (8, 10) and the new tonality conception which had already been evolved by the composition of the seventh piece, where B major is coloured by C major. József Újfalussy has already pointed to the important role played by 'semitone tension bitonality' in the musical idiom of Bartók in connection with the analyses of *Bluebeard's Castle* and the Dance Suite.[115]

Similar phenomena can be observed in numerous chamber works dating from the twenties. For example, at the beginning of the First Sonata for violin and piano, which comes closest to the 'free atonality' concept, the violin melody moves around a C centre above broken triads consistently based on C sharp in the piano part.

149

♩ = 72 -80

B: Sonata no.1, 1st movement

Approaching this same method is the return of the principal theme at the end of the Prima parte of the Third Quartet, where the melodic material, which belongs to the Key of C major, is supported by a C sharp–G sharp bass.

162

And in the Seconda parte the 'revolving theme' centred on E flat is accompanied by a harmonic basis formed by D Dorian triads which at the same time provide the thematic counterpoint (for the cello triad progression is actually the further development of the initial folksong theme).

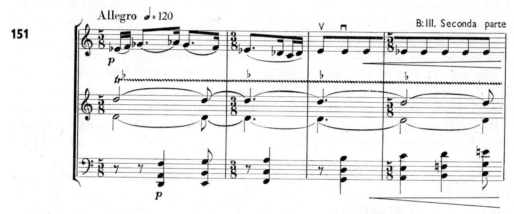

This series of examples can be completed by a phenomenon already discussed: semitone bitonality is likewise concealed in the inner structure of the Fourth Quartet's 'Arab theme' and the Fifth Quartet's scale themes.

In the light of all this it may well be asked why, of all the many possibilities offered by bitonality, it was precisely these three tonality combinations, employing the tension of the semitone, the diminished fifth, and the augmented fifth, that Bartók favoured? This question may be approached from two angles. First it is necessary to examine what it is that is individual in all three of these bitonal combinations, and secondly we must investigate what it is that gives to these interval relationships the tension which is so characteristic of them.

By the first approach we once again arrive at the technique based on the complementary principle. We have already established that in Bartók's various methods it is chiefly the combination of unified systems which are complete in themselves that is common. Of the possible polymodal combinations, for example, it is the pairing of the Lydian and Phrygian which stands out because, related to a common base, without any artificial intervention whatsoever, this leads in a natural way to twelve-degree chromaticism. Now a virtually completely analogous method can be provided by the combination of two tonalities.

Firm believers in atonality consider bitonality a compromise between tonality and atonality. In certain cases this is undoubtedly true, mainly when the two contrasted tonalities do not lose their individual tonal character, and so it is as if the two tonal centres exist independently alongside each other within the piece. Such methods are to be met with in Bartók, too, principally in the form of combination of relative keys. The best example of this is the Marcia movement of the Sixth Quartet, where the major form of the theme is accompanied like a shadow by its relative minor version (B major–G sharp minor). The two do not merge into each other: each retains its own independent modal and tonal character.

As opposed to this we found in the case of bimodal methods that although the individual modes may appear as relatively self-contained, independent systems, they do lose their independence either partly or completely in the complex material of the musical fabric, and, producing a new quality, merge into one another. The typical examples of bitonality demonstrate essentially these same characteristics; Bartók selected and preferred the three tonality combinations analysed above because they contain the pentatonic complementary basis with the help of which the seven-degree system becomes twelve-degree. This means at the same time that with these tonality combinations the two tonalities no longer exist in parallel with each other but neutralize each other. The most 'economic' use of this technique is represented by the detail already quoted several times from the Fourth Quartet where C major and G flat pentatony are combined. In the other cases, however, when each tonality is represented by a complete seven-degree system, there are, apart from the five-degree complementary basic notes, two 'superfluous' notes in each which are identical with two notes from the other tonality, or their enharmonic equivalents. That is, the C major–A minor tonal plane can most easily be complemented into a twelve-degree system by the C sharp major–A sharp minor, F sharp major–D sharp minor, and B major–G sharp minor tonal planes since the F sharp–C sharp–G sharp–D sharp–A sharp pentatonic group of notes is common to all three. The 'superfluous' notes appear on one side or the other side or on both sides of the fifth column.

F	C	G	D	A	E	B							
							F♯	C♯	G♯	D♯	A♯	E♮	B♮
						B	F♯	C♯	G♯	D♯	A♯	E♮	
					E	B	F♯	C♯	G♯	D♯	A♮		

The three complementary seven-degree systems contain three major and three minor tonalities. Combined with the C major–A minor tonality, these tonalities produce the relations which have crystallized as the most typical Bartók bitonalities. This is also why bitonality with the tension of a semitone, a diminished fifth and an augmented fifth dominates.

This explanation of Bartókian bitonality, based on the complementary principle, shows the importance of adjacent chromatic note relationships as opposed to polar relationships. The polar relationship is also valid but its content has an 'adjacent note' quality: it is a question of the mistuning by a semitone of the nearest, that is the fifth, relation

164

(dominant) of an initial tonality. In the same way the augmented fifth relationship is explained by this same principle: this is the chromatic displacement of the dominant tonality in a different direction. With this we have come to another aspect of Bartók's mistuning technique, or to the recognition of a new system of relationships which is also connected with mistuning. As the perfect octave-fifth relations were replaced by mistuned relations in melodic and harmonic structures, so in the pairing and combining of tonalities it is likewise these non-perfect octave and non-perfect fifth relations which play the decisive role.

With this we have strictly reached the other approach to the problem concerning why it is precisely these interval relationships which characterize Bartók's bitonal technique. The system of functional tonality is based on the most immediate and strongest relationships appearing in the acoustic overtone series: octave identity (numerical relationship: 2) and fifth relationship (numerically 3). Thus the natural relationship of all other notes to the fundamental note can be measured partly by reference to the overtone series (relating them acoustically) and partly by reference to fifth relationship (relating them tonally). The chromatically adjacent notes to the fundamental note, however, can be regarded as the notes most alien to it, for they come in the uppermost section of the overtone series where the notes are so to speak indistinguishable, and taken on the basis of fifth relationship the chromatic adjacent note is separated from the fundamental note by seven fifths, and the diatonic semitone neighbour comes at a distance of five fifths from the fundamental. In this way the adjacent chromatic note relations really mean the negation, in the philosophical sense of the word, of the acoustic–tonal order, the greatest possible antithesis to the thesis of tonality. Bartók carried out the act of discontinued preservation by making the adjacent chromatic note relations, which 'disrupt' these fifth relationships, a connecting link in the chain of tonalities connected on the fifth-relation basis, while at the same time alongside this he retained the fifth relationships of tonality.[116] His new kind of tonal system is also built on the *non-perfect octave* and *non-perfect fifth* relationship of tonalities in the earlier sense of the word—consisting of perfect fifths.

This is therefore the other explanation of the matter: the 'non-perfect' octave (that is, the octave mistuned in two directions) is actually the augmented or diminished octave which is the same as the two chromatically adjacent notes; and the 'non-perfect' (that is, mistuned) fifth is none other than the diminished or augmented fifth. In other words, we are once more faced with the three basic forms of Bartókian bitonality, combining tonalities with semitone, diminished fifth or augmented fifth tension between them.

In Bartók's bitonal methods, however, it is not only the quantitative relationship between the two keys, or their distance from each other, that has to be examined but the inner qualitative structure of the relationship between these two tonalities. Indeed it follows more or less naturally from what has been said so far that with Bartók bitonality is only an idiomatic process in the interests of enrichment of the tonality principle without its actually influencing the strictly 'monotonal' unity of the works. That is, in the great majority of cases where bitonality is used, one of the tonalities has a dominating role in the tonality complex, and as a result the two tonalities which come together are not by any means equal: in

165

comparison with the one which dominates and has also a structural role to play, the other fulfils a 'mistuning' complementary function.

Valuable information is offered on this topic from the composer himself in a late study which dates from 1945 and was to have been a foreword for the piano anthology planned for publication by the E. B. Marks Corporation. Referring to the early piano works and the already familiar explanations of these, Bartók writes among other things: '...The tonality of the first Bagatelle is, of course, not a mixture of C sharp minor and F minor but simply a Phrygian coloured C major. In spite of this, it was quoted several times as an early example of bitonality in the twenties, when it was fashionable to talk about bitonality and polytonality.'[117]

This of course does not at all mean that Bartók dismissed once and for all with this one sentence the possibility of using polytonality in connection with his art. The quotation rather underlines that we are to notice in the occurrence of bitonality a special tonal relationship which is in the end, like polymodality, a means, a component in Bartók's complex conception of tonality.

As far as the Bagatelle referred to is concerned, the composer is undoubtedly right in stressing that the key to the tonality of the piece does not lie simply in the simultaneous presence of the tonalities indicated by the two different key-signatures. On the other hand it cannot be denied that the musical fabric of the piece is composed of two separate tonal and modal layers—C Phrygian and C sharp minor. Thus in the whole complex two tonal levels, C and C sharp, and also two modes, Phrygian and minor, confront one another. At the same time, through the different modes coming together in the different tonalities, there arise even more modes, since the third of C sharp minor appears to be major in relation to the likewise minor third of C Phrygian. Similarly the fourth degree of the minor scale is an augmented fourth when related to the Phrygian keynote, and thus represents a Lydian level, and the minor sixth of the minor scale is the alien major sixth alternative in the Phrygian scale. So it is easy to see that certain degrees of the C sharp minor scale appear as the chromatically adjacent notes in the Phrygian scale on C, primarily the third, but also the fourth and sixth. Taking all this into consideration we can scarcely feel even Bartók's expression 'Phrygian coloured C major' to be satisfactory from absolutely every point of view, for it might also be put the other way round: major coloured C Phrygian. But in place of using very categorical descriptions it would be more to the point to come to thorough understanding of the principle behind the phenomenon—namely that here we are dealing with an unambiguous C tonality, the polymodal character of which has been achieved by the composer through bitonality.

152

166

It is the combination of different keys that produces polymodality in the piece 'Minor and Major' (no. 103 in *Mikrokosmos*). B major, which appears alongside the left hand's A minor part, obviously represents more than just another tonality: in relation to the minor third and perfect fourth of A minor, it brings a Lydian colour into the piece.

153

On the basis of all this it has perhaps become clear what is meant by saying that Bartók's bitonal methods are not tonal ambiguities but special structures in which the individual factors produce a new quality.

Having looked at some of the simpler examples we must now investigate the more complex phenomena, too. One typical bitonal structure with Bartók is a tonal divergence between the harmonic foundation and the melody belonging to it. The closing theme in the first movement of the Second Quartet, for example, may be divided tonally into two levels: the cello's fifths have without any doubt an F sharp tonality whereas the first violin's melody comes to rest on the note C sharp and this C sharp is further reinforced by a codetta.

154

While in the example just given there is a perfect fifth relationship between the tonality of the harmony and that of the melody, it is a mistuned relationship that binds harmony and melody in the majority of cases. It has already been possible to note this tendency in some of the examples of diminished fifth and semitone bitonality; confrontation of melody and harmony in a mistuned relationship. Or, put another way—bitonality comes about as a result of the mistuning of the perfect octave-fifth relationships. And with this we have reached a very important point in the argument: recognition of the special dialectics of *idiomatic polytonality and structural monotonality*. As Bartók himself stressed when explaining polymodality, in his works we should not look for instances where one part is constructed from one mode from the beginning of the piece to the end and the other part from another mode likewise throughout, it is in a similar way that we have to interpret the phenomenon of polytonality. It is not a matter of tonal duality or plurality extending over the whole work but of the breaking up of tonality in certain larger or smaller units within the musical fabric as a whole, which can be regarded as an idiomatic phenomenon, and this does not

167

preclude tonal unity from reigning in the works from a structural point of view. Thus when we say that in Bartókian bitonality one of the tonalities has a dominating role, this does not refer to the given detail (in which it would be difficult to decide which of the tonalities used is the dominating one and which is the one with a colouring function) but to the whole work, movement or formal unit. Once again we can refer to the Fifth Quartet as being the best, but by no means the only, example. In the theme based on a G flat–F tonal duality it would be senseless to regard either one tonality or the other as the dominating one, the decisive one. But when at the end of the work this same material meets on a tonal central note, approaching it from two different directions, there can no longer be any doubt as to the tonal unity of the movement and at the same time of the work.

This monotonality which is produced by way of polytonal material provides not only the structural unity of the work but also its structural differentiation. In other words the tonal unity of the work is secured not only by the framework tonality but also by the complex of different tonalities which appear in the various formal sections of the work. Here is further evidence that Bartók endeavoured to preserve the form-building principles of the tonal era, and it was only with extension and revaluation of concepts that he produced new qualities.

In the tonal plan of the works it is quite conspicuous how the perfect octave-fifth relations are replaced by their mistuned versions. This is, for example, how the peculiarly Bartókian structure is produced in which the second most important tonality is on a level a diminished fifth (augmented fourth) higher than the basic tonality of the work. What else could this be but the displacement of the dominant key in functional tonality—that is, the mistuning of the tonic–dominant relationship. In an unfinished draft Bartók analyses the Fifth Quartet and in connection with the B flat–E–B flat tonal structure of the first movement he actually states that in relation to the B flat tonality the tonality of E 'plays the role of dominant'. He also draws attention here to the fact that the themes of the movement come in ascending major second levels—that is, on the degrees of the whole-tone scale, the main theme being built on the B flat–E–B flat outline just mentioned.[118] Striving in the direction of halving the octave can be seen here—that is, the possibility of 'exact' halving offered by distance division, as opposed to the asymmetrical fifth–fourth division of diatony.

Besides the 'mistuned dominant' the 'mistuned tonic' also appears in the tonal plan of Bartókian forms. The best examples of this are provided chiefly by the Third Quartet, where the second part has D tonality and later E flat tonality after the C sharp tonality of the first part, obviously displaying an effort on the part of the composer to construct the tonal levels on the basis of the adjacent chromatic note principle.

We can now attempt to make a summary of the characteristics of the many aspects of Bartók's conception of tonality. Its starting point, its natural basis, is the European functional tonal tradition. Retaining the fundamental elements of this tonal tradition and developing them further, he supplements them with the modality of different kinds of folk music and the art music of the East. But by simultaneous combination of them he enriches both tonality and modality in particular directions so that the tonal system may in a complemen-

168

tary way reach, or at least approach, the twelve-degree tonal ideal produced as an inevitable development of the tonal tradition. This is polymodality and polytonality. The two are not separated from each other: the essence of polymodality is simultaneous use of different divisions of the octave right up to complete exhaustion of the whole chromatic range of the octave, and the essence of polytonality is the combination of different tonal levels, likewise in the interests of twelve-degree chromaticism. The two can appear separately, but polymodality is generally supplemented by polytonality. The tonality or modality complex which thus comes about is bound together by a common centre-note or framework-note which includes the content and—chiefly—the structural function of the keynote of tonal significance and the final note of modal significance. Bartók's tonality can thus in the last analysis be summed up as *polymodal polytonality related to a common centre.*

A striving towards synthesis, as we have already noticed, is the most important and most firmly fixed feature of Bartók's creative activity. The presence of this can be observed not only in the new combination of tonality and modality and the re-establishment of tonal duality, freely extended and created anew, but also in the way that Bartók took over and transformed *all* the ready-made elements provided by tradition. That unlimited desire to take in and the ability to take in with which Bartók strove to merge into one all useful results—the centuries of experience of European art music and the experiments of his contemporaries, the material and methods of primitive folk music and ancient art music of the East—is in itself something quite unique. It was only possible, however, for this large-scale reception to become the source of a large-scale synthesis because he transformed every element he took over; he took nothing over and used nothing in its original form, in its original capacity. Bartók's whole creative art is characterized by transformation and merging different factors into one. Its special quality and its greatness partly lie in that it exists on so many levels and can be explained from so many angles. It is a rich growth, the innumerable roots of which are nourished by the whole of human culture. It is not a simple continuation but a free and humanistic re-creation of everything ancient, of everything preceding it.

PART TWO

Analyses

The First String Quartet

The history of the writing of the First Quartet is closely connected with that of the post-humous Violin Concerto and thus although the year 1908 is generally taken by the literature as the date of the composition of the quartet, we can justifiably presume that various sketches for it reach back into 1907, and it assumed its final form in January of 1909. Clarification of these problems has chiefly been due to the work of Denijs Dille, who extracted the complete picture from various documents preserved in the Budapest Bartók Archives and from information obtained from Stefi Geyer.[119]

In the score of the Violin Concerto a note in Bartók's own hand shows that he began to compose the work on 1 July 1907, in Jászberény and finished it in Budapest on 5 February 1908; along with this information goes yet another supplementary note in the score which indicates 28 June 1907, Jászberény, beside the humorous quotation of the children's song which begins 'Der Esel ist ein dummes Tier'. From Stefi Geyer we now know that this is a reference to the happy days spent in Jászberény when Stefi Geyer and her brother entertained Bartók as a guest at the home of their Jászberény relatives. It was obviously at this time that the young composer fell in love with the young violinist and the two-movement Violin Concerto composed for Stefi Geyer became the direct expression of his feelings: the first movement is the portrait of the 'young girl' and the second movement depicts the 'violin virtuoso'.

There is a manuscript preserved in the Budapest Bartók Archives on one side of which three themes from the Violin Concerto are sketched in pencil, while on the other side there are four theme sketches for the First Quartet, these latter being written in ink. The violin concerto sketches are accompanied by humorous drawings and notes from which it can justifiably be concluded that they originated during the happy time together in Jászberény. Although it is not certain, it may nevertheless be supposed that the quartet sketches also date from that time.

Actual composition of the work, however, began only in 1908, presumably in February or March, at the time when the relationship with Stefi Geyer came to an end. From the information obtained from the violinist we know that Bartók wrote as follows in his last letter to her: 'I have begun a quartet; the first theme is the theme of the second movement (that is, of the violin concerto): this is my funeral dirge.'

It is shown by the above mentioned theme sketches, which presumably date from 1907, that at that time Bartók still intended to construct the first movement from the introduc-

173

tory theme of the second movement in the final form, and so the use of the Violin Concerto theme is a later idea which, according to the evidence in the letter, obviously finds its explanation in the breaking off of the relationship. But from all this it does not follow that the second and third movements of the final form were finished earlier than the first, as Denijs Dille supposes. It is more probable that Bartók structured the earlier theme sketches (which incidentally do not show that the composer intended them for a string quartet) even in the course of 1908 into a conception in which the role of opening movement is played by the slow polyphonic material with an altered version of the theme taken from the Violin Concerto. Thus this summarizes the Violin Concerto since in its structure and character it is related to the first movement of the concerto, while its theme relates it to the second movement. This was Bartók's first reaction to Stefi Geyer's rejection and her finishing the relationship. (It should be noticed that the second reaction, that is anger and caricature, became embodied later in the 'Grotesque' movement of the *Two Portraits*.)

Writing was interrupted in the summer of 1908 by lengthy tours abroad; in June he went to Germany, where he introduced the Fourteen Bagatelles to Busoni, and in July he went through Switzerland to the south of France. After the earlier visits to Paris in which his programme was very bound, this was now free roaming in the most beautiful parts of France, in the Haute Savoie and on the south coast. He wrote to Etelka Freund on 2 September 1908: 'At last, via Lyon, Vienna, Valence and Avignon, I have reached the *ne plus ultra* of my desires: the sea. It's only the little Mediterranean Sea, but a *sea* it is nevertheless. Now I'm in the village of Les Saintes Maries, not far from Arles. It's wonderful! I walked for 7 hours without meeting a soul. Here I have bathed in the sea for the first time, walked barefoot for the first time, and seen a mirage for the first time. For these three 'first times' it's been well worth making such a long detour.'[120]

A true complement to this tour was provided in the autumn of the same year by a trip to Transylvania and concerning the joyous discoveries he made there he wrote as follows on this occasion to Irma Freund: 'Yesterday I went along the Torda Gorge; today I'm making merry at Torockó below Székelykő. In some ways this famous Székelykő reminds me of the Grand Salève, except that there's no *funiculaire* here! Of all the villages in Hungary which I've visited so far, this one is certainly the most beautifully situated.'[121]

From Transylvania he travelled on to Bucharest and from there he wrote to his mother on 3rd November 1908: 'I've made a bit of an excursion to the Balkan peninsula! I've made friends with the Rumanians (since I can't make friends at home).'[122]

It can be assumed, therefore, that he continued writing the string quartet when he returned from this journey at the end of 1908, and according to the note in his own hand in the 'Stichvorlage' sent to the Rózsavölgyi company, he completed it on 27 January 1909. This is also supported by the postcard he wrote to Etelka Freund on 28 January 1909. 'I am happy to announce that the quartet got itself finished yesterday and would be pleased to visit you on Saturday evening (in my company). Would you be kind enough to receive it? If not, then perhaps on Sunday, after lunch...'[123]

This jocular announcement was thus probably followed by a performance before a closed circle of friends—for the time being, only on the piano. It can be assumed that it

174

had an immediate success, for the Waldbauer–Kerpely String Quartet, consisting of young artists, began studying the work in that very year.

The 'Stichvorlage' preserved in the Budapest Bartók Archives offers a few important details concerning the gradual evolution of the work's final form. The score is in an unknown hand, Bartók in all probability having had it copied by someone, and later he introduced some alterations to this copy. The central section of the first movement was originally five bars longer, but the composer erased the last five bars and this is how the form evolved in which, after the colour chords appearing at **10**, a cæsura leads to the return of the theme— now an octave higher.

Evidence of the gradual development of the special connection between the first and second movements can be seen in that Bartók had the copyist leave this part empty (the first fourteen bars of the second movement) and only wrote in the final solution during correction of the finished copy. This detail is all the more interesting since the material of this part, the 'winding theme' moving in parallel thirds, had already appeared among the very first thematic sketches. Is it possible, therefore, that the composer originally imagined the join between the two themes in a different way? Or is Denijs Dille's hypothesis concerning the reversed order of writing true after all?

Another correction is also instructive: in the section between **17** and **20** in the second movement Bartók erased an earlier version which did not contain the great dramatic tension of the final form.

A further point which concerns the evolution of the final version of the First Quartet is that in 1931 Bartók adjusted the metronome indications given in 1909 and printed in the first Rózsavölgyi edition. For on 19 October 1931, Max Rostal, the English violinist and quartet leader, wrote to Bartók concerning the correct tempi of the work.[124] Bartók replied in his letter of 6 November. '... I am very sorry that I haven't been able to reply earlier; in order to be able to do so I had to study thoroughly the tempo and MM signs, especially of the First Quartet, and I've only now found the necessary time. Let's hope you will have an opportunity to play the works in other places, too, so that when you do so, you will be able to consider the contents of this letter, but perhaps it won't reach you in time. *Quartet I.* In the first movement, the MM sign is indeed quite impossible and incomprehensible, and in the 3rd movement, too, I find many misplaced MM figures. I should add at this point that in my early works MM signs are very often inexact, or rather they do not correspond to the correct tempo. The only explanation I can think of is that I metronomized too hastily at the time, and perhaps my metronome was working imperfectly. I have phonogrammes made 20 years ago of some of my piano pieces played by myself and they show that I play them today in exactly the same tempo as I did then. Now I use a balance metronome which, of course, cannot show any considerable differences from the correct oscillation number. Let me give you all the tempi exactly.'[125]

After the work was completed more than a year passed before Bartók's First Quartet was given a performance. The première was given in the programme of Bartók's first composer's evening in the Royal concert hall on 19 March 1910. This was a memorable date in the history of Hungarian music: Bartók's composer's evening was preceded two days earlier by a similar introductory concert by Kodály. These two closely connected concerts were like the unfurling of the flag of new Hungarian music.

At his composer's evening Bartók himself played a series of his piano pieces, and alongside these the Piano Quintet dating from 1904 and the First Quartet were also performed. A large part in the success of the concert was played by the extraordinarily talented young Waldbauer Quartet, who from this time onwards became permanent and perhaps the most devoted interpreters of Bartók's chamber music.

To judge the significance of this introductory concert it is absolutely necessary for us to look into the contemporary criticism which, quite typically, contains the two basic ways of receiving Bartók: the rejection of conservatism, and approval and enthusiasm which does not yet fully 'understand' but rather 'feels' in advance and has favourable presentiments. Thanks to the investigations carried out by János Demény, we have before us today a virtually complete documentation of the criticism of both concerts.[126] Some of the critics, those who around 1903 and 1905 had celebrated the 'true Hungarian national genius' in Bartók after the arrogant nationalism of the Millennium, now give expression to their disappointment. For by this time the shouting emphatic Hungarian quality, the romantic way of being Hungarian, had disappeared from Bartók's music and was replaced by a more refined Hungarian tone which strove towards the essence of the matter. This, however, was naturally not noticed by the critics—*could* not have been noticed by them since the basis of it was the area of folk art which was just then being discovered in the course of Kodály's and Bartók's first journeys in the interests of investigating folk music.

Of the newspaper criticisms perhaps it was only the opinion of the *Népszava* which approached Bartók's string quartet with sympathy and understanding. The article, although it is not signed, was probably written by Béla Reinitz, later to become Bartók's enthusiastic devotee and friend. The critic does not stand unequivocally beside Bartók; he has indeed numerous objections to the quartet, but his tone is free from all preconceived ideas, and what is most important, he makes no attempt to pit the earlier Piano Quintet against the new tone of the string quartet.

Two more lengthy essay-type pieces appeared on Bartók's quartet, both in periodicals. One was Sándor Kovács's study in the periodical *Renaissance* under the title 'Socialist Music'.[127] With a somewhat simplifying method, it is true, the writer does, however, establish well intentioned æsthetic and sociological parallels between the polyphony of Bartók's music and the democracy of the society of the future. The other large study, by Antal Molnár, was published in the columns of the *Zeneközlöny* (Music Gazette) about a year after the first performance.[128] Antal Molnár, who was at that time the viola player in the Waldbauer Quartet, wrote *from within* concerning the work, with more authority than any critic, uniting as he did in his own person the active musician's ability to perceive with the professional knowledge and objective perspective of the scholarly composer-musicologist. At the same time complete identity with the composer and the ability to enter a conceptual alliance with him can be read in the lines of his study.

First movement: Lento

Beginning a string quartet with a fugue—it was certainly Beethoven's C sharp minor Quartet which provided Bartók with an immediate example for this. Giving this kind of opening–starting function to the fugue was new in Beethoven's time, for until then it had usually had a finishing function, or at least required something before it as an introduction (prelude, toccata, French overture, slow introduction, etc.). This is how it usually was with Beethoven as well, for in both the late piano sonatas and the *Diabelli Variations* it comes as a climax, a crowning finish. The change in position of the fugue naturally had some effect on its inner character, too. In the C sharp minor Quartet Beethoven forms the unfolding organism, the new world being born, by gradually increasing the number of parts. The inner transformation of the fugue becomes evident above all in the formation of the themes: the closed Bach type of fugal theme, sometimes concise in the style of an epigram, is replaced by open, gradually unfolding themes. When he begins his string quartet with a fugue, following Beethoven's example, Bartók takes over the inner characteristics which go with the formal conception: on the one hand the gradually unfolding, open character of the theme and its weaving continuation, and on the other hand the fact that the movement is formally not a fugue—merely in its opening and closing parts.

In examining the fugal technique of the First String Quartet we can take the fugue theme and fugal structure first: the question of form will in any case be discussed separately. A special technique is in evidence above all in that the four parts do not enter at equal distances from each other in time as in the majority of fugues, but two at a time in stretto.

The two pairs of parts correspond to one another in no more than a unit of five notes (that is, with minor deviations, to which we shall return later); the following part would thus—on the basis of strict fugal structure principles—be a codetta leading to the next entrance. This explanation, however, obviously does not work: at most it is possible to call the three bars before the entry of the third and fourth parts (cello–viola) a codetta, a tail-piece. The characteristic method of the fugue, therefore, lies in that the two upper and two lower parts are closely connected to each other—it is two parts together which give the so-called fugue theme. We might even simply call it a double fugue in which the countersubject is a transposed imitation of the subject (there are examples of this in Bach, too).

The two parts are so closely related both melodically and harmonically that to imagine them as having independent lives is virtually impossible. The motif consisting of a downward sixth and a fifth which turns back on this is a melodic unit more or less complete in itself, a characteristic type in Wagnerian and late Romantic melody, but it is self-evident in connection with this late Romantic character that without a harmonic context it is somewhat meagre. The mature art of the young Bartók is characterized by the way in which he weaves the two melodies into one another and through the stretto entry constructs what amounts to another opening motif, a melody which is closely linked to the theme of the second movement of the early Violin Concerto published posthumously, and which, in a wider sense, is related to a constantly recurring theme type (leitmotif) in the compositions dating from his youth.

177

The tense seventh chord is, incidentally, an important element in the theme: after the entry it appears three more times, on different degrees, forming tonal islands in the wavering tonality. This interlinking of the component parts of the seventh chord, on the other hand, draws attention to how much the two parts, with regard to their position, are composed in one; the 'space' between the larger melodic leaps is consistently filled out by the other voice. This is how Bartók's inclination towards complementary structures makes an appearance even here, in a late Romantic setting.

And the 'inexact' imitation of the downward sixth is explained by the harmonic demands of the structure: the first violin's F–A flat motif is answered not by C–E flat but by C–E, which ensures principally the tension of the F minor seventh chord, and also makes it possible for the ascending fifth G–D to be answered not by the neutral fifth D–A but by the melodic leap E flat–B flat which produces a new seventh chord.[129]

The fugue subject is thus a combined texture composed of the two voices, over four bars; after the imitation of the first motif of five notes the free counterpoint which follows also enters with thematic claims: here the material consists of descending fifths and small cambiata figures. The contrapuntal character of the two parts ends in the fifth bar and changes gradually over to parallel movement. This really is a codetta; the two lower parts take over only three bars without any alteration, and then the movement of the parts becomes free, preparing the way for a new formal section. It should be noticed that the roles of the two lower parts interchange in an interesting way: the cello plays the first violin's part, which means the cello moves in a higher register than the viola.

That Bartók was by no means striving after the revival of Baroque fugue form here is indicated by the small syncopated motif which comes into the foreground after the fugal exposition being made to appear as a secondary theme, and by the disappearance of the contrapuntal nature of the structure. The varied development of the small sighing syncopated motif makes a formal middle section which is followed at **5** by the reminiscent return of the fugue theme: neither the whole theme nor the accompanying contrapuntal texture returns, only the characteristic sixth leap bending downwards, embedded in harmonic blocks. Here the two important motifs join forces: the sigh motif gives a direct answer to the gesticular sixth-motif of the fugue theme.

A sharp formal cut is produced by the sudden break in the upward moving fabric of the three upper voices. A trio section follows which is evolved from the uniting of two motifs: there is a passionate, occasionally interrupted rubato melody (viola, joined later by the second violin) which is developed from the rhythm of the sigh motif above a fifth organ point on C–G; and meanwhile above this there is a thin violin melody flying in a strongly contrasting high register. The trio itself is also in three parts; in the central section the spirit of Debussy and Ravel is evoked by an impressionistic first and second inversion chord mixture, with which the cello's solo melody woven from Hungarian folksong phrases goes very well. This whole section radiates an atmosphere which was later to become characteristic of Kodály's cello and chamber works. The last two bars of the trio round off the section with a poetic sound effect and this leads back to the fugue theme; each component of the B flat major triad is coloured by adjacent notes—the B flat by A, the D by C sharp and the F by G flat.

The trio breaks off just as suddenly and remains as open as the section which introduced it. Leading note relationship is, however, present in both: in the former the lowest part moves from C sharp to C, the keynote of the trio, and in the latter the E in the highest part leads to F, the opening note of the returning fugue theme. Thus even here one characteristic method of Bartók's later form structuring is already present: the sharp cut which does nevertheless connect organically interrelated sections by invisible threads.

The recapitulation which starts at **11** recalls the two-part texture from the beginning of the movement an octave higher but note for note (only the codetta becomes shortened to one bar), but the entrance of the two lower parts is merely hinted at over the extent of a single bar. After that the central part of the first section is replaced by six bars of polyphonic texture with a rising tendency, and still later the rounding off motif is also presented in a condensed form: the four-syllable line of downward sixth returns in a harmonized form, touching on the same harmonics as those after **5**—that is, A, F sharp, E flat, and C. There is, however, an essential transformation in that the downward sixth motif here takes a major form throughout (A–C sharp, F sharp–A sharp, E flat–G, C–E). This transformation to the major is nevertheless present only on the melodic level, for the chords below the individual notes are mostly minor in content. This minor character is reinforced by the five bar coda following it, which in both its tonality and in certain fragments of its melody recalls the opening of the movement; but instead of F minor it is A flat minor which dominates.

The key to the deliberate tonal ambiguity of the movement is to be found in the augmented triad consisting of the notes E–A flat–C. The two sixths heard at the beginning of the movement—as has already been pointed out—produce a chord which is the third inversion of F minor seventh. The E–A flat–C augmented triad is present here, too, but the note F quite unequivocally determines its tonal affiliation. In the fifth bar before the end of the movement this characteristic augmented triad is heard once more (supplemented by the degrees of a whole-tone scale), but its tonal tendency is determined by the very next bar: it resolves onto A flat minor. It is not insignificant that on this occasion Bartók writes the E as F flat, by which he expresses the tendency to resolve onto E flat.

156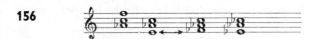

On the basis of all this it can be taken that the movement is tonally determined by F minor–A flat minor duality, and not founded on the relative key relationship as later is the case with the D minor–F major of the Sixth Quartet, but through the centrality and tonal ambiguity of the augmented triad mentioned.[130]

Second movement: Allegretto

The attacca connection between the first two movements is a somewhat external point. If we are to believe Denijs Dille's already mentioned assumption, maybe Bartók wished in some way to compensate for the fact that he added the first movement later to the already finished second and third movements. He brought about the combination with particular care, partly motivically and partly by the gradual acceleration of the tempo.

This writing of two movements as one, however, is likewise a reference to Beethoven's C sharp minor Quartet: there, too, the C sharp minor first movement is closely connected to the D major second movement. This structuring of the movements in one is a typically romantic phenomenon which in fact disappears from Bartók's later string quartets, with the exception of the third. In the Piano Quintet preceding the First Quartet, however, we find similar form-building methods.

The structure of the whole movement is characterized by organic writing taken virtually to extremes, just like the majority of later Romantic works: the chamber works of César Franck, Reger's string quartets, or Schoenberg's First and Second String Quartets. And so, although the outlines of classical sonata form can clearly be recognized, every single detail of the movement is pervaded by one of the few thematic or motivic ideas which are taken as a basis. In spite of even the functionally static exposition being more dynamic, more development-like, with Bartók than with earlier masters, orientation in the formal construction of the movement is provided clearly by the relative dynamics of the music.

At the beginning of the exposition a winding melody appears, arranged in consistent parallel thirds. It is only later that it becomes clear, however, that although this theme stands at the start of the first group of themes, it is to be regarded rather as a framework theme which has a smaller share in the movement's thematic work than those which follow it.

The role of principal theme is thus filled by the motif which is heard after **1** in the second violin, accompanied by the first violin's ostinato figure. This drooping gesture, just like the majority of the melodic elements in the movement, represents the late Romantic amorphic melodic type: somewhat asymmetrical, tonally indecisive and open at almost every point, easy to break up into parts and fit in elsewhere.

At **3** transitional material begins which, with the help of a little rhythmic element, leads organically into the secondary theme at **6**. As regards texture, this theme comes very close to the former one; it is heard in the middle parts while the outer parts accompany it with an ostinato motif. As opposed to the warm expressive theme, the closing theme consists of cold whole-tone scale motifs above knocking, drum-like pizzicato on the cello (**9**). The appearance of the closing theme, however, presents no barrier to the reappearance of the earlier secondary theme (at **10**), which is very typical of this late romantic structure. The return of the framework theme shows that the exposition reaches a conclusion at **11** and the development section begins.

After the considerably dynamic exposition the development holds even further dynamism. In the first part of the variational–dissecting development process the principal theme and its accompanying motif play the leading role, while later (at **20**) the secondary theme

180

becomes the centre of the thematic work. After an organically developed process of leading back, it is the framework theme which recapitulates first—indeed, it is displayed more broadly here than anywhere else in the movement. And after **28**, at the Poco sostenuto, the drooping gesture of the principal theme also returns—accompanied by the scale motif familiar from the closing material. This dense combination of the principal theme and secondary theme material is a typically Bartókian technique: a beautiful example of the abbreviated recapitulation later to become even more frequent. The recapitulation is also more concise on this occasion because the second theme, which played such a large part in the development, is now omitted. The coda gives the framework motif one further hearing but in augmented rhythm, in high position on the two violins, above a softly resonant accompaniment.

The tonality of the movement is not completely unambiguous here either, although the B major closing chord leaves one in less doubt than the A flat minor ending of the first movement. The framework function of B major does in any case become clear from the fact that at the beginning of the movement the half-closes of the framework theme, always remaining open—A sharp–C sharp, F sharp–A sharp, C sharp–E sharp—represent an unstated B tonality. This is later borne out by the framework theme's second appearance at the end of the exposition; the winding parallel thirds resolve in C flat major (fifth bar after **11**), which is obviously the enharmonic notation of B major and is justified only by what precedes it. The third appearance of the framework theme presents a C sharp minor resolution at the border between the development and the recapitulation, but this is obviously an interrupted cadence. Its fourth occurrence is once more unambiguous: the coda closing in the already mentioned B major.

It is understandable that it is only by the appearance of the framework theme that it is possible to expose the tonal structure of the movement. The other themes are indeed considerably uncertain as to their tonality. The drooping motif of the principal theme contains no tonal character whatsoever—at most, the accompanying ostinato points towards F sharp tonality. The secondary theme's tonality floats likewise; here, too, it is only the accompanying ostinato that forms a relatively firm framework (E flat). And the closing theme is constructed from a whole-tone series, and it is only the repeated notes of the cello's pizzicato motif (D sharp and C) which offers any tonal basis. In the recapitulation the principal theme returns in C sharp instead of F sharp, while the closing theme comes with F sharp and D sharp as points of support. Even though all this does not follow the customary arrangement of keys of the sonata strictly, it can be fitted into the B major framework of the movement.

Third movement: Introduzione — Allegro vivace

In the small-scale independent introduction preparing the way for the final movement, rhythmic–chordal elements and melodic–soloistic elements are contrasted. After the wild anapaestic rhythm of the opening comes a rubato melody of an improvisational nature on the cello, filled with inner calm. Its motivic elements assume an important role in the last

181

movement. The cello monologue of the Introduzione is continued by a violin monologue, its lonely melody climbing up into the highest regions of the instrument and there fading out. After this the actual movement itself begins, with a decisive, energetic theme under a repeated organ point. The theme consists of two parts which are organically connected and yet quite clearly separate: the first part is a closed, emblem-like motif heard twice, closely akin to the main theme of the second movement, and the second part, a melody in Hungarian folk rhythm, is developed from the first:

157

With the exception of one single episode-melody the thematic material of the whole movement is developed from these two elements of the principal theme. The first section—we can call it the principal theme group—uses the first element, and indeed in two different characters: from **4** as a light, scherzo mood, and from **7** its hard, emblem-like nature is emphasized. Here, in the shape of a small motif of wilful character, some new material is slipped in, which plays an important part in Bartók's life-work; it also appears in no. 83 of *Mikrokosmos* and in the *Music for String Instruments, Percussion and Celesta*. Strictly speaking not even this is 'new' material since it is related to the principal theme of the preceding movement, too.

158

The whole of the second half of the exposition is filled with the second theme, syncopated and in folk rhythm, developed from the second element of the theme, and here, too, some new material is slipped in—an adagio melody with a strongly folk character (**11**). This melody, coming close to pentatony, is incidentally one of the first signs that even as early as

182

this the more ancient kind of Hungarian folk music had already exerted some influence over Bartók.[131] The syncopated fast theme and the adagio melody together form the movement's so-called secondary group of themes. The closing theme is evolved from the syncopated rhythm.

The development section begins at **14** and mainly makes use of the first element of the principal theme. After a calm, ironically commonplace variation, a scherzando–grazioso fugato is rolled off as the centre of gravity of the development, as it were. The carefree tone almost changes, as later so often with Bartók, to hard, deadly sarcasm. Attraction between similar characters is displayed in that the sarcastic tone of the fugato is followed by the likewise sarcastic tone of the 'wilful' theme, and it is only then that the recapitulation begins (at **28**). The basic tone of the recapitulation is now influenced by the tension of the development: the extreme tension extends into this section, too.

Like that of the preceding movement, the structure of this movement is also characterized by all the thematic material being, so to speak, on the surface all the time, and since all the elements are organically related to one another, their appearance is understandable at virtually every point in the musical development. It must nevertheless be added that this technique is later present in only the second of Bartók's quartets, and after that it almost completely disappears. Organic structuring later becomes associated with greater economy and stricter formal discipline.

On this occasion, too, it is the outer points which help to clarify the tonal structure. The repetition of E at the beginning of the movement and the banal A major cadence in the bar before **1** together with the A fifth-chord at the end of the movement ensure an unambiguous tonal framework. Within this, the first part of the principal theme is considerably uncertain as to tonality; in the folksong theme it is at most the first note that provides the tonal point of support (B flat in the exposition, A in the recapitulation), while the syncopated theme is ambiguous—melodically it moves around a C sharp centre (at **12**—that is, in the exposition), whereas on the basis of its harmony it represents an F sharp minor tonality. This is transposed in the recapitulation to F sharp and B minor respectively. The tonal accompaniment of the coda is very characteristic: the tonality of A has become more or less established when it is suddenly changed by the repetition of B flat, generally speaking creating the same sort of impression as the weighty subdominant stretch at the end of Baroque works, after which the return to the basic key is even more effective. But here this B flat introduces a whole-tone scale which, extending from B flat to C sharp, has a sort of dominant effect and prepares for resolution on to A.

B: I.3.

159

183

The final chord places two fifths on top of one another which indicates on the one hand that the specificity of the tonality (major or minor) remains open, and on the other hand that the second fifth (E–B) does not detract from the determinative tonal strength of the fundamental note (A).

The Second String Quartet

There is little information concerning the origins of the work. Very wide limits are indicated by the composer's dating noted at the end of the score: '1915–1917'. At this time Bartók lived in Rákoskeresztúr and the general worries of the war-torn world made his life difficult. Perhaps these external circumstances also contributed to the writing being protracted over such a long period; during this long time Bartók was obviously compelled to stop working on several occasions.

There is evidence of this vexed life in a letter Bartók wrote to his mother on 16 September 1916. 'The following "official" announcement arrived yesterday (the 14th) about Márta in Szalonta: they have set out from Vásárhely together with three companies of soldiers, the soldiers on foot, with them in cars and on carts. One can imagine they are now progressing slowly but at least in safety, and that they are now on this side of Kolozsvár (this is also in the official news). In other words they are moving under permanent armed guard. Now that I know this I almost envy them; it might be quite an entertaining business taking an active part like that in one of the minor scenes of the war... But it's fortunate that with the help of the lieutenant general dignitary we can get news of the various stages of their "flight". It would be wretched to be in complete uncertainty for so long!'[132]

It is obviously to these vicissitudes that this remark refers in a later statement by Bartók: 'I went through a great deal of excitement...'[133] But we also know that in spite of everything he did work during the war years, indeed a surprising number of compositions came from his pen then. 'I have even found the time—and ability—to do some composing: it seems that the Muses are not silent in modern war,' he wrote in 1915 to his Transylvanian friend, János Buşiţia.[134] In this period, the Sonatina, the *Rumanian Folk Dances* for piano and the two series of *Rumanian Christmas Songs* (Colindas) were written and then he began work on the Five Songs of op. 15, but by the spring of 1916 he finished not only these five but also a further Five Songs written to poems by Endre Ady (op. 16), and composed one of his most significant piano works, the Suite, op. 14. Besides all this, two large-scale works were also in preparation in parallel—the Second String Quartet and, from 1914 to 1916, *The Wooden Prince*.

In connection with the creation of the Second Quartet, important information is offered by an interesting document which is rare in Bartók research; from the estate of Zoltán Kodály the Budapest Bartók Archives obtained a two-page sketch in pen and pencil which contains, with the exception of the last seventeen bars, a rough draft of the third movement

185

of the quartet. There is no date on it and it is impossible even to presume during which part of the known period of composition (1915–17) it was actually put to paper.[135] On another, fuller sketch preserved in the New York Bartók Archives the date of completion is given: 'Oct. 1917'.

The Budapest Bartók Archives' draft conceals valuable information concerning Bartók's method of composition: the draft contains the material of the third movement of the work virtually in its final form, and where it is incomplete, the composer left precisely the amount of space (bars 43–49) into which the appropriate part of the completed composition fits—that is, when he put the draft to paper Bartók already had the musical process of the whole movement in his mind. It can also be noticed that it is primarily the thematic sections which crystallized in his imagination, and so it is chiefly the connecting material which is incomplete.

Just as with the First Quartet, the final tempo indications for the Second Quartet also came only later. The history of the alteration of the tempo indications is briefly as follows. In 1935 André Gertler turned to Bartók requesting him to write a brief analysis of the Second Quartet and to re-examine the metronome indications in the work.[136] In answer to Gertler's prompting letter, Bartók wrote on 31 January 1936: 'Now at last I can send you a list of corrections to the metronome numbers. Unfortunately, however, I cannot undertake a detailed written analysis of the form; there is in any case nothing special in the form. The first movement is a normal sonata form; the second is a kind of rondo with a development-type section in the middle; the last movement is the most difficult to define—in the last analysis it is some kind of augmented *ABA* form...'[137] The list of corrections enclosed was published in 1948 by István Barna, with André Gertler's permission; in the more recent scores and parts from Universal Edition it is these corrected metronome indications which appear.[138]

The first performance of the Second Quartet was given on 3 March 1918, at a concert by the Waldbauer–Kerpely Quartet. This ensemble, who had also introduced Bartók's First Quartet in 1910, also carried the Second Quartet to success and from then onwards took Bartók's chamber music all over the world more and more intensively. Bartók knew the talents of the group and he composed the Second Quartet expressly for them and it is also dedicated to them. Thus Bartók's compositional activity became interwoven with the activities of this excellent group; this relationship remained close later, too, although by then several other world-famous quartets undertook performances of Bartók's works.

Bartók's new string quartet was given a more unified reception than the first. Even the opposing or restrained critics were much more respectful than in 1910. János Hammerschlag's criticism in German in the columns of the *Pester Lloyd*, for example, doubts the genre characteristics of the quartet, meanwhile paying great respect.[139] A less technical and analytical but generally more enthusiastic account of the work was written by Béla Reinitz, who also remarked how Bartók's chamber music had become one with the group of talented young musicians.[140] But on this occasion the finest and deepest account was written by Zoltán Kodály in the periodical *Nyugat*, going beyond the limits of the simple concert criticism, making a comrade-in arms statement, as it were.[141]

186

First movement: Moderato

The movement's principal theme is heard above a harmonic accompaniment in a swaying rhythm. It is sensitive, a true violin melody, and the similarity of its character to some melodies of the two Sonatas for violin and piano written a few years later is very striking. The first two bars are a real foundation element for the whole movement: the ornamental element running upwards in fourths appears as an important motif in the course of what follows (a); the three-note unit following this (b) provides the material for the development section; and the arching fourth-model (D–C sharp–G sharp–G) takes on importance when the principal theme appears in the recapitulation (c).

160

Once the six-bar unit of the principal theme is completed, motivic work commences immediately, using the first opening motif (a): the 'Auftakt' motif consisting of two fourths begins to expand, and indeed with great rapidity. At **2**, the first violin part is already moving over a range of three octaves. The first tension is followed by a quick calming: the 'Auftakt' motif is tamed within the limits of an octave and is extended in the course of imitative playing by a new descending element. It is typical of the organic writing of the movement that this triplet extension (it might also be called a variation) of the principal theme later becomes joined to the secondary theme starting at **5**.

The secondary theme, formed from a single augmented triad, leads through a long chromatic transition to the calmingly closed final theme which is periodic in structure. Once again it is organic structure that is indicated by the fact that the minor trichord motif from which the final theme is formed has already appeared in the chromatic transition section.

The development section (at **10**) begins with a motivic transformation of the characteristic opening motif, but the real tension of this formal section is created when the three-note unit (b) from the principal theme becomes an independent motif.

It is real virtuosity in Bartók's development technique that after this extraordinarily dynamic exposition he can increase this dynamism even further in the development. Accompanied by the dense parallel third movement of the inner parts, the two outer parts stretch out the motif in a varied form to its most expansive form. This dramatic climax is followed by a slower sostenuto section. The second violin rises above a block of augmented fourth chords with a repeated-note melody with a lament character, into the end of which is built the varied motif. This sort of passionate lament interpretation on repeated-note melody is borne out by several analogous melodies from *Bluebeard's Castle* and *The Wooden Prince*.

After the sostenuto section—although the volume diminishes—we come to another melodic climax; then the parts, closely intertwining, fall back down and grow quiet. This line which calms down and becomes smoothed out is also emphasized by the clarification of chromaticism into pentatony.

187

The quieter, more relaxed tone is continued by the recapitulation: the opening motif returns unchanged but its continuation is somewhat modified. In place of the chromatic descending melodic line, outwardly calm but inwardly tense, comes a melody in a swaying rhythm, waving upwards and downwards in a 1 : 5 model. The gentle arches outlined by its melodic line—by a certain inner emotional intensification—become more and more heated. The individual swelling of the melodic arches reminds one of the quartet's most directly related compositions, the Suite for piano.

After an abbreviated recapitulation of the secondary theme it is surprising to find the principal theme coming into the foreground once more—to be precise, the motivic development of the 'Auftakt' thematic motif, but in a transitional function. After a general pause the final theme's minor trichord appears—unisono—in a weighty, emblem-like form. (Does this replace in some way the long transition developed from the minor trichord in the exposition?) The whole final theme period returns in a more relaxed, quieter character, also changed melodically, the two violins playing the melody in parallel octaves while the cello accompanies them with harp-like pizzicato chords.

In the coda of the movement there is a detail which is typical of Bartók's instrumental 'dramaturgy': it turns out that the principal and final themes, which so far have been set in contrast with each other, are actually related. Bartók 'unmasks' the thematic work here when he begins gradually to expand the dolce theme, which covers a range of a minor third, and suddenly there it is before us—the opening motif of the first theme has developed from it.

The coda, however, not only unmasks but also summarizes: with Wagnerian technique all the thematic material of the movement is used on top of each other: first the principal theme and the secondary theme (five bars after **21**), then in the last seven bars the secondary theme and the final theme.

One may try to analyse the movement's considerably ambiguous tonal structure by considering the final theme, that being the only definite tonal focal point. But even this

188

periodically closed theme conceals some tonal ambiguity, for its harmony does not coincide with the tonality which is naturally to be felt from its melody. The melody's keynote, which is reinforced by the period's imperfect cadence–perfect cadence relationship, is C sharp in the exposition, and A in the recapitulation. But Bartók interpreted this melodic keynote as a fifth, and in the exposition he harmonized the C sharp based melody in F sharp minor. This is modified to a certain extent in the recapitulation when the melody's A minor trichord is accompanied by A major harmonies; but in the last analysis the inner contradiction mentioned above evolves here, too, when a final D major chord is attached to the melody ending in A.

The phenomenon is naturally by no means extraordinary. Even among Bach's chorales we can find melodies given harmonies which can be interpreted in different ways. With Bartók this happens even more naturally since the modal principle stemming from the melody is almost always obliged to join forces with the tonality systems originating in European traditions. There is no reason for us to lay emphasis in a mechanical way on either element in this tonal duality. We have to accept the ambiguity which goes with it: in the exposition the final theme is in C sharp and F sharp tonality, and in the recapitulation it is in A and D.

With the secondary theme the source of the ambiguity is the augmented triad. Here, however, the matter is settled more unequivocally by the chords used in conjunction with it: in the exposition F sharp minor is built under the augmented triad as a tonal basis, and in the recapitulation this tonal basis is D major. The agreement between this and the harmonic level of the final theme is not to be neglected; it indicates that the movement's harmonic profile, coming close to late Romanticism, is a homogeneous unit. But even though the tonal traditions of sonata structure would permit us to do so, we can scarcely conclude from this that we should regard the tonality of the secondary and final themes in the recapitulation—that is, D—as being the tonality of the whole movement.

Nor is any help offered in the matter by the principal theme. There can be no question here of tonality springing naturally from melody. In the exposition melody and harmony together make one feel a vague B flat minor tonality. In the recapitulation this same theme becomes even more doubtful tonally as a result of a peculiar circular movement in the chord progression which turns back on itself. The chord leading back to the recapitulation is the dominant seventh of the key. But instead of E, it resolves onto F, indeed onto a chord which is similarly dominant in structure, which would in turn demand resolution onto B flat. Instead of B flat it is again a tonality one semitone higher which appears—that is, once more a dominant seventh chord based on B. Just as with an interrupted cadence, as a result of the substitutional or 'mistuned' resolution the two chords move in a 'shortened' circuit until a 'proper' resolution does in the end lead to B flat. This suspended B flat tonality, however—even though it does in the last analysis agree with the opening tonality of the movement—can not be made valid for the whole movement. Or at most it can only be considered as one point of support.

So let us consider the end of the movement, being the principal tonal point of support. In the two bars before **23** the A minor tonality of the cello part, taken in the melodic sense,

189

is supported on the one hand by A minor VII$_3^4$, and after **23** the same inverted seventh chord from A minor is coloured by a B flat minor seventh chord. This sort of semitone bitonality is no rare phenomenon in Bartók, but the two notes are never equal in importance —one dominates, the other provides colour: here it becomes clear from the double support of A minor that it is not A that colours B flat, but the other way round.

But the A tonality is reinforced by melodic phenomena as well. Before, the cello laid stress on the A–E fifth, and in the two penultimate bars—rhythmically rhyming with the former case—it increasingly comes to end on A. Before and after this, however, it repeats on no fewer than three occasions the little melodic fragment which unambiguously has its origins in the final theme. The melody does actually descend onto E, but this has a subfinal effect and does not destroy the feeling of A minor tonality which has already taken root in our minds.

And finally what does the secondary theme's augmented triad contribute to all this? As we know, this chord is in itself neutral but in association with some other element it can become unambiguous. And this is what happens here: the feeling of A tonality which has evolved melodically is reinforced by the notes A and C sharp in the chord, especially when A comes in the uppermost part in the last chord. And in the cello part the final E comes as the fifth of A and the adjacent F from the augmented triad has only a colouring function. In other words, the augmented triad in the upper voices is coloured into A tonality by the little

190

melody in the cello. The notes A and E dominate, and they are given colour by C, C sharp and F without any feeling of the tonality disintegrating.

165

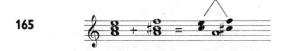

After all this, one still queries how the A tonality coda is to be reconciled with the B flat tonality of the opening of the movement and with the tonality of the other themes. The B flat tonality of the principal theme, however, is not so strong or firmly established as to stand with any force as a contrast to the movement's A tonality. Furthermore, this sort of semitone duality is not alien to Bartók's compositional technique, particularly in the creative period around the Second String Quartet, at which time the closed and, from a tonal point of view, decisive tonal system which he was to use later had not yet evolved. And as far as the tonal connections of the other themes are concerned, the tonalities of F sharp, C sharp and D can easily be fitted into the system of interrelationships belonging to A.

Second movement: Allegro molto capriccioso

This movement belongs to the garland-like formal types. Two traditional forms, a rondo and a variation series, are united in it: for the rondo theme produces more and more variations at its every appearance—that is, in place of a simple recapitulation we are faced with a higher level recapitulation on every occasion.

At the opening of the movement there is a hard barbaric tritone motif which has a kind of framework function. Its melodic character, consisting of upbeat quaver movement rhythm and the repetition of one single interval, paves the way for the rondo theme.

The rondo theme belongs among Bartók's characteristic barbaric ostinatos and is a close relation of the minor third theme of the second movement in the *Dance Suite*. Arab folk music is evoked by both the drum-like accompaniment and the melody of the theme. The structure of the theme is extraordinarily clear: it divides into two almost identical melodic lines which correspond to each other. The second line differs from the first only in that the melody darts higher than in the first line by a major second, which is a simple but effective means of extension. The inner structure of the melodic line is three-part: the line is opened by third repetition, in the centre there is a 'revolving motif' which turns back upon itself, and the line is completed by a scale-like descent.

166

B: II. 2.

191

The first appearance of the rondo theme is immediately followed by a variation: the theme moves from the first violin down into the two lowest instruments. The variation makes use of the first and third parts of the theme.

The framework motif is wedged in between the first and second variations, a fifth higher and in inversion. Then follows another variation of the rondo theme, more remote in comparison with the preceding one. Accordingly the ostinato accompaniment also changes: as well as the repetition of the single note, the upper changing notes also appear.

At **9** the rondo theme moves over through organic texture into the framework motif, which is not in such a static form as in the two previous occasions: it is now broken up motivically. At **11** the cello plays a new motif with the rhythm of a folksong line and with this the first episode begins. After the new motif has been divided up, a big chromatic intensification leads to the other new material of the episode (**13**). The new motif consists of a downward seventh in restrained tempo (Sostenuto) and an 'a tempo' ending added onto it immediately. These two elements in the motif are related to one another as question and answer. At **14** the rondo theme returns in a new guise in keeping with the variational process. On this occasion it is the first and second elements of the basic theme that form the centre of the variational work.

192

This is immediately followed by a new variation in which one of the theme's motifs is arranged as a small period:

170

Further variations of the framework motif introduce the second episode. The motif in folk-song line rhythm appears once more, and open motivic work is evolved from its three-note cadence and the semiquaver figure of the framework motif (21). The whole episode is very dynamic in character—just like the development section in a sonata movement. In the middle of this (25) we witness a peculiar dramatic detail: the minor third motif of the rondo theme collides as rhythmic element with the dolce melody developed from the motif in folksong line rhythm. Dark rhythm blocks become wedged in between the individual sections of the melodic element. From this battle it is the melodic element that emerges victorious: at 27—to a fine pizzicato accompaniment—the melody is at last able to unfold in its entirety. (Its final element unmistakably refers to the augmented triad motif which has a secondary theme function in the first movement.) After 29, the first four-note motif of the melody, after a gradual increase in speed, joins with the elements of the framework motif and a strepitoso ascent (31) leads to the question–answer motif, in a way which is analogous to the chromatic intensification before 13 in the previous episode. The amplitudinous question motif rises in terraces and reaches its climax in the third bar before 33; after that the accelerating elements of the answer motif lead to the next big junction in the form, the return of the rondo theme.

This latest version of the rondo theme also contains metrical transformation: as opposed to the even metre ($\frac{2}{4}$) which has obtained so far, it now moves over to uneven ($\frac{3}{4}$) (Allegro molto, before 34). On this occasion the variation makes use of spring-like expansion of the theme.

171

We are reminded of the so-called proportion of the old dance forms by this transformation of the rondo theme into an uneven metre. Here, too—as in the dances—the change from even to uneven is a method of intensification.

This more tense variation of the rondo theme, on a higher level, leads to similar transformation of the episode elements. In the four-note chromatic figures beginning at 37 there is a return of the apparently disappeared framework motif, a further variation of the variation, when the two elements—original form and variation—are so remote from each other that their relationship is scarcely recognizable.

The episode closes by evoking the rhythm–melody battle which took place in the earlier episode. What appeared there in the form of a third motif now returns in darkly snapping chords with an element from the lonely melody wedged in here and there.

At 🅼 a *ff* pizzicato chord introduces the last return of the rondo theme, and also the large-scale coda.

Although it does include yet further variations of the rondo theme, the coda, as regards function, is nevertheless rather in the nature of a summary. The acceleration in tempo produces a transformation of the basic character of the rondo theme to a prestissimo which has the effect of a stretta: the fairly robust, angular dance character which has prevailed so far becomes replaced by a gliding–rushing tone. The metre changes from $\frac{3}{4}$ to $\frac{6}{4}$, which likewise has significance as a summary, as in this kind of metre binary and trinary elements appear together. The horizontal summary in the metre is aided by the polymetrics evident vertically: for a large part of the coda the cello accompanies the upper parts in $\frac{4}{4}$, so that duple note-groups are heard simultaneously with the triple groups.

The coda is also a summary in the melodic sense: it travels once more the road of expansion covered by the other variations so far, and indeed the expansion is in this case even more extreme: the original minor third theme first assumes an even narrower form, and it is from that that the most spacious melodic arch evolves. The coda is a summary as regards the structure of its melody, too. In the rondo theme and in the first four variations of the rondo theme there was a dome-shaped melody and in the fifth a spring-like stretching melody. Now both occur at once: the various units produce a dome-shaped outline, but at the same time the repeated return to the D starting point and the gradual augmentation of the individual arches contain the spring movement principle. Naturally in the process the line structure of the theme disintegrates and is replaced by homogeneous connection of smaller units of one or two bars.

The harmonic and tonal character differ considerably from that of the first movement. In the latter it was the chromaticism characteristic of the post-Romantic tonal world that dominated, and it was possible to establish the tonality largely on the basis of criteria appropriate to that world. Here chromatically woven melody virtually completely disappears (traces of it are at most to be found in the episodes), and it is replaced by hard interval-repetitions. The framework motif is characterized by a diminished fifth and the rondo theme by the initial minor third and its different extended variations. In keeping with this the tonality of the formal sections is also determined by the 'plane' of the drum-like note-repetitions and interval-repetitions. In this way the framework tonality of the movement evolves on the plane of D: the rondo theme opens out of the D–F minor third and comes to a close on this same minor third at the end of the movement. The fourth and fifth appearances of the rondo theme between **14** and **18** in the centre of the movement are also built on this tonal level of D.

The disappearance of the late Romantic harmonic background does not, however, mean that functional attraction has been entirely eliminated from the tonal relationships.

194

The survival and transformation of functional attraction appears very characteristically straight away in the movement's framework motif. The tense character and leading-note resolution of the diminished fifth and augmented fourth intervals is a phenomenon which has its roots in classical harmonic order. This is what Bartók uses and breaks down to a purely melodic level when he leads to the movement's basic tonality with a chain of diminished fifths and augmented fourths.

172

The essentially harmonic process appears in its purely melodic projection, so much so that the melodic elements take on an independent life of their own and an independent system of attractions with the adjacent semitones evolves—in both directions. For in the melodic projection the third of the resolving tonality comes as the root (for example: of the B flat–D which resolves the tense A–E flat dominant it is not the B flat which remains as the root but D). This is how it comes about that the C sharp–D dominant–tonic progression can also be replaced by E flat–D, and yet with exactly the same dominant–tonic attraction content.

Third movement: Lento

The movement is introduced by mistily rolling dissonances coloured by sordino. The melodic event is provided by consistent augmentation of two-note downward curving melodic fragments. Starting out from an augmented second, the motif assumes the form of a major third, fourth, fifth and minor seventh.

From **1**, complementary rhythm polyphonic writing unfolds in the lower voices and above this there is a gesticular fourth motif (a). The melodic outline is unmistakably related to the opening of the first movement's principal theme, but what was earlier a fast run upwards of an ornamental nature now appears as a weighty, gesticular character. This formal section is completed by a slow, rhythmically even emblem motif consisting of chord blocks. Its melodic line refers back to the fourth motif; its harmonic content on the other hand is reminiscent of the first movement's augmented triad motif (b).

173

In the formal section beginning at **2** it is an emphatic melody which has a descending line and an anapaestic rhythm that plays the most important role. It can be compared with a dirge collected by Kodály: its plaintive tone comes across very penetratingly here, too.[142]

195

Disregarding its first two notes, a note for note quotation of the first movement's principal theme is concealed within it.

Lengthy motivic development work leads to the third theme in the movement (**4**), which melodically is characterized by movement in two directions round a steady axis-note. The melody is consistently heard with fourth-chord harmonies, sometimes with precise mirror-symmetry. Its subdued colours, with *pp* dynamics, lend it an awesome, mystic atmosphere. This formal section is separated by the emblem motif from the section which follows in the nature of a development. A real combat evolves between the emblem motif and a third-motif which has not played any part so far. After this dramatic clash, there begins a formidable intensification using *pp* dynamics and sotto voce colour, in which a minor third projection of the first fourth-motif and variations of the fourth theme moving round this axis become used simultaneously in counterpoint. After the culmination at **8** the recapitulation begins, and this brings back the themes of the movement in abbreviated form and in a different order. The gesticular fourth-motif returns only in its third form. Immediately after that follows the fourth-chord theme on the steady axis, and the movement is ended by recalling the battle between the emblem motif and the exclamatory third-motif. Before the tragic close which falls back into *pianissimo* the dirge melody makes one more sorrowful appearance. This ending is just as dramatic and open as that of *The Miraculous Mandarin* or that of the Suite op. 14.

The closing chord, consisting of the third A–C, which is also the closing chord of the emblem motif which appears at the main formal junctions in the movement, determines quite unambiguously the tonality of the movement. In this light it then also becomes obvious that the A above the G sharp–F motif in the rushing dissonance of the introduction is likewise a tonal framework. Apart from this in the tonally fairly indeterminate movement it is only the third theme moving on a steady axis which represents a definite tonality: E in the exposition and C in the recapitulation. It should be added that even though the steady axis note would in itself be enough to determine the tonality of the theme, the E is further supported here by the cadence of the theme which evokes a typical closing phrase in Hungarian folksongs.

The unambiguous A tonality of the closing movement incidentally bears out in retrospect our claim regarding the tonal position of the first movement. Thus the three-movement symmetrical tempo structure of the work has a corresponding symmetrical tonal structure: A–D–A. The point does arise that in the First String Quartet we did not discover any such tonal unity, but there the tempo structure is also open, not symmetrical, since it gradually progresses from slow to fast.

196

The Third String Quartet

In the summer of 1927, immediately before the time at which the Third Quartet was written, Bartók was in Germany on a concert tour; at the I.S.C.M. festival arranged in Frankfurt he introduced his First Piano Concerto under the baton of Furtwängler in July, and then on the sixteenth he introduced his Piano Sonata in Baden-Baden at a concert arranged within the framework of the Deutsches Kammermusikfest. At the same concert Alban Berg's *Lyric Suite* was also performed. That Bartók gained interesting impressions during this concert tour is also shown by a letter dated 22 July, written from Davos to his mother: '...on the sixteenth there were three different concerts; at 11 in the morning was the one in which I also played; at 5 in the afternoon there was a performance introducing works written for mechanical piano and mechanical organ; and at 9 in the evening Lichtbild (film) performances with music recorded on film to go with it (this is a new invention, and it already sounds just as good as the better gramophones). Then on the screen appeared, separately, Schreker (composer), Kerr (critic) and finally Schoenberg. Each of them spoke about this new invention, their voices naturally being co-ordinated most precisely with the movement of their mouths.'[143]

Bartók travelled from Davos in Switzerland to the performances and also returned there, where his wife was being treated in a sanatorium. On 7 August he wrote to József Szigeti: '...according to the doctor my wife's condition is so favourable that she will be able to come home to Pest at the end of September.'[144] We do not know how long his wife actually did remain there, but this much is certain that Bartók returned earlier to compose. He wrote a letter from Budapest to Universal as early as 10 September, and on the 13th he gave a radio concert in Budapest. At the end of the Third Quartet score the composer indicates September of 1927 as the date of the work's composition.

Bartók sent the work in to the Philadelphia Musical Fund Society's competition. We have no information as to precisely when this happened and what the events leading up to it were, but we can presume that it was connected in some way with the two and a half month concert tour he began in America in December of 1927. Either his attention was drawn to the competition in the United States, or the friends and concert organizers who arranged the tour urged him to take part in the competition. And so we do not know whether he composed the quartet expressly for the competition or whether he sent in the already written work, making good use of the opportunity offered.

For almost a whole year there was no news at all about the result of the competition.

197

This may explain why Bartók sent the 'Druckvorlage' of the quartet score to Universal on 13 September 1928, and began to make enquiries by letter as to whether the Wiener Streichquartett—Rudolf Kolisch's quartet—might like to play it. But not much later, on 27 September, he sent a pressing letter to the publishers to say that he needed the parts, for the time being only written out by hand, since the Hungarian Quartet (the Waldbauer Quartet) wanted to give the first performance of it in Budapest.[145]

After this, on 2 October, news arrived from the United States that the work, along with the Serenata op. 46 by Casella, had won first prize in the competition.[146] Bartók then wrote another letter to Universal Edition: 'Yesterday morning I sent you the original manuscript of my third string quartet instead of the photocopy, since the making of the reproduction would have taken some more time. Then in the afternoon I heard—for the moment just from the Budapest newspapers and Reiner and Murray's cable from New York—that I have won the Philadelphia Musical Fund Society's prize with the work. As a result (that is, in accordance with the Prize specification) the manuscript is the property of the Society mentioned')... (3 October 1928, Budapest, from the original German).[147]

In his letter to Frigyes Reiner, dated 29 October, we learn in more detail how he received the news of his winning the prize. 'My Dear Friend! Many thanks for the congratulations cabled jointly by you and Murray. Don't think, however, that you were the first with the news: you were outstripped by the paper *Az Est* which, on the afternoon of Oct. 2, reported that I had won 6,000 dollars! I read this with suspicion and calmed down a little only when I got your cable in the evening and was able to say to myself that, after all, I really had won something. Within a few days I had learned from foreign newspapers that at least four of us had won something; who had won how much we couldn't discover from the many conflicting reports. So I waited patiently until at last, a few days ago, the letter from Philadelphia arrived, telling me exactly what had happened (and including the check of course). There is no need for me to stress the fact that the money 'came in handy'; we are able to breathe more freely now, to say nothing of the publicity we've had... It had been such a long drawn-out affair that I didn't count on winning anything and only the day before I received the news I had sent the 'Druckvorlage' to Universal Edition in order that they might get it printed.'[148]

Universal—obviously under the influence of the international prize—set to work on the quartet very quickly, which did not please the composer very much, as became clear from his letter of 12 October. 'When I got back from Prague I learned from your letter of 6 October that you wish to put my third quartet to press—or may even have already done so. This was not my intention when I sent you the photocopy four weeks ago. For the fact of the matter is that I have first of all to hear the work since it is possible that various smaller details (bowing, too difficult chords and such like) will have to be changed. In any event I think that these possible alterations will be of very little significance. So if the score is now being engraved you must know that such alterations to the block may have to be carried out later. If you wish to avoid this, the engraving should be discontinued...'[149]

From all this it can be seen that Bartók only felt the composition to be complete once he had also tried it out in performance. For this reason, too, he pressed for the first performance. In his letter of 16 October to Universal he acknowledged receipt of the parts, and he then forwarded them to the Waldbauer Quartet, and also connected with this is the fact that the Wiener Streichquartett also received the parts for study purposes in spite of the Philadelphia Musical Fund Society, who had arranged the competition, having exclusive performing rights on the work for three months.

In the end it was the Waldbauer–Kerpely Quartet which gave the first performance of the Third Quartet on 19 February 1929, in the Wigmore Hall in London. But two days later it was performed by the Vienna Quartet in Frankfurt within the framework of the I.S.C.M. concert series. From then onwards the excellent Vienna Quartet (Rudolf Kolisch, Felix Khuner, Jenő Lehner and Benar Heifetz) became, like the Waldbauer ensemble, enthusiastic propagandists of Bartók's chamber music. The group led by Kolisch made even greater and more consistent efforts than the Waldbauer group to play the new chamber music as widely as possible. It is with their name that the premières of most of the chamber works of the new Viennese school are connected, and it is very typical that alongside the works of Schoenberg, Berg and Webern, Bartók's quartets also frequently appeared in their programmes. At the Frankfurt performance mentioned above along with the Bartók quartet, Schoenberg's Third Quartet and Berg's *Lyric Suite* were also performed.

The first performance in Hungary took place in the Music Academy's main hall on 6 March 1929, at the concert given by the Waldbauer–Kerpely Quartet. Bartók was not present since he had a BBC concert in England on the previous day. Two pieces, which might also be called studies, stand out from among the criticisms: that of Sándor Jemnitz (*Népszava*) and that of Aladár Tóth (*Pesti Napló*). These two—they can be justifiably called the greatest—figures in the history of music criticism in Hungary warmly received Bartók's new work in the spirit of progressive aesthetics.[150] Both pieces are characterized by critical courage, confidence and a sense of responsibility. To take a stand right at the outset beside this truly new composition, difficult to understand, and to explain it with depth—this required a truly great spirit and courage, coming close to that of the composer himself.

The formal plan of this work is even more individual than that of the Second String Quartet. The external division presents two basic formal units with the inscriptions 'Prima parte' and 'Seconda parte'. To these movements, fundamentally different in both their material and their character, are added two other smaller sections—the Ricapitulazione della prima parte, that is an abbreviated recalling of the first movement, and then the coda, which, as far as its material is concerned, is really the Ricapitulazione of the Seconda parte. The four formal units are written completely as one, to be played without any break—in the manner of Romantic sonatas written as one movement. Here, however, all this can scarcely be said to contain any Romantic features, especially considering that this work by Bartók—together with the piano works dating from the year 1926—displays a decidedly anti-Romantic attitude.

199

Prima parte: Moderato

Above static harmony a sensitively unfolding violin melody starts the movement. Functionally it is rather a framework theme than a principal theme, but virtually every important motivic element of the movement is contained within it. It is a rhythmic and melodic 'ancestral figure' which is sufficient for the development of a complete organism. The most striking point is the survival of the two kinds of rhythm pattern:

It is from the extension of the first melodic motif that the first theme develops—the three-part motif consisting of an upward fourth and a third which turns back. It is not difficult to recognize in this one of the characteristic cadence types of pentatonic Hungarian folk-songs.

175

It is from the extension of the second phrase that one of the most important parts of the development section material in the movement is constructed: the melodic element set against harmony blocks.

176

The theme's third, melodically arching phrase assumes importance in the development process of the movement, and not merely in the parts which continue the writing in closer relation to the theme but also in the development section where it has a considerably independent setting.

177

200

b)

p mf

Finally the little trichord scale which completes the melody is the embryo from which the scale motifs of the development section grow. At first sight this system of interrelationships may appear exaggerated, but it will be justified in the analysis which follows, for all the elements in the movement can be fitted into a closed organism.

After the framework theme, a contrapuntal section begins with more or less precise imitation of the opening motifs of the themes. The fugue-like entries are somewhat obscured by the cello playing a supporting part—even before its own thematic entry—to the two violins' counterpoint. This is the plan of the entries:

178

From the entry of the two lower instruments onwards the rhythmically moving motifs increasingly expand, and at **2** there is a return of relative calm with the narrower elements of the framework theme being recalled. At **3** the imitation work is continued on a *forte* dynamic level right up to the summarizing of the theme's opening motif, harmonized with fifth-chords.

Further proof of organic development is that the bitonal ostinato of the new formal section beginning at **4** stems from the opening motif of the first theme. The ostinato serves as a background for the new thematic element, which is composed of capricious little melodic gestures. Bartók had already experimented with this effect, reminiscent of natural sounds and noises, in the First and Second Sonata for piano and violin, and then later, just before this string quartet, he also found it justified in a programme music way in the piano work *The Night's Music*.

At **6** the flexible, intertwining polyphonic writing once more comes into the foreground. Behind the four-note motif, tensed out spaciously, we can recognize a variation of the first part of the framework theme, which appeared at **2** (a). The imitational development of the motif brings the opening movement of the First Quartet to mind; in both, the intervals of the theme's opening motif combine to make seventh chords (b).

179

a)

$\stackrel{\text{♩}}{=}88$

più f

più f

B: III. Prima parte

201

b)

In the looser development-like section beginning at **7**, melodic and harmonic elements confront each other. It has already been mentioned that the melodic motif is a broad variation of the second phrase of the framework motif. If we take the fact that the theme's third, arching element also appears here into consideration, we come to the conclusion that the hard chord blocks are really breaking up a related melody into pieces. We have already encountered this kind of Bartókian dramatic development technique, based on a contrast between melody and chord, in the middle of the central movement of the Second Quartet, in a similar development-like episode.

The chord sequence also displays individual features. There has already been mention of a part where the three-note motif was outlined by fifth-chords. Triads outline the melody here, too—indeed two of them in counter-movement. This polyphony between two chord layers is naturally scarcely very successful in actual sound since the two simultaneously sounding triads merge into a single dissonant mass. This is not a rare phenomenon in Bartók's works dating from between 1926 and 1931, especially in piano works. It must be added, however, that this sort of polyphonic use of chords comes over much more plastically on the piano than on string instruments.

After the hard triad-blocks—a peculiar paradox—an enormous chord piling eight fourths on top of each other takes shape with pleasing gentleness from the melodic motifs. The three last notes of the four-note motifs produce this fourth-chain using nine different notes, and the first notes of the motifs give another fourth-chain which supplements the figure into twelve-tone chromaticism.

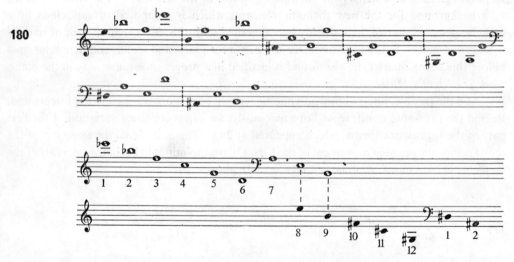

180

At **9** a three-note motif with a diminished octave framework unfolds from the fourth-chords. The motif presents apparently new material but it is actually no more than the further extended closing section of the broad four-note motif which appeared at **6**. Through dynamic intensification the diminished octave motif leads to the little scale motif which is heard in a framework similar to the earlier chord blocks, and while from one angle it refers back to the dome arch of the framework theme from another angle it anticipates one of the principal ideas of the Seconda parte.

181

In place of a real recapitulation it is only the first theme which returns with that kind of reminding function. The other themes familiar from the exposition are missing: only the first two phrases of the framework motif appear—inevitably, since we have arrived at an important formal junction: the Seconda parte is to begin.

The tonal framework for the Prima parte is provided by C sharp. This is the basis for the second-pile in the introduction and the organ point in the return of the theme. The C sharp tonality first appears melodically at **2** unambiguously on the stressed notes of the framework theme. Otherwise long stretches are dominated by the ambiguity of semitone or polar bitonality. Thus even in the recapitulation indicated the C sharp–G sharp basis is coloured by G–D–A, and indeed this is more than colouring here, for the melody itself fits into this tonal layer.

On the border between the Prima parte and the Seconda parte there is a process which is interesting from the tonal point of view: a simple slide from the keynote C sharp leads to the keynote D of the Seconda parte—completely like Beethoven's method (even the notes are the same) between the first and second movements of his op. 131 quartet.

Seconda parte: Allegro

The movement begins with projecting the colouring 'background' into the foreground: above an organ point trill on D–E flat a glissando-like melodic fragment appears which here and there enriches the music like a pinpoint. This technique was later to play an important role in the fourth movement of the Fifth Quartet. The first theme, divided into folksong-like lines, is built into the triad mixture of the cello's pizzicatos; the top part shapes the melody in the D Dorian mode. It is worth comparing it with the central theme of the piano piece *With Drums and Pipes*; it would appear that the series *Out of Doors* (from which *The Night's Music* also comes) has strong threads connecting it to the compositional world of the Third Quartet.

182

At **3** a polymetric, barbaric folk dance theme with a rolling character appears. On account of its being composed of scale-arches it may also be compared with the first theme, but whereas in the latter the keynote is the lowest point in the scale-arch, here the theme has a firm axis lying on E flat, around which the melody weaves a winding line upwards and downwards. From the melodic structure aspect the theme reminds one of the theme of the Second Quartet's last movement, based on the E axis; but in character—even if only because of the difference in tempo and rhythm—they are very different. As regards rhythm the theme may be compared with the principal theme in the first movement of the Second Sonata for Violin and Piano. Both are characterized by a combination of $\frac{5}{8}$ and $\frac{3}{8}$ units. Here, however, there is a very considerable difference in melodic line.

183

This second theme's accompanying material—as in the first movement—is connected with the preceding theme, and in this way the musical structure is made even more organic: unbroken ascending scales evolve from the triad mixtures of the theme. The trill organ point is also heard—its basic note D supports the tonality of the accompaniment, while its adjacent note, E flat, supports the central note of the movement. The second theme continues dynamically straight away: it appears in inversion and many rhythmic variations.

At **10** the cello and viola give a third theme which makes a rather sharp contrast to the preceding one in rhythm and melodic line, but at the same time it displays close relationship to the first theme of the movement. Bartókian organic structure is once more eloquently proved by the transitional section between the second and third themes (between **7** and **10**); the elements of the former theme are gradually broken up and at the same time the rhythmic conception of the new theme appears and with it one or two fragments of the melody.

While in character it reverts to the first theme, the third theme follows the dynamic pattern of the second theme in its development. Its melodic and rhythmic disintegration flows into a section which is even more open and relaxed than what has preceded it, a true development. At **23** large-scale, lengthy thematic development of the second theme begins, and at the beginning of this the third theme is also woven in.

At **31** a fughetta starts from a more distant variation of the second theme. The fast semiquaver theme, leggerissimo in character, is accompanied by a simplified outline of itself in quavers, by way of a countersubject as it were. The sparkling fughetta rolls off *piano* and *pianissimo* throughout, coloured at its climax by sul ponticello. This is a splendid example of Bartók's flitting-scintillating scherzo-atmosphere; it is the descendant of the coda of the Second Quartet's second movement and the forerunner of the glistening scherzo in the Fourth Quartet.

After the fughetta the return of the first theme (at **36**) suggests the beginning of a recapitulation, but this is merely a pseudo-recapitulation, since the development work is now continued even more dynamically. At **40** the third theme appears contracted into a completely chromatic projection, structured in canon and mirror-canon, and after **41** the composer's 'scalpel' continues to strip off the thematic and motivic layers—penetrating right down to the 'skeleton' of the themes. Of the scale-like melodic arch—the melodic material common to all three themes—no more remains than the basic gesture divested of all concrete melody and rhythm: the glissando. After this complete—and, it may safely be said, dramatic—demolition of the material used in the music, we expect a static point of rest, a recapitulation, but surprisingly it is not the movement's own recapitulation which appears but that of the first movement.

In the *Ricapitulazione* there are two structural principles at work—actually striving in contrasting directions. One stems from the nature of the recapitulation: the task of rounding off the material exposed, arranging things reassuringly, to make things stop statically. The tempo is actually faster here since the composer here prescribes Moderato with ♩ = 96 as opposed to the first part's Moderato with ♩ = 88; in reality, however, it is still a deceleration which takes place because the rhythmic values are increased; the principal theme, for example, returns in a rhythm augmented to three times the original values. The other trend shows Bartók's tendency as a composer (he himself also made a statement concerning this) never to make anything reappear in an unaltered form. This recapitulation is an extreme example of a transformed recapitulation because it is necessary to carry out real detective work in order to identify the returning themes at all.

The first surprise: from the slow counterpoint of the two lower parts unfold the outlines of the first and third themes together. The cello brings back the four-note third theme. Above this the viola plays the first theme with augmented rhythmic values and in crab.

184

The downward bending three-note motif which comes into the foreground at **1** may be the crab of the opening melody just heard on the viola, but at the same time it also refers back to the final element of the dome motif in the first part. The micro-melodics of the second theme, evoking nocturnal sounds, returns relatively briefly—only one melodic detail is given a larger role in a mirror inversion variation. It is only after this (at **3**) that the true recapitulation of the first theme follows—that is, the crab quotation concealed in the counterpoint to the third theme proves to have been no more than a vague reference. But the three-note opening motif does not come in its original form here, either, but in a so-called permutational variation (giving numbers to the notes of the original motif, in the order 2–1–3):

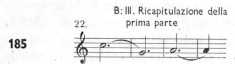

Thus the thematic material of the first part returns in essentially reversed order, which is very significant from the formal construction point of view, since it conceals within it the basic principle behind Bartók's symmetrical, bridge-form sonata movement which was to become firmly established later.

After all this the recapitulation briefly evokes the second part of the development section, and then brings back in a virtually unaltered form the small Lento codetta which prepared the way for the recapitulation of the theme in the first part, and here for the transition to the coda.

The *Coda* is in its entirety constructed from the material of the Seconda parte and for this reason it, too, is really a recapitulation, like the part which precedes it. In the middle of it comes the second, E flat centred theme of the Seconda parte which played such a large part in the development, too. Of the three themes this is obviously the most suitable for varied motivic development. Apart from this the whole coda is like a stretta; its fast tempo (Allegro molto), much changing of the metre, and accumulation of motifs make it extraordinarily animated. In the first part of the coda the scale elements of the theme are in the foreground. Then rolling evolves between the various motifs of the theme. The climax of the stretta's rushing excitement comes at **10** where a version of the theme which is straightened out into scale form is played by the two violins in second canon using extreme diminution (displaced by a quaver), while the two lower instruments provide a counterpoint, likewise in canon form, in the shape of enormous glissandos over a range of two octaves. At **11** the third theme also returns and then the work is closed by excited series of trills and roughly snapping chords.

The two movements of the work display a considerably individual structure, both separately and together. The Ricapitulazione and Coda at the end of the work have undoubtedly a closing function: they do not by any means make the form three-part as some analysts have interpreted it. In the case of the Second Sonata for Violin and Piano the two movements really do become a three-part structure as a result of the material of the first movement being recalled at the end. Here, however, it is not of secondary importance that it is the material of *both* parts that returns in the closing section: the two-part form is thus not completed by *one* third part but by a complex consisting of *two* parts—that is, the binary structure remains binary.

The little section which has a finishing function really has the purpose of inwardly welding the two movements together. For if we consider that neither movement has a real recapitulation (in the first the first theme does return but just as an indication, and in the second the first theme makes only a pseudo-return), then it is obvious that the Ricapitulazione is the *real recapitulation* of the first part and the *coda* that of the second.

186

Prima parte			Seconda parte		Ricapit.	Coda
Exposition	Development	Abbreviated recapitulation	Exposition	Development	Recapitulation	Recapitulation

The amazing economy of the composer is also evident in this individual construction. Since the first theme of the first part has already made a signal return in the first part itself, it is given a relatively small role in the recapitulation. And the first theme of the second part can be omitted from the coda because it has likewise already been used in the pseudo-recapitulation.

Reference has already been made to the fact that it is a slide from the C sharp tonality of the first part that leads to the D tonality of the beginning of the second part. This D tonality, however, which is also borne out melodically by the D Dorian theme, is soon replaced by a new chromatically raised level: the E flat axis-note of the second theme suggests an E flat tonality, especially since the melody—similarly to the first—is likewise in the Dorian mode. But this second theme really represents a tonal accumulation: the E flat tonality melody—as a continuation of the first part—is accompanied by D tonality chords. This D–E flat duality can be observed at the end of the exposition as well: the bass, establishing the D tonal level at **21**, slides up to E flat once more by the beginning of the development. At **26** there is a repeat of the exposition's semitone-bitonality: the E flat centred melody is accompanied by D tonality chords. The Seconda parte is ended by this D tonality when the cello part, resolving from C sharp, settles for a considerable time on D, so as later to move on from there and gradually lead over into the ensuing formal section. There can naturally be no question of a firmly established final effect here (the analysis of the form has emphasized precisely its open character), but it can be no accident that the movement set out on a D tonal level and breaks off on a D level.

From a tonal point of view the Ricapitulazione is even more loose than the main section itself, since here the basic points are missing which earlier were pointers in determining

207

the tonality. The Lento codetta, however, which returns unaltered, is very characteristic. The bass changes precisely at the point where, because of the consequences, it resolves not onto C sharp but onto C. 'In theory' it ought to have led to C sharp here, too—this should determine the tonality retrospectively—but because of the coda's E flat centre the melody finally goes to C.

Since the coda's thematic material is provided by the E flat centred second theme it is quite regular that its tonality should evolve according to the original tonality of the theme. But E flat is only one component of the tonality of the movement, for alongside it an important role was also played by D tonality in the main section. At the same time the coda is the closing section of the whole work and so it is necessary to bring back the C sharp tonality of the Prima parte in some form—at least according to the compositional technique which had evolved with Bartók by this time and which makes for unity tonally, too. Whether this C sharp tonality does in fact return can be decided by a glance at the closing chord of the work. But the genius of the composition is seen in the way in which this closing C sharp tonality is added earlier to the E flat tonality of the coda's material.

The already mentioned climax of the excitement in this formal section is prepared by accumulated repetition of tetrachords in the framework of a diminished fourth. Notice the target-notes of the two outer parts:

Between the E flat and C sharp which have been reached melodically there lies the static D, which played such an important part together with E flat in the Seconda parte. The exciting final moments thus really combine three tonalities. Then in the stretta intensification beginning at **10** these tonalities also appear separately. The upward striving scale developed from the E flat centred theme sets out from E flat and at **11** arrives at D sharp (which is of course equal to E flat). The second violin part, moving in canon in diminution with that of the first violin, starts from D, and so the accustomed D tonality once more joins E flat. To all this the glissandos on the two lower instruments contribute by preparing C sharp tonality, which finally and emphatically enters the scene with a relatively new theme, the third theme, which has not been heard for so long. This theme, which originally remained considerably open from the tonal aspect and always changed its position, now emphasizes the C sharp tonality both in its ascending form with fifth-mixtures and also in its descending form with fourth-mixtures. This accumulating of tonalities and the final selection of one single tonality from among them shows how great a part is played by tonality in Bartók with regard to formal structure.

The Fourth String Quartet

According to the date written at the end of the score by the composer, Bartók started to write the Fourth Quartet in July of 1928 and completed it in September. As we know, during this period there was still no news of the Third Quartet, which the composer had submitted to the Philadelphia Musical Fund Society's competition. Then when the prize did finally arrive, attention was directed on the Third Quartet, and it was chiefly in that connection that Bartók corresponded with Universal Edition in the interests of publication and the first performance. And so there is scarcely any trace of the birth of the new quartet, except the following reference which appears in a letter written on 22 December. 'Some time ago I brought to the notice of Mr. Hertzka, director, the fact that I have also a fourth quartet which is now finished in manuscript. I think it would be wise to publish this latter a little later (perhaps only early in the autumn).'[151]

Bartók was patient because on this occasion, too, he wanted the work to be performed before it would be printed. And so it happened that not long after the first performance in Hungary of the Third Quartet, the Waldbauer Quartet performed the Fourth Quartet on 20 March 1929, in the course of Bartók's composer's evening, in a programme which also contained the Third Quartet, some pieces from *Out of Doors*, the cello version of the First Rhapsody and the vocal solo version of *Village Scenes*. Aladár Tóth and Sándor Jemnitz this time also wrote about this truly very important musical event—the first performance of a new Bartók composition—in splendid studies.[152]

As well as the Hungarian string quartet group, a foreign quartet also played a serious role in gaining international recognition for the Fourth Quartet—this time not the Kolisch Quartet but the Pro Arte ensemble from Brussels. Their impresario, Gaston Verhuyck-Coulon, with whom Bartók was already in contact in connection with the Prévost arrangement of Allegro barbaro for wind orchestra, introduced the young group, who were nevertheless already world famous, to Bartók in his letter of 22 February 1929, and referring to information obtained from André Gertler, requested the parts for the Third and Fourth Quartets.[153] The Pro Arte Quartet had already played the First and Second Quartets on several occasions—the first, for example, in July of 1927 in Frankfurt, just after Bartók's appearance there. Whether Bartók heard the Quartet's performance at that time we do not know. In any event he quickly complied with Verhuyck-Coulon's request and thus the group performed the work early in October of 1929 in Berlin and on 21 October in Vienna.[154] The performance in Vienna was preceded by an interesting exchange of letters. Paul Bechert, director of the I.T.H.M.A. theatrical and musical agency, wrote to Bartók forwarding the Pro Arte's request that the master should dedicate the Fourth Quartet to them.[155] Bartók complied with the request although he scarcely knew the ensemble personally. So in all probability it was Paul Bechert's emphatic request and the international reputation of the Quartet which prompted him in this decision and possibly also the hope that in this way an even wider international audience might be secured for his work. And so on 14 October he wrote the following letter to Universal. 'I do not know what stage the publication of the fourth quartet score is at. If, however, it is at all possible I would ask you to add the following dedication: Au Quatuor Pro Arte, and after that the names of the gentlemen concerned (which I cannot give you exactly but which you can certainly find out)...' On the same day he wrote a favourable reply to Paul Bechert. Thus when it came to the first Viennese performance on 21 October, the Pro Arte ensemble played the work as 'their own'.

It must be added straight away that the ensemble proved truly worthy of Bartók's apparently somewhat trusting confidence. In their letter of 23 October, Universal Edition talk of a 'particularly great success', and this is further underlined by the criticism. The Brussels impresario, Verhuyck-Coulon, thanks Bartók for the dedication on 15 November and writes, among other things: 'The Pro Arte Quartet like your work very much indeed and consider it one of the fundamental pieces [une des pièces capitales] of modern chamber music literature.' The draft of Bartók's reply to this letter, presumably written at the beginning of December, is preserved in the Budapest Bartók Archives: in it he expressed his delight that the ensemble like his work so much and writes that he would like to hear their interpretation. With this, and later, too, the Pro Arte Quartet rendered imperishable services in introducing Bartók's quartet art internationally.

Another detail which belongs to the history of the Fourth Quartet is that the publishers, as in the case of the Third Quartet, asked Bartók whether he would undertake the preparation of the formal analysis usual in the Philharmonia miniature score series. At first Bartók refused and trusted the publishers with the writing of the analysis. But with the Fourth Quartet—it would appear—he was not satisfied with the introduction printed at first, although it is known that it, too, appeared with his consent, and in the end he himself wrote a short analysis of the individually structured work.[156] This analysis—which incidentally is to be found in the scores put out more recently—is nicely complemented by what he wrote to Max Rostal concerning the work's tempi in his letter of 6 November 1931. 'While in Quartet I the tempo should be very elastic all through, in Quartet IV it is much more even and machine-like (except in the 3rd movement). But even here the chords, for instance, in the 37th bar of the 1st movement can, and, indeed, should be played more forcefully, making the tempo, of course, rather drawn out. To indicate the change of tempo at this point (and in similar places) would be confusing; the tempo changes of itself, so to speak, if one correctly grasps and interprets the character of these 'pesante' chords.

All the MM figures are *correct* here.

In the 2nd movement the main tempo should, if possible, be $\downarrow. = 98$ or even quicker, not slower (of course with legato bowing... and *on no account spiccato*!); from bar 78 to 101 (of the middle section) ♩.= 88 is better; from 102 on, the main tempo again. The 5th movement can perhaps be played somewhat quicker than indicated by the MM figures.'[157]

First movement: Allegro

The formal construction of the work has been outlined by the composer himself in the fore-word to the pocket score (Universal). This truly authentic explanation is also followed in this analysis, but further clarification has been put forward with reference to one or two points. Bartók does use the customary terms of analysis somewhat mechanically in a few cases, and strictly speaking he himself is not aware of the new elements in his own formal construction.

The first 13-bar unit undoubtedly has the function of a principal theme: Bartók calls it a 'group of principal themes'. This really is a multi-layered principal section, actually composed of three different kinds of material. The first is a vigorous opening gesture of two bars which is then answered by a second gesture of similar length. In the period-like relationship between the two elements the special point is that in the first the parts close in together while in the second they open out. This opening outwards naturally serves the dynamism of formal construction, for it is very difficult to continue a thematic unit which is closed within a period. In Bartók's theme-development and form-building technique, how-ever, an essential role is played by the organic continuation of the parts and building them into each other, even when the material is apparently broken up. Here, too, in the first 13-bar unit of the Fourth Quartet the continuity is interrupted by five cæsuras. These inter-ruptions, however, influence only the atmosphere, for from a purely musical point of view there is an organic inner relationship between the parts which are separated from one an-other. In the first four bars, as has been mentioned above, the first gesture is answered by the second gesture.

After the first 'period' with its broad movements there appears material which is narrower in its movement. Its motivic basic element, however, is none other than the closing trichord just heard. The parts enter in a terraced way and a characteristic 'note-cluster' is produced by their being closely built upon each other. The layers of the first cluster are built from below upwards and those of the second from above downwards, in a close minor second pile. The end of the second cluster—corresponding with the second gesture of the beginning of the work—opens out and the parts, crossing each other, become rearranged into a major second pile.

At the end of the first cluster, hidden away as it were in the cello part, a little rhythmic motif with a chromatic melodic arch appears. This motif—we may anticipate—is the basic element, the proto-motif of the movement, and indeed of the whole work. Its importance soon becomes evident: after the opening out of the second cluster the principal theme is brought to a close with it. Now the emblem-like, terse motif appears in a mirror canon arrangement.

A new trend in Bartók's development technique is already in evidence in these first

211

thirteen bars. In the earlier string quartets after the exposition of a theme or motif, dynamic thematic development work began, which was, however, essentially writing which continued according to traditional principles. The material of the principal theme in the Fourth Quartet is fundamentally different from this: the continuity is divided into relatively static blocks, and it is within these blocks, almost in micro-structures, that dynamism develops. The music is more concise and compact than anything preceding it and can really only be compared to the development technique of Webern.

The formal section from bars 14 to 29 is a transition according to Bartók's analysis. Its material is a wave-line motif consisting of four notes which unfolds polyphonically at three levels above a bitonal basic texture. This motif is so characteristic and plays such an important role in the movement—and even more so in the work's final movement—that we might be better advised to regard it as a second principal theme and not a transition. This is also supported by the reappearance after it of the proto-motif's mirror canon, so that the two similar blocks surround fairly firmly the section regarded by Bartók as a transition, but as a result of this it scarcely possesses any transitional character. It is rather the proto-motif canon which may be regarded as transitional material, for here, it leads to the new formal unit beginning in bar 30.

Concerning the four-note motif it has been shown elsewhere that it is a mistuned tetratonic melody, a form of an imaginary fifth framework which has been distorted into a diminished fifth. This is best proved in the last movement when it becomes clear that the motif s the central 'section' of a mistuned pentatonic system. Thus the motif is in itself bitonal, in an individual linear form of bitonality (see *Ex. 121*). But the motif's accompaniment, as has already been referred to, is likewise bitonal: a C major trichord level is heard in the viola's ostinato while the cello accompanies this with G sharp minor second inversion chords. These two tonal levels are not alien to the bitonality of the melodic levels above them, for the notes they use can also be separated and divided into two pentatonic systems at a distance of a diminished fifth from each other.

This stratum, which from the tonal point of view is double (C–F sharp) is, however, divided by Bartók into three layers in the texture: for the motif sets out from C sharp and is then continued by a canon on a level one fifth higher, and then a new part joins in on a level which is in a diminished fifth relationship to this latter. This third and uppermost part produces a double tension in the texture because it progresses in a tense, anti-acoustic relationship not only with the part immediately below it but also with the lowest part.

The most characteristic melodic element of the secondary theme beginning in bar 30 is derived from the proto-motif. The whole-tone scale motifs along with it make the theme group considerably vague from the tonal aspect. On the basis of the beginning and the stronger cadence of one of the scale motifs a feeling of A flat tonality evolves—even if only faintly. Seen from this angle Bartók's analysis becomes more understandable with regard to the function of the preceding section. The part which shows C–G sharp bitonality is 'transitional' in function because one of its levels points back to the C tonality of the principal theme and its other level (G sharp) forward to the A flat tonality of the secondary theme which agrees with it enharmonically. This aspect, however, does not diminish the particularly important role played by the motif in question.

The downward chromatic gesture in the beginning of the secondary theme later turns round—just as it has the same value both upwards and downwards in the proto-motif—and in this way a folksong-like, more closed theme of fifth-structure evolves from it. But the melody is only relatively closed, since there is no natural feeling of cadence because of the double fifth-answer, and so the cadence—mistuned in relation to the fifth levels—is only created by recalling the chromatic opening motif. This theme section starts from A flat and arrives at E—that is, its mistuned dominant.

The six-bar final theme beginning in bar 44 is born from an extension of the proto-motif. The broad downward arch of the motif is accompanied by straightforward melody-axes repeating the same note. This type of theme plays an especially important part in Bartók's works which display neo-Baroque aspirations. Its closest relation from the First Piano Concerto can be seen in Example 30.

The tonal position of the final theme is likewise not unambiguous. Since it is directly connected to the secondary theme ending on E, it is possible to regard E as the tonal centre here, too. There can, however, be no question of a 'keynote' since this E axis is placed at the uppermost point in the texture. The exposition is concluded by a minor second cluster. Its tonal definition is provided solely by the chromatic tetrachords moving towards E in the two lower parts.

189

The development section begins with a combination of the secondary theme's chromatic gesture and the trichord of the note clusters. From the changing note motif originate demisemiquaver trills, the same kind of musical picture as in the Musette from the suite *Out o Doors* dating from 1926. The repetition of the trills, starting with a sforzando, has a shivering effect. To this 'shivering' background large-scale development of the four-note mistuned motif begins; the small motif, which at its first appearance (bars 14–24) continually turned

213

back upon itself, here comes in a broadly arching melodic form. Behind its melodic development it is, however, quite apparent that its roots reach back into the development of the diminished fifth canon.

Together with the unfolding of the melody there also starts a variation process the tendency of which is to expand the motif structurally. It is to be noticed that it goes through a similar expanding process in the last movement. In bar 75, as the final result of the motivic dissecting work which has taken place up to this point, the musical texture disintegrates into its most basic elements: every melodic element disappears and only broad glissandos and trill motifs remain. This part is very similar to the end of the Third Quartet's Seconda parte.

But after this great 'demolition' we can also witness the reconstruction process: a struggle begins between the shivering trills and the proto-motif, which once more steps into the foreground. The two different kinds of material are almost 'brutally' confronted with each other: the proto-motif or an occasional fragment of it breaks open and wedges its way into the closed blocks of the trill motif.

The end of the development section and at the same time the beginning of the recapitulation is indicated by the basic motif appearing unisono. From the recent battle this was the motif which emerged triumphant so it is logical for it to come now not as a secondary element as at the beginning of the exposition but to be given greater emphasis. For this reason it is also wedged in between three appearances of the returning opening motif using three different instrumentations.

The recapitulation continues in a perfectly regular manner, although more or less each individual theme and motif is transformed. This transformation is also accompanied by a certain condensing: as opposed to the 48 bars of the exposition, the recapitulation has only 42, and within these there is a significant decrease in the first and second theme groups, the final theme being the only one to grow and that only because the coda of the movement develops from it.

Interrelationship between the development section and the coda is a phenomenon already familiar from formal structure in Beethoven. We meet the same thing in this Bartók movement, too, but it is characteristic of Bartók's economic structure that only the dynamic closing and returning section from the development is used for the coda—that is, the battle between the two contrasting motifs. The melodic element is represented here, too, by the basic motif, but contrasted with it on this occasion is not the trill motif but rising and augmenting melodic blocks unfolding out of a mysterious *piano*. Their victory appears inevitable at first, but after a climax (bar 152) the basic motif appears again and now it comes out triumphant. This triumph is reinforced by a canon in diminution and a melodic extension which lends an even more closed character to the motif.

B: IV. 1.

190

The position within the recapitulation of the section which we have called the second principal theme group also proves that it is more than transitional material: it returns on the same tonal level, only transposed down an octave—that is, it belongs unequivocally to the principal theme group. On the other hand, the other themes, in keeping with the sonata principle, appear in a different tonality. The secondary theme ends in C, and this same C tonality is then continued by the final theme, too. In the dramatic struggle of the coda, the melody—climbing higher and higher out of the depths—contrasting with the proto-motif, rests consistently on F sharp and G sharp—that is, on the Bartókian (mistuned) dominants of C; in other words, on the adjacent chromatic notes of the acoustic dominant. This same melodic preparation precedes the motif which ends the movement; the contrapuntal game breaks off on A flat—that is, the augmented fifth of C. From there it 'resolves' into C; in the summarizing emblem motif the melody's minor third is coloured by a major third, and indeed in a structure which is different from that of the alpha chord: the minor third is underneath and the major third is above.

191

B: IV.1.

Second movement: Prestissimo, con sordino

It has already been mentioned that the direct antecedents of this movement can be found in the Second and Third Quartets. An extension of this kind of tone to cover a whole movement is presented with particular emphasis in Berg's *Lyric Suite*—the composition which inspired Bartók in other respects as well. The connection with Berg is indeed strengthened by yet another element: in the fifth movement of the *Lyric Suite* (Presto delirando) there are the same kinds of light, flitting glissando effects as in this movement by Bartók (bars 136–145, and at the end of the movement). There are, of course, glissandos in the Third Quartet as well, and also in the first movement of the Fourth, but there they have a weighty 'clinging' character. Here these light glissandos, stemming from the tone of the movement which is in any case light and fleeting, are the final variations of the chromatic upward and downward melodic lines.

'The second movement has a scherzo character and is in three sections', writes Bartók in his outline of the form. Its theme is an arching melody which rises and falls back chromatically—within the framework of a perfect fifth, in the tonality of E. It is first heard on the two lower instruments and then on a level a fifth higher on the two violins. The theme is accompanied by point-like chords on the two other instruments, each joining on two adjacent notes of the chromatic theme. By the time the melody arrives back at the starting note, E, the accompaniment rises as far as A sharp and, by means of a direct leading-note step, reaches the basic note of the level beginning a fifth higher.

The harmonic profile of the movement is also determined by the superimposition of two perfect fifths. In a chordal form, however, semitone displacement makes the sound tense.

215

In the scherzo theme the first fifth wave-arch has really been answered by a wave measuring a fourth. This fourth also has some influence on the chords in the movement—fourth-chords become constructed from it.

The first part of the scherzo form is also tripartite within itself. The theme returns in bar 54 in a four-part canon at the octave in diminution, and at bar 62 a sixteen-bar transitional section begins which prepares for the trio. A motif using complementary writing and weaving two major seconds into each other, anticipates the second-piles of the trio.

In the trio section a large part is played by the clusters composed of various melodic repetitions. Bartók's organic and economic structuring is characterized by the melody and the accompanying background fabric being built from the same material; the parts—filling each other out, that is in a complementary way—add up to second-piles. At the same time the theme starting in bar 78 also refers back to the first movement's note clusters. In the centre of the trio section the cluster remains alone and its moving parts fill out two fifths chromatically. We will meet with a similar cluster effect in the trio of the Scherzo movement in the Fifth Quartet, too.

193

The colour technique of the clusters suddenly changes in bar 136 to light glissandos, and then sul ponticello playing lends an even more individual, an even more colourful sound to the end of the trio.

As a result of the tonally neutral character of the clusters and other note piles, it is not possible to determine the tonality of the trio. The tonal character is gradually restored in the closing section, however, when the fifth-chords are brought back. Chromatic raising of the fifth-chords leads back to the tonality of E which on this occasion comes only at the melodic level, for the other parts add colour to this with adjacent notes and fifth-chords on other foundations (bar 189). This recapitulation, however, is anticipated by a clever pseudo-recapitulation: from bar 175 the parts throw the scherzo theme's opening motif to each other in its original form and in inversion. Adjacent chromatic notes already appear here to mistune and colour the tonality.

In the middle of the scherzo recapitulation an interesting combination of the theme and the complementary transitional motif appears as new thematic material. This is accompanied by the cello's pizzicato-glissando fifth-chords.

194

The animated movement is ended by an even more animated coda. The glissando motifs come into the foreground once more, and to these a colourful background is provided by fast scale motifs, chains of trills, pizzicato and sul ponticello playing. The musical material, completely dissolved as it were, quietens down to *ppp* and then on the wings of major ninth glissandos really does fly off. The closing harmony rounds off the movement tonally: airy E harmonics join an E–B–F sharp fifth-chord.[158]

Third movement: Non troppo lento

In the movement which occupies the central position in the symmetrical construction of the work it is principally the change in texture that is conspicuous; up to this point counterpoint has dominated, or at least been mixed in with homophonic elements. Here it is homophony that reigns supreme; the whole movement is characterized by static harmonic blocks with melodies unfolding under them, above them, or among them. The key to the movement lies in the structure of the harmonies and their relationships to the melodic elements.

The opening chord and the closing chord, containing the same notes but not structured in the same way, offer very important guidance in the analysis of the harmony of the movement. In the opening structure major seconds dominate, and in the closing structure the same is heard but laid out in fifths.

195

The opening out of this closer structure into something wider shows that both have an imaginary common basis, the chord consisting of five interrelated fifths.

217

196

Harmonic movement between the outer points is generally of a slower nature; each chord-block is spread out over a lengthy area as the static basis behind the melodic action. This slow melodic action is essentially no more than a variation of the fifth-structure basic chord—coloured with adjacent chromatic notes. Thus the second chord beginning in bar 13, for example, has two notes from the perfect fifth-structure surrounded by chromatic colouring notes.

197

Tension grows in proportion to the disintegration of the fifth-structure and the enrichment of the melodic elements. In the third formal unit, starting in bar 22, the fifth-structure is already incomplete, the missing notes being replaced by chromatically adjacent notes.

198

When the melody calms down, the harmonic structure rests on a perfect fifth-chain in bar 33 and then similar 'alien' notes again make the musical texture tense.

We reach a point of rest in bar 41: the perfect fifth-structure changes over to a perfect fourth-structure. After this comes a climax in the excitement (the tempo also changes to Agitato), and the chord structure is once more coloured by 'alien' notes. In bars 47–51 the wave motion of the two outer parts seems to introduce a new harmonic element into the movement, but this, too, is actually a continuation of the earlier chord forming principle: the two-phase chord change uses a complete pentatonic system—but of course pentatonic systems form a chain consisting of four interrelated fifths.

In the harmonic action of the movement, therefore, quite independently of the melodic process, a special tension wave can be observed. This is made even more interesting and complex by the combined movement of the two dimensions. For the melody consistently complements the chords. The first chord, still arranged in seconds, is filled out in the middle by the melody.

Similarly the second melodic unit beginning in bar 14 is built into the chord block. And the third, in the highest register of the cello, even rises above the harmonic block. By the time it comes to rest, its final note, A, becomes an organic part of the fifth-structure sounding above it.

199

This complementary process is finally tensely extended by the violin melody which appears at the climax in the movement's excitement in such a way that the notes of the melody are fitted in among the notes of the chord virtually like cog-wheels.

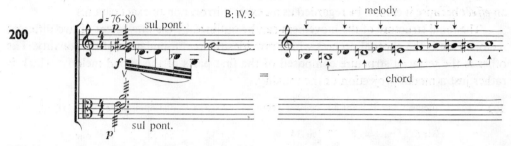

200

This is the climax in the tension curve of the movement, but the complementary process reaches its peak on a yet higher level in the most complete complement possible: G flat pentatony and C diatony (the black and white keys on the piano) are fitted into one another and this produces a complete chromatic scale.

After this there is nothing surprising in the fact that the final chord of the movement is supplemented by the note D, with which the whole process began.

All this combined harmonic and melodic action encloses within a firm formal framework a gradual unfolding of a single melody with a Hungarian folk character, and its variation. The closed eight-bar theme is divided into two equal parts: the first is considerably improvisational in character, consisting of movement around a single centre note; the second part is a parlando–rubato monologue, with a more expansive melodic arch. The first part is chromatic, the second diatonic. The repeated notes of the first part create tension not only through their excited rhythm but also through their complementary relationship with the accompanying chords. On the other hand, the second part is related to the harmonic accompaniment in a similar way when it comes to rest: the final note is no longer a complementary note but a component part of the harmony.

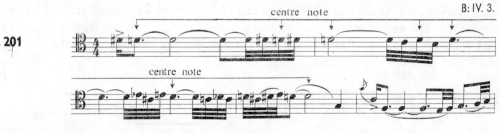

201

219

final note

The central section of the movement evolves in a diff e rent way; here, when the melody reaches the extreme point of the variational process, it breaks up into tiny fragments almost like bird-twittering (bars 35–40). Then at the Agitato climax the melodic character reciting on a single note (first part of the theme) returns, in relation to which the following eight bars make a variation of the calming (second) part of the theme. In bar 55 a tranquil summary begins; the diatonic monologue melody returns to the cello while the violin accompanies it with a counterpart which has a mirror canon effect. (This can only be called an *effect* because it cannot be regarded as an exact mirror, nor an exact canon.)

The tonal structure of the movement can be outlined by the movement of two different factors. One is the chordal process which provides the real foundation of the tonality. The other is the terraced structure composed of the first parts of the varied melody, which is rather just a modal projection of the tonality.

202

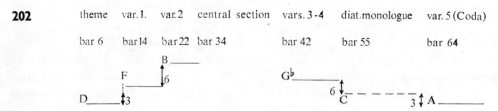

Fourth movement: Allegretto pizzicato

This second scherzo-like movement is strongly related to the Prestissimo which corresponds to it in the symmetrical order of the work. In the Prestissimo it is the muted tone-colour that gives a special tonal character to the music, and here this is provided by pizzicato. The relationship, however, is even deeper than this; Bartók himself draws attention to the fact that the movement's 'theme being identical with that of the second movement; there it moved within the narrow realm of the chromatic scale—here it is extended over the diatonic scale; accordingly its range in the former is a fifth, while here it is an octave'.[159] It is characteristic of Bartók's primarily musical thinking that he does not carry out the extension of the chromatic arch-melody mechanically, and thus as opposed to the chromatic melody moving in minor seconds, he does not apply the whole-tone scale moving in nothing but major seconds, but the augmented fourth–minor seventh so-called acoustic scale of Rumanian origin. The basic unit's tendency towards logical extension, however, is apparent in the Lydian opening of the theme, which uses a group of major seconds, and in the last part of it, which comes nearer to the whole-tone scale:

B: IV. 4.

203

The movement is also characterized by expansion in the tonal sense. The theme of the second movement was played in two fifth layers; here the theme is heard in a four-part fugato arrangement, and on four different fifth levels. This sort of fugato arrangement, which later assumes an even more consistent form in the *Music for String Instruments, Percussion and Celesta*, obviously produces greater tonal breadth than the two-level answer at the fifth.

It is worth following the relationship of the theme entrances to the accompanying harmonic basis. The tonality of the movement is A flat which in the fugato arrangement agrees with the first entry of the theme. It is, however, very characteristic of Bartók's harmonic world that the melody based on A flat has an accompanying chord based on G—to be precise, a chord which, along with a G–D–G perfect octave layer, contains another A flat–E flat layer which in relation to the first is mistuned. It is out of this mistuned level that the melody appears. The entry of the second part—on a level a fifth higher, that is starting from E flat—is accompanied by similar tonal ambiguity. Here the melody does appear out of the fifth-chord based on E flat, but the chord's fifth and octave are coloured by adjacent chromatic notes here, too: A is heard beside B flat, and E beside E flat. And the E also colours chromatically the second fifth of the E flat basic note, that is F.

The third part enters from the same background as that which preceded it, but a fifth higher—that is on the B flat level. The B flat–F–B flat octave framework is coloured in the same way here by A and E, but their functions are different: the A colours the basic note and the E colours the fifth. From the tonal point of view, the fourth entry is the clearest of all: the melody's F level is supported by an F major triad, but the third and fifth are alternately coloured by adjacent chromatic notes—B flat and B.

There is a peculiar polymetric relationship between melody and accompaniment. The eight-bar melody, regular in construction, is accompanied by 'guitar-like' chords which are asymmetrically divided. The asymmetry of this accompaniment appears even within the $\frac{3}{4}$ metre, but there are even more complicated metrical displacements to notice than this. The sforzato accents of the individual chords produce larger metrical units, and the peculiar thing is that these larger metrical units are different and continually alternate. In the first nine bars, for example, $\frac{5}{4}$, $\frac{6}{4}$, $\frac{7}{4}$ and $\frac{8}{4}$ divisions appear in a consistently increasing order within the $\frac{3}{4}$ notation.

The relationship between melody and accompaniment is thus characterized not only by simple polymetrics but by complete metrical independence, for which it is primarily Arab folk music that may have served as an example to Bartók. It will suffice to document the metrical contrasts of a single line. (Notice that only in one case does the accent of melody and accompaniment coincide, and this merely increases the strange feeling of deviation in the other accents.)

B: IV.4.

204

221

The thirty-six bar formal section structured as a four-part fugato—the first part of the three-part scherzo form—ends in A flat tonality at the end of the significantly augmented fourth entry. From this close, however, by means of further motivic use of the theme, a transitional section begins without cæsura, providing a continuous bridge over to the trio, which begins in bar 45.

The theme is a close variant of the trio theme in the second movement. The hard pizzicato effect of banging on the fingerboard prescribed by the composer lends it an individual colour. The background is provided here, too, by cluster-like colour-chords.

A free recapitulation of the scherzo theme begins in bar 88. The fugato structure is here replaced by a two-part octave canon in diminution, in the first violin and the cello, the guitar effects of the two parts between them continuing the character of the trio. The thematic material, closed to start with, is broken up as in a development by means of inversions and rhythmic imitations, and then closes like a fan (bars 102–112) and, settling into the A flat major level, moves into a small coda (bar 113). The material broken into scale motifs which mirror one another and into rhythm imitation is very closely related to the pizzicato episode in the second movement of the *Music for String Instruments, Percussion and Celesta* (from bar 242). The motivic material of the coda on the other hand, which has derived from the last part of the scherzo theme and taken on an independent life, anticipates no. 124 of *Mikrokosmos*—'Staccato'. After a momentary suspension of the rhythmic progress another fan-like closing gesture leads to the final chord of the movement. Only the A flat at the top and bottom of the chord represents tonality, for the 'area' between them is filled out by the notes of the theme's scale, further coloured by two adjacent chromatic notes.

205

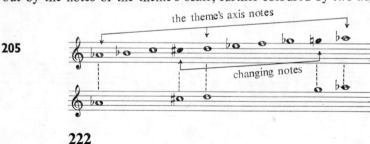

Fifth movement: Allegretto molto

While the relationship between the second and fourth movements rested on the principle of variation, the first and last movements of the work—that is, its pillar movements—are connected by the cyclic principle. What played a relatively subsidiary role in the first movement (Bartók describing it as no more than transitional material) here appears as a principal theme and plays a dominating role in the whole movement's thematic work.

The whole movement is a sort of 'Allegro barbaro'. The four-note motif appearing as principal theme bore certain traces of Arab folk music even in the first movement; these come forward now even more unambiguously as a result of the transformation of the rhythmic character and the drum-beat accompaniment.

The appearance of the theme—to quote the composer once more—is introduced by 'chord beats (chords of fifths obscured by seconds)'. We have already seen how important fifth-chords are in the work's harmonic system. It is, therefore, to be expected that the fifth movement should summarize and condense from this aspect as well. In keeping with the movement's C tonality the central layer of the fifth-chord is the fifth C–G, to the basic note of which D flat is added as an adjacent chromatic note, and to its fifth F sharp is added. The tonally decisive C–G plane is, however, veiled by the cello's F–C–G fifth-chord broken in a downward direction which sounds, precisely because of its being broken downwards, a little like a G–C–F fourth-chord. As a new note the F also clashes with the adjacent chromatic note F sharp, thus intensifying the hard, raw quality of the chord.

206

It is out of this introductory chord repetition that the theme's drum-like ostinato accompaniment develops. Here the C–G fifth becomes the sole basis of the music, but the number of adjacent chromatic notes increases, for the D flat and F sharp which create tension from within the fifth are now joined by A flat in the form of an acciaccatura. From the metrical point of view it is very important that the even quavers of the viola are divided by several interrupting chords on the cello—reinforced by *sf*—into metrical units of three and two. The groups of three and two combine consistently into larger 3+3+2 units—that is, into a kind of asymmetrical accompaniment form which is a very frequent phenomenon in Arab folk music. Note that Bartók modified the even quaver accompaniment of the piece 'Ostinato' from the series *Mikrokosmos* when he transcribed it for two pianos, in such a way that similar 3+3+2 metrical units are produced (see *Ex. 55*).

The short barbaric theme develops with the help of inversion, expansion and changes in register. After its first appearance, it is heard two octaves higher in bar 23 in mirror inversion. It must be stressed that this is not a note for note mirror inversion, but a version in which the melody progresses along an unaltered interval structure in the opposite direction.

223

B: IV.5.

In the other variations, however, (bars 31 and 37) the interval structure is also expanded; this is how, for example, a perfect fourth model evolves from the mistuned tetratonic melody. It is, however, characteristic of all the various versions that they fit perfectly into the ostinato chord of the accompaniment.

208

B: IV.5.

In the course of further development of the theme when more remote motivic combinations also appear, the accompanying chord slips down to the A–E fifth level (into which, however, the form of the theme which has an A sharp–D framework fits) and then, as the most important modulatory section, the F sharp–C sharp fifth level assumes supremacy and this, on the other hand, is now coloured by the adjacent chromatic notes C and G. Although the set of notes used is in itself virtually unchanged, its application indicates that the musical process has arrived at a higher tonal plane, to a 'Bartók dominant' level, as it were, while the theme returns in its original form. This is no static recapitulation with any settling tendency, but a bridge to another dynamic turning point when the first three notes of the theme break away from it and carry on as an independent motif with a scherzando character. The fifth-structure which has reigned so far is now supplemented by fourth-structure:

209

B: IV.5.

As a result of the gradual break up of the melodic elements the bare fifth-chords once more come into the foreground—even rhyming with the introductory section, only in a different tonality. An interesting point is the confrontation of fourth-chord and fifth-chord: in the upper parts there is an E flat–A flat–D flat fourth chord, to which the cello plays a D–A–E fifth chord. Just as in the introduction, the breaking of the chord in a downward direction gives the impression of a fourth-chord on this occasion, too, as a result of which the upper and lower chord levels clash in semitone bitonality. But the tonal withdrawal is only temporary, for after the parts move chromatically in different directions, a unisono leads to the C cadence of bar 148.

The border between two large formal units is indicated by the sharp cut of a general pause. The new section is not a development section but a central section like a trio, which has completely new material. This 'new' material, however, is an undisguised reference to the first movement. For the light grazioso theme beginning in bar 156 is none other than the folksong structured closing melody of the secondary theme in the first movement. There the melody was played in three fifth layers and here it is heard on three fourth levels and finished with a mistuned cadence.

210

The emblem-like proto-motif also returns from the first movement, setting a hard marcato character against the grazioso theme. The whole central part of the movement is taken up with these two materials and rich development of them, and then in bar 238 the beginning of the recapitulation of the first part arrives with the appearance of the Arab theme. The drumming accompaniment is now omitted, though the hard grating fifth-chords play a part here, too, but just between the various appearances of the theme. Instead of simultaneity it is now placing things side by side that dominates. Here also the contrasting keys, displaced by a semitone, appear side by side laid out in a linear way. The placing of the C sharp and C tonalities alongside one another chordally is followed by linear spreading out of the whole melody's bitonality (see *Ex. 121*).

After the scherzando motif is recalled in G sharp tonality, the coda begins in bar 365 and this ascends, through building up the Arab theme, to the bringing back of the first movement's emblem-motif. A contrapuntal accumulation of the emblem-like proto-motif—almost identical note for note with the end of the first movement—closes the movement, and at the same time the whole work, with a *ff* marcato character.

The Fifth String Quartet

Bartók wrote this work as a commission from Elizabeth Sprague-Coolidge. This American patroness, famous for her support of contemporary music, commissioned works from numerous significant composers of the period; among them, Schoenberg's Fourth Quartet was also written in 1936 as a result of a request from her. When and how she came to be in contact with Bartók is not known, but since Bartók was permanently represented at the I.S.C.M. festivals from the twenties onwards, he was obviously held to be one of the leading European composers in the United States as well, at least in more expert professional circles.

Interesting information on this question, however, is provided by a letter dated 16 November 1935, from Gaston Verhuyck-Coulon, the above-mentioned Brussels impresario, in which he tells Bartók that Mrs. Coolidge had handed over the parts of the Fifth Quartet to the Pro Arte Quartet and entrusted the group with a few performances. 'It will probably be of interest to you,' Verhuyck-Coulon adds, 'that this work was ordered on the recommendation of our friends the Pro Arte Quartet.'[160]

The composition was completed extremely quickly on this occasion, too: Bartók began work on it on 6 August 1934, and finished it precisely a month later, as is shown by the usual note at the end of the score. It must be added that this was the sole composition written in that year, and the preceding year yielded no more than orchestral arrangements (*Hungarian Peasant Songs* from the *15 Hungarian Peasant Songs* written originally for piano and the *Hungarian Folksongs* from the series of *Twenty Hungarian Folksongs*). Thus the Fifth Quartet is the first great creative achievement after a short period of 'silence', the 'first chord' in the great works of the thirties.

The first performance of the Fifth Quartet, in accordance with the wishes of the commissioner, took place in Washington on 8 April 1935, at the Viennese Kolisch Quartet's concert. The other works in the programme were Beethoven's great B flat major Quartet op. 130, and Alban Berg's *Lyric Suite*.[161]

Mrs. Coolidge, to whom the work is dedicated and who, as the commissioner, possessed exclusive performing rights on the work for almost nine months, also asked for a performance from the Pro Arte Quartet, as was mentioned above. From Verhuyck-Coulon's letter already quoted we know that the group performed the work in Marseille on 13 December 1935, and the impresario asked Bartók for a short introduction and formal analysis for this concert. It is not known for certain whether Bartók did actually send what was requested to the Pro Arte Quartet, but some evidence is offered by an incomplete draft preserved in the Budapest Bartók Archives and published by László Somfai. This is once more a document as valuable as the analysis of the Fourth Quartet published later in Universal Edition, and indeed in certain respects it is even more valuable than that, since it affords a glimpse of the new individual conception of Bartók's tonal thinking.[162]

After the first performance in Washington almost a whole year passed before the work was first performed in Hungary. The interpretation on this occasion was given by the successors to the Waldbauer Quartet—the New Hungarian Quartet.[163] They first played it in Vienna at the concert of the I.S.C.M. Austrian section on 18 February 1936, and then it was heard in the main hall in the Music Academy in Budapest. It is typical that the *Pester Lloyd*, the Viennese correspondent of which had received Bartók's new work in February with rapturous adjectives (it is true that the critic was no less a person than Ernst Křenek), reported on the Hungarian performance almost sourly.[164] The paper's *home* staff obviously represented the conservative upper middle class attitude which did actually 'bow' before Bartók's greatness on the basis of his success abroad, but they were unable to understand it.

The finest critical study was Sándor Jemnitz's piece in the *Népszava*. Jemnitz, who not much later published a long and penetrating study on the Fifth Quartet in German in the periodical *Musica Viva*, gave a shorter account of the musical event in the Budapest paper, but with great enthusiasm and expert understanding, and also laying stress on the progressive political significance of the performance.[165]

First movement: Allegro

The process of the theme's birth and development has emerged from the composer's workshop to the listener, the public. The melody evolves before us through a hard hammering, almost clattering, note repetition, just as in the first movement of the First Piano Concerto, except that the directions of the two melodies are different.

The theme started by the two lower parts is answered in octave canon by the two upper parts. As has been explained earlier, the theme itself has a mistuned octave structure—that is, it is built on a B flat–E–A framework, in which the E–A level is produced by downward displacement of F–B flat by a semitone. When the two upper parts enter an octave higher, the lowest part is already moving in the mistuned plane, so that the combined sound is made tense by semitone bitonality. And when the upper parts also reach the E–A level, the lowest part's tetratonic motif slides down another semitone, and thus the bitonal tension is not relieved. The two parts woven in a contrapuntal texture eventually meet and with a leading-note type of semitone step this leads to a playful transitional section. At the end of this short transition the clattering motif which opened the movement reappears. It can already be sensed that this clattering motif is to fulfil the function of framework motif in the movement; it appears at almost all the junctions in the form. Here it is heard in a grating mass of D and C sharp notes, which already secures the tonal transition as well: C sharp resolves like a leading-note on to C, and D on to E flat, and in this way the following formal section evolves, the C minor tonal plane of the secondary theme.

This secondary theme is characterized by melodic leaps over wide intervals and by polymetric displacement. The theme is played by the two violins, while the two lower parts accompany with a rhythmic counterpoint.

An important melodic feature of the secondary theme is that it moves in the two-line octave and continually jumps back to the one-line C as a steady support note. This characteristic Bartókian melodic type—with one side fixed and steady and the other expanding—might also be called a 'spring melody', indicating in this way the inner dynamism of the melodic type.

212

The melody, which is written in $\frac{4}{4}$ but actually moves in units of $\frac{3}{8}$, $\frac{4}{8}$, $\frac{5}{8}$, $\frac{6}{8}$ and $\frac{7}{8}$, stretches higher and higher, and when it reaches its climax it suddenly breaks off—interrupted by the clattering framework motif. This is a marvellous moment in Bartók's instrumental dramaturgy, when the two materials struggle dramatically: the melody interrupted on A flat (G sharp)–B still cries out repeatedly, but it is the framework theme, appearing on the C tonal plane, that is victorious (bars 36–44).

This appearance of the clattering framework theme signifies the start of a new formal section. But from the tonal point of view it is the G sharp–B surviving traces of the preceding theme that prepare the tonality of the new theme, and indeed by means of the leading-note method of the preceding formal boundary, except that whereas in the earlier case the second opened out into a minor third, here the minor third closes in, the G sharp leads to the melody's A tonality, and the B prepares the steady B flat bass.

The formal function of the new dolce character theme is a final section. The soft, waving melody represents a significant contrast to the hard energetic tone which has dominated so far. Its structure is an inversion of the principal theme: the latter rose from B flat through E to A, but here there is a descent from A to B flat. The mistuned octave framework is reinforced by the pedal notes, squeezing the melodic movement between B flat and A.

The texture of the final theme is also different in character; the first two themes were treated contrapuntally and drawn with considerably broad 'brush-strokes'. As opposed to these, the new theme is homophonic, and the melody always appears in only one part, above or below a thin harmonic support. The whole thematic section is characterized by a fine texture almost like a spider's web and by 'durchbrochene Arbeit'.

The B flat–A tension is gradually relaxed with the lower level leading chromatically through B, C, C sharp and then settling in a D–A–D perfect fifth-octave framework. The perfect octave framework is, however, filled in by two tetrachords of which the lower is tuned up a semitone. This is the first appearance of the mistuned major and Phrygian scales to play such a large role in the final movement. The two tetrachord layers together exhaust the whole twelve-note range (see *Ex. 102*).

The final theme ends on an F major second inversion chord; we might almost think that in this way the dominant level of the development section is being prepared on the basis of the regular modulation design of the classical sonata structure. This is indeed an important formal turning point; the appearance of the clattering framework motif also indicates that the development section is beginning. The F plane just reached is, however, suddenly slipped by the composer down to E; just like the themes, the whole movement has a mistuned fifth-structure. Thus the development section begins in E—that is, on the level of the characteristically mistuned dominant.

The two elements of the principal theme take on independent life: an ostinato evolves from the first expanding motif, and above this what was originally its melodic continuation, the pentatonic fourth-motif, sounds as a counterpart. The virtuosity of the first section of the development can be seen in the way in which three different motifs become fitted together in the characteristic common rhythm pattern of the movement. The fourth-motif becomes traced onto the clattering framework motif, and then with the same beat the 'upbeat' part of the final theme also takes part as an independent motif in the musical process and leads organically to the second development section beginning at E.

In this section the secondary theme's characteristic accompanying element assumes importance, but above it it is not its own melodic material that is heard but the tetratonic motif broken off from the end of the principal theme. In bar 97 the two pairs of parts exchange roles: the syncopated chords move up into the two violins and the tetratonic motif is continued in the two lower instruments. In bar 104 exciting intensification begins: the parts throw the tetratonic motif to each other in a diminution imitation, slipping increasingly higher and higher chromatically. At the climax of the development section—in keeping with the beginning—in the tonal plane of E a rhythmic variation of the clattering theme and an ascending form of the tetratonic motif are placed together (bars 111–114) and then the tetratonic motif, supplemented so as to become pentatonic, settles into a consistent wave-line in parallel octaves. Here it is easy to see the mistuning of the octave in two directions: the E plane of the upper part is imitated by the lower parts in the E sharp and D sharp planes.

229

The wave-line pentatonic theme is finally transformed into scales which rear upwards, and this leads to the recapitulation of the framework motif, which signifies the formal boundary of the development section. This is the point where, according to the traditional sonata principle, the principal theme ought to return. But Bartók chooses a special method whereby the principal theme returns only fragmentarily—only hinted at, as it were, building it into the material of the framework motif (to be precise, that is what it developed from at the beginning of the movement), and then, to our surprise, it is the final theme which returns first.

It is worth devoting special attention to the ingenious tonal methods. Since the principal theme is not really brought back yet, it would be premature to bring back the B flat tonality. The development ends with the tonality of E, but we should remember that at the beginning of the development, before the framework motif, the final theme ended in F. It signifies the symmetrical rounding off of the development that it is now the tonality of F that appears first in the framework motif and the fragment of the principal theme. In the clattering framework motif, however, E is also present alongside F for a time, as a memory of the key of the development just finished.

It is of great importance that the signal principal theme's direction is altered: it does not come out of the framework motif's note repetition by arching upwards, but downwards. This same change in direction also characterized the final theme and—to anticipate—the return of all the other themes as well.

The final theme is prepared by the same material on this occasion as in the exposition, only its direction and tonality changing. Earlier the melody moved downwards in a major seventh framework bounded by A and B flat, and here it moves upwards within an F sharp– E sharp framework.

After the final theme it is the secondary theme which returns, and only after that does the principal theme appear in its complete form—that is, the themes, in keeping with a certain symmetrical structural principle, return in a precisely reversed order. The inversion technique is thus valid in both 'time' and 'space', the only reservation being that the 'crab progression' does not refer to the themes themselves but only to their order. The spatial inversion of the themes, however, is consistent: in the recapitulation all melodic movement appears in its mirror form, in the same way as may be observed in the outer movements of the Second Piano Concerto.

It is typical of Bartók's structural economy that the pentatonic fourth-motif is omitted from the recapitulation of the principal theme, obviously because it played a particularly large role in the first part of the development section.

In the coda, which has the effect of a stretta, the main role is played by the tetrachord motif at the end of the final theme. The composer uses with incredible richness the tetrachord's 'upbeat' character which seems to be 'leading to something'. These tetrachords, leading upwards and downwards, point like so many arrows at different tonal planes—some transitional, some final. In bar 209 they once more lead, in a summarizing way, to the framework motif, which appears in the B flat plane. But one further little diversion leads out of the tonality of B flat to D flat in the upper parts and to the plane of E in the lower parts. This is an increase in tension before the cadence, a sort of dominant (mistuned dominant) detour, so that the feeling of having arrived at the closing tonality may be all the stronger.

The parts, closing fan-wise from two directions, display clearly the summarizing nature of the major and Phrygian tetrachords playing such an important role in the coda, and at the same time they already create the foundations of the close relationship with the final movement.

Second movement: Adagio molto

The movement is introduced by amorphous, almost pointillist material. Its tonality, too, solidifies only in the fifth bar on the basis of the cello's held D. The first closed formal unit is prepared by major second motifs which fit into one another chromatically and then by augmented fourth motifs.

Above consonant triad blocks little five-note melodies open out which are obviously extensions of the melodic fragments in the introductory section. In this part special attention is called for by the individual complementary technique which Bartók—among others— already used in the second movement of the First Sonata for Violin and Piano. The melody above the chords never fits into the chord but uses primarily the adjacent chromatic notes of the notes in the chord. The melody above the C major triad consists of the upper adjacent chromatic note of the root, and the lower adjacent notes of the third and fifth. And the A minor seventh chord in bar 15 is complemented by the root's upper and lower, the fifth's upper, the third's lower and the seventh's lower and upper adjacent chromatic notes.

At **B** a new formal section begins in the tonality of G: a 'background fabric' is evolved from a tremolo organ point, pizzicato glissandos and fast scale fragments, behind a folk character melody structured on a mistuned fourth. Considering the melodic material of the movement so far it can be established that this melody, which settles into an interrelated, clear, four-line structure, has evolved through gradual organization of the fragmentary melodic world. Then this melodic world is once more broken up: beginning at **C** melodies consisting of fourth-chains rise up and lead with increasing expressiveness to the largo climax in bar 43, from which the melody winds downwards, with the tension of continual parallel diminished octaves (major sevenths), to the calming tonal plane of D. Consonant chord blocks appear once more, evoking as it were the movement's first closed formal section, but the five-note little melodic units are now replaced by a mere complementary note here and there. In bar 50 the introductory material also returns—actually in inverse order, in keeping with the bridge forms, and in this way the movement ends with the same trill motifs as it began. The last trill is extended by a little 'quasi glissando' scale motif and the movement ends 'perdendosi' with the deep D on the cello. (For further analysis of the movement see p. 236.)

Third movement: Scherzo alla bulgarese (Vivace)

This movement forms the symmetry-axis of the five-movement work, and for this reason it has naturally no counterpart, no corresponding movement, as the other movements in the work have. The use of the word 'bulgarese' is somewhat misleading, and refers exclusively to the metrical character of the movement, since the melodic world displays principally Hungarian and, to a lesser extent, Rumanian folk elements.

The first scherzo theme is built on the dome-arch, fifth-layer strophic structure of the new-style Hungarian folksongs. Bartók uses an individual technique here in that the fifth-structure is complemented by third-structure in the melody, and, as a result of this, in the verse as well. This combined third-structure and fifth-structure is clearly shown in the diagram below. The individual lines are indicated by their first and last notes. It is interesting to compare this scherzo melody with the principal theme, likewise of folksong structure, in the second movement of the *Music for String Instruments, Percussion and Celesta*, and its close relative, no. 130 from *Mikrokosmos*: 'Village Joke'. Apart from the already mentioned dome structure, the breaking up of the third line into two smaller units characterizes all three pieces alike.

Line	I	II	III	IV
Fifth Quartet	1–1	3–5	9–7/5–3	9–1
The *Music*	1–1	5–4	7–10–4/3–7–2	1–1
Mikrokosmos				
no. 130	1–1	5–5	10–6/6–2	2–1

232

The third lines which are broken into two parts are further characterized by the fact that they represent the climax of the melody, and the second half-line is always placed one level lower down, as if it were an organic return to the fourth line.

Bartók evolves the diatonic set of notes in the Dorian scherzo theme from a chain of minor and major thirds, or viewed from another angle, from two parallel fifth-chains. This is no new phenomenon in Bartók, since the leitmotif of his early works also contains a similar melody forming principle. The theme here is a development of this to an extreme. The comparison with Alban Berg's Violin Concerto presents itself almost involuntarily: there the abstract note-row and the theme formed from it are both produced by the towering of thirds upon each other. There is a characteristic difference, however, in that while Berg uses this method to extend diatony (the third-chain uses up nine degrees of the twelve-note scale), Bartók forms a Dorian-mode diatonic scale from it.

215

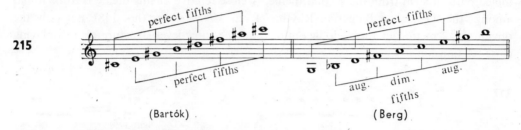

(Bartók)　　　　　(Berg)

The C sharp Dorian theme's accompanying harmonies appear in a D sharp layer, which displays a surprising bitonality. The solution to the chords based on D sharp, however, is to be found in the melodic third-structure of the theme: C sharp is here not a keynote, but a centre-note, and the harmonies are no more than the downward mirror reflections of the thirds towering upwards. This is also proved melodically in the closing part of the movement.

216

B: V. 3.

Another point in the structure of the scherzo theme is that each of its lines is followed by an imitating line—like a somewhat distorted shadow. From these 'shadow parts' grows a three-bar transition after which a verse is heard again. Its structure resembles that of the earlier one, only the melody of the single lines is changed: each line comes in a mirror

233

inversion, but there is no question of precise inversion, merely the 'contours' of the melodic lines are inverted.

In bar 24 (**A**) a new theme appears in the first violin, with a sharper and more differentiated rhythmic profile. Its structure is likewise strophic, but as opposed to the earlier four lines, this is divided into three lines. To this structural difference is added a contrast in tone, too: as opposed to the first theme's light rolling character, this one is harder, more energetic, more angular. But the inner relationship between the two themes soon becomes apparent. With the appearance of the second theme the first does not disappear—it merely becomes an accompaniment. Its subsidiary role does not, however, last long; very soon, in bar 30, a new thematic form appears which is a characteristic combination of the two earlier themes. It is related to the third-structure theme by its rhythm pattern which has an unstressed beginning, but the semiquaver revolving motif in the middle and the ending joined on to it stem from the second theme. A close relative of this theme is to be found among the 'Dances in Bulgarian Rhythm' from *Mikrokosmos* (no. 148), not only the obvious $\frac{4+2+3}{8}$ metre but the melodic outline and the three-level structure also displaying close relationship.

From use of one little motif (a minor trichord) of the theme which has come about from this combination, a longer and more relaxed section results (bars 36–49). After the climax in dynamics and in tension (bars 42–44) a gradual abatement and calming leads to the return of the first scherzo theme (bar 50). But the theme does not return unaltered: the first and third lines of the melody arch upwards, and the second and fourth lines downwards—that is, the recapitulation summarizes, as it were, the two strophic structures at the beginning of the movement.

The trio is connected to the scherzo by a long held third pedal on the viola. This third organ point is joined by an ostinato motif repeated every bar (first violin), securing a colouring background, so to speak, for the theme to be heard later. In the fifth bar it becomes clear that the metrically stressed principal notes of the ostinato motif, which has a chromatic character and narrows in like a cone-shaped funnel, support a melodic tetratonic motif. The trio's eight introductory bars, together with the presentation of the colouring background, also form a bridge over the difference in tempo between the scherzo and the trio: the tempo gradually accelerates to vivacissimo. The hitherto asymmetric pattern is replaced here by a symmetrical $\frac{3+2+2+3}{8}$ metre.

The theme of the trio begins in bar 9. Its structure—like that of the scherzo themes—is strophic; indeed the folk character is even more conspicuous and unequivocal. On this occasion there is a perfectly simple Hungarian bagpipe tune hidden behind the guise of the complicated Bulgarian metre. The even rhythm of the bagpipe tune is made infinitely alive and interesting by the refined alternation of the proportions between the notes corresponding with the individual syllables. The skeleton of the pattern, consisting of even crotchets, appears in a choriambic and antipastic version, similar to the adaptable rhythm of the Hungarian folksong. A particularly interesting point in this rhythm is that the ratio between the long and the short notes is not the ordinary 3:1 or 2:1, but 3:2.

After the first verse, generally choriambic, another verse starts immediately which is similar in character but antipastic in rhythm and different in structure (bars 17–24); the first verse is closely related to the descending structure of the old style of folksong, and the second to the dome-shaped structure of the new style.

After the introduction of the two folksong verses, a real battle begins between another similar folksong-like motif and a dissonant 'choking' motif. In bar 41, the dissonant 'choking' motif (which is none other than the ostinato which has been accompanying up to this point) becomes victorious, is augmented by a precise mirror reflection counterpart, and for nine bars the texture of the music contains a colour effect devoid of any melodic element. We encountered a similar effect in the second movement of the Fourth Quartet (bar 113), where there was similar parallel movement between several chromatically-filled-in fifth-layers. The relationship between the colour effect of the two sections is further reinforced by con sordino playing, and also by the pedal technique supporting the moving parts.

After the *fortissimo* colour effect quietens down, the melodic elements begin to appear 'shyly', uncertainly, like people creeping out of their hiding places when a storm moves away (from bar 50). The two elements continue to struggle with each other for a time but the folk motif more and more decisively regains supremacy. It is a striking point in Bartók's organic structural technique when the trio's bagpipe theme returns in third progressions which refer to the scherzo and, without any obstacles, lead directly back to it.

The Scherzo's first theme appears in the recapitulation doubly extended: that is, the two verses are here actually built into one another, and in such a way that every single line's basic and mirror inversion and the 'shadow imitation' of each of them all stand alongside one another. Thus here the summarizing technique which characterized the return before the trio is used even more consistently.

The second theme returns in bar 30 of the scherzo da capo, in a significantly extended form: the individual melody lines are given a cadence, and the descending verse consisting previously of three lines is now supplemented into a four-line dome-shaped folksong structure. The scherzo recapitulation then continues in accordance with its first appearance but enriched with numerous further alterations. The central section, based on the development of the minor trichord motif, is here even more dynamic: it switches into an Agitato stretto

235

in bar 58. This tempo then remains to the end, except that two bars in a somewhat restrained tempo are wedged in between the question—answer kind of recalling of the first scherzo theme (after bar 85)—an intensification of the tension before the resolution, as it were.

Fourth movement: Andante

The key to the symmetrical construction of the whole composition is that the movements which correspond to each other are connected not only by relationship in their tone and atmosphere but also by concrete thematic interrelationship. In the case of the second and fourth movements this interrelationship is more than mere thematic reference: every element in the two movements is common, and the formal application of them also follows the same principles. For precisely this reason the fourth movement can justifiably be regarded as a fuller and more developed variation of the second movement.

The fourth movement is introduced by the same sort of open pointillist material as the second movement. Here a pizzicato motif corresponds to the earlier trill motif, and the interconnected major seconds grow into a slow rhythmic trill.

218

The extending, broadening tendency is shown by the increase in the extent of the introductory section: the second movement's nine bars are answered by twenty-two in the fourth movement. It must be added, however, that this increase is present only in the quantity of the material, for the time taken up by the two formal units is virtually identical, since the tempo of the second movement is Adagio molto ($\downarrow = 40\text{--}38$), that is almost twice as slow as the Andante. The consonant harmonic blocks are also responded to by static harmonic blocks in the fourth movement, although the way they are played is different; these take on a special colour by means of saltato note repetition in sextuplet rhythm.

Whereas in the second movement the complementary melodic fragments appeared above the held chords, here they are wedged in between the chord blocks. The descending monologue melody unfolding from theme is also a close relative.

236

219

In the centre of the movement it is the broadly arching theme of folksong structure that appears here, too. It is developed—as is generally the case with all the variations in the fourth movement—more richly and more melodically, but this cannot conceal the completely consistent relationship between the two melodies. If the difference in tonality is disregarded, the precise note for note agreement between the themes becomes obvious by appropriately placing one above the other.

Incidental to the richer development of the melody is the fact that it is heard in an octave canon between the first violin and the cello (strictly speaking, at a distance of two octaves). It is particularly worthy of attention that the effects accompanying the melody are also

237

related: the second movement's tremolo organ point is here responded to by the viola's held notes coloured with dissonances, whereas the little scale fragments are replaced by little wave motifs.

It is from the chromatic scale fragment of the 'colouring background' in the second movement that Bartók has developed the next formal section in the fourth movement, which has a transitional nature (bars 55–63). The last three bars of this transitional section, however, introduce an apparently new motif into the musical process. But the iambic minor third motif embedded in the chord blocks does have its own antecedent in the twenty-second bar of the movement, immediately before the sextuplet chord blocks.

This minor third motif then becomes connected to the long fourth-chains already familiar from the second movement. The fourth-chain broadens into an exciting formal section here, too; above the ominous murmuring of the chromatic 'wave motifs' in the two lower parts, the fourth-chains produce real storm music. An occasional natural scene was by no means alien to Bartók's apparently abstract musical thinking. Listening to the great celesta–harp–piano waves in the third movement of the *Music for String Instruments, Percussion and Celesta*, Bartók once whispered to his neighbour: 'Listen, the sea!'[166] The 'storm' abates from bar 80, and the calm after the storm, the quietening of the tormented soul, is depicted by a peaceful series of harmonies—quite reminiscent of Beethoven's Sixth Symphony.

This is where the fourth movement essentially differs from the second; in the earlier movement the musical process does bring back the amorphous material from the beginning of the movement, even though in a significantly abbreviated form, and at the same time the broken, tragic tone. Here in bars 95–97 only the chord blocks return, in a very abbreviated form, only as a token as it were, and instead of the introductory material it is the hushed calm after the storm which puts the final full stop to the movement. Underneath the held B on the first violin the cello arrives, by pizzicato glissandos and rising by thirds, at the closing chord of the movement's tonality, the G minor triad. Its minor character, however, is coloured with major by the violin's held B.

Thus Bartók does not use symmetrical bridge form at every point and 'at all costs'. The symmetrical structure becomes healthily relaxed in the fourth movement, thus becoming more organically connected with the final movement. But there is something else which precluded the use of the recapitulating symmetrical form. As has already been mentioned, the fourth movement really differs from the second and moves beyond being a simple variation in that whereas the atmosphere of the second movement returns to the amorphousness, the darkness, the fragmentation of the beginning, the fourth movement becomes smoothly continuous—it opens out and moves through a large and passionate crisis to a harmonic calm and catharsis.

238

Fifth movement: Allegro vivace—Presto

In the complicated structure of the movement the framework motif, the new Bartókian formal element, serves as an important guide, just as it did in the first movement. Its triplet, upbeat rhythm and tetrachord structure is often a guiding principle with regard to tonality. This function appears straight away in the introduction as it leads, after some diversions, to the dominant of the movement's B flat tonality.

But the Presto theme, the first thematic material in the movement, does not start from this F just reached, but from a mistuned dominant—that is, from E. The repeating note first section of the theme refers on the one hand back to the beginning of the opening movement, and on the other hand it rather reminds one of the start of the First Quartet's finale. From the repeated E the melody slides down by means of a Phrygian tetrachord to the first melodic terrace of the theme, and then from there it descends further in a similar way to the terrace below that. The characteristic fifth-structure of Hungarian folksongs can be found here in a mistuned form; the B flat level is answered by an E level. When the lower layer is finished (the descending tetrachord is not only an opening element but also a closing element), we would expect a B flat cadence, but this comes only after a suspension and not even in the soprano melody but in the bass, and then the long continuation of the melody leads to the tonal plane of F, and it is only a somewhat forceful 'appendix' which restores the feeling of B flat tonality (bars 50–54).

After this junction in the form, as a contrast to the hitherto descending theme, an ascending theme starts. This ascending theme, however, can scarcely be regarded as new material; although it is not a precise inversion of the earlier theme, it is nevertheless closely related to it on the basis of its tetrachord units and its structure: it is an inverted variation of it.

After this Bartók makes thorough use of the possibilities offered by precise inversion and varied inversion. In the first 149 bars of the movement he forms a closed unit from the two related themes thus presented, and in such a way that he brings back the two themes so far introduced in precise mirror inversion, too, and in inverted order. In this way evolves this individual formal unit considerably rare in sonatas:

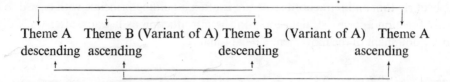

Theme A   Theme B (Variant of A) Theme B   (Variant of A)   Theme A
descending ascending   descending   ascending

It is also worth observing the structure of the themes. The first has already been mentioned: mistuned fifth-levels above and below each other. Mistuning plays an important role in the second, too: the two tetrachords of the major scale are slipped close to one another, and so for example in the ascending form it sets out from G flat and arrives in G. On the basis of this the tonal plan of the four-part formal unit can also be outlined:

Framework	Theme A	Theme B	Theme B	Theme A
	E–B♭–E–B♭	G♭–C–F	G–D♭–A♭	B–F–B–F
B♭–F		F	A♭	C	B♭

The upper line shows the inner tonal structure of the closed thematic units, and the lower line the tonality of the material wedged in between them. It is noticeable that each new starting of a theme is combined with displacement by a semitone; just as within the themes, the technique of mistuning is always present between the themes as well.

This first large formal unit in the exposition, as well as introducing the two basic themes, or to be precise by doing exactly that, throws light clearly on the melodic and rhythmic proto-motifs of the whole movement. The melodic proto-motif is, as has been mentioned, the tetrachord, which is built into the musical material mirror-wise; in its ascending form it is major in structure, and in its descending form it is Phrygian (see *Exs. 102–103*).

In the rhythmic variation process two motifs move into the foreground conspicuously; one stems from further development of the first theme (a), while the other is a fundamental gesture of both the first and second themes (b). The upbeat motif produced by the two, which was introduced in a triplet form in the framework motif, lies at the heart of all the rhythmic movement, and so we can see in it the rhythmic proto-motif corresponding to the melodic proto-motif (c).

After the appearance of the framework motif (**D**), indicating a formal boundary, new material appears which has a 'quasi-secondary theme' function. It has no special melodic character, although the tetrachord motif has a role here, too, even if only temporarily. From a melodic extension of it alpha chords appear opening upwards, there is a dynamic intensification reaching *fff*, and then the four instruments construct homogeneous minor second piles one upon the other, each consisting of ten chromatic degrees. This is a good example of Bartók's individual cluster technique (bars 183–200).

From **E** a freely written contrapuntal section begins which has the function of a final theme, and which takes its motivic material from the tetrachord elements and rhythm motifs of the first two themes. The changing note opening motif of the imitational section does, however, create the impression of new material. A very similar start and way of writing can be seen in no. 128 of *Mikrokosmos*.

With regard to tempo, too, Bartók tried to make the character of a faster section (più presto, ♩ = 144) even more unambiguous for the performers by the indications 'scorrevole' and 'leggerissimo'. As a result of the incredible animation and contrapuntal complication of the musical material, a flitting, scintillating musical picture evolves. At one point the chromatic 'durchbrochene Arbeit' of the tetrachord motif refers back to similar development of the tetratonic motif in the first movement.

From the multicoloured whirling of the tetrachords a two-direction scale motif eventually evolves, as a kind of summary; the two violins move upwards scale-wise and the two lower instruments downwards, broadening the music out like a fan, rushing forward into the appearance of the framework motif in the tonality of F sharp.

The scale motif summarizes the most important elements in the exposition's material with classical conciseness. It consists of two tetrachords—indeed, two mistuned tetrachord layers; the upward moving one starts from F sharp and arrives at F, and the downward one goes from A to A sharp. These eight-degree scales are not just summaries in principle, for both can be extracted from the fundamental form of the first two principal themes. It can be seen that the descending form builds Phrygian tetrachords upon each other, and the ascending does it with major tetrachords.

The mistuning technique is most brilliantly proved when the repeating scales, which have a diminished octave framework, open out at the end and lead in a form which is not mistuned to the tonality of F sharp.

225

The framework motif appears at this point in a significantly altered form: it takes on the melodic profile of the opening motif in the recent contrapuntal section. Its dynamics suggests the beginning of a development section.

In place of a development section—obviously because the material presented has already been through abundant elaboration and development earlier—new material appears: new, that is, in relation to this movement—it is the principal theme of the first movement. The tempo is increased to prestissimo ($\downarrow = 152$), and to an excited, ominous 'background texture' (col legno drumming in the two violins and mistuned glissandos in the cello) a fugato starts with the first movement theme just mentioned. In keeping with the spirit of the whole work, the theme entrances are built not on a perfect but on a mistuned fifth-structure (on the E–B flat–E–B flat tonal levels).

From the continuation of the first movement theme it is eventually the tetrachord motif that crystallizes here, too, and the material thus flows organically into the latest appearance of the framework motif. But it seems that on this occasion the framework motif is not used to indicate any formal division but becomes itself the object of development work. Moving through different metamorphoses, a humorous, capriccioso variation is evolved from it. From the changing note opening motif are born bald glissandos; the so far largely motory rhythm also relaxes, and the melodies appear in capriciously changing tempi until in the end the framework motif, now in its original form, pulls together the virtually disintegrating material. And so we come to the important formal division: the beginning of the recapitulation.

As is general with Bartók, the recapitulation is abbreviated. Thus the double principal theme appears without repetition, the first theme returning only in a descending form, and the second theme only in an ascending form. But between the cluster material, which has the function of a secondary theme, and the tetrachord counterpoint, which has a closing function, is now wedged a strange section. A banal melody is played in A major on the second violin, and this is accompanied on the other instruments by stereotyped I–V harmonies. When the melody reaches the top finishing note, the same melody is heard a semitone

242

higher, slipped into B flat major. Meanwhile, however, the accompanying chords remain in A major. The 'out of tune' barrel-organ effect produced by this bitonality indicates that here we are faced with one of Bartók's bitter jokes. We are reminded of Mozart's *Dorfmusikanten Sextett*, or Stravinsky's accumulation of functions in the fair in *Petrushka*.

The solution to this quotation-like detail, however, lies hidden in the work itself. For the A major melody is no more than a non-mistuned, diatonic version of the second principal theme. It is as if Bartók wants to point out that this melody would be so very banal and flat in a perfect octave-fifth framework without mistuning. And then when he displaces it bitonally—this is also mistuning—the unaltered accompaniment makes it ridiculous. This is the difference between organic mistuning, the inner transformation of material, and external manipulation.

The quotation cannot last for long, the original form of the theme sweeps it away 'con slancio', and the tetrachord motif rushes into the same scales, having a closing function, as we encountered at the end of the exposition. There this led to the tonality of F sharp, but here it races into the imaginary E tonality of the coda, which is marked 'stretto'—that is, into the mistuned dominant of B flat.

226

The accelerated ostinato repetition of the tetrachords piling on top of each other—above the E organ point coloured by D sharp—increases the tension so much that in the end the approach, opening out fan-wise, to the final B flat represents a calming solution, with one last accented summary of the tetrachord motif.

The Sixth String Quartet

Bartók began writing the Sixth Quartet in August of 1939, immediately after completing the Divertimento. As is well known, Paul Sacher, who commissioned the Divertimento, put his wooden house in the Swiss Saanen at Bartók's disposal. Completely alone and withdrawn from the world, he completed the Divertimento in a brief two weeks, and he might have finished the quartet as well had he not been forced back to Hungary by the tension of war and his mother's illness. It is not possible with any of the other quartets to see into Bartók's thoughts at the time of composition so well as in the sixth. This is principally due to correspondence. In the letter written on 18 August 1939, to greet his son Béla on his birthday, we can read what follows. 'Somehow I feel like a musician of olden times, the invited guest of a patron of the arts. For here I am, as you know, entirely the guest of the Sachers; they see to everything—from a distance. In a word, I am living alone—in an ethnographic object: a genuine peasant cottage. The furnishings are not in character, but so much the better, because they are the last word in comfort. They even had a piano brought from Berne for me... Recently, even the weather has been favouring me—this is the 9th day that we've had beautifully clear skies, and not a drop of rain has fallen since the 9th. However, I can't take advantage of the weather to make excursions: I have to work. And for Sacher himself—on a commission (something for a string orchestra); in this respect also my position is like that of the old-time musician. Luckily the work went well, and I finished it in 15 days (a piece of about 25 minutes), I just finished it yesterday. Now I have another commission to fulfil, this time a string quartet for Z. Székely (that is, the 'New Hungarian Quartet'). Since 1934, virtually everything I have done has been commissioned.

The poor, peaceful, honest Swiss are being compelled to burn with war-fever. Their newspapers are full of military articles, they have taken defence measures on the more important passes etc.—military preparedness. I saw this for myself on the Julier Pass; for example, boulders have been made into road-blocks against tanks, and such little attractions. It's the same in Holland—even in Scheveningen.—I do not like your going to Rumania—in such uncertain times it is unwise to go anywhere so unsafe. I am also worried about whether I shall be able to get home from here if this or that happens. Fortunately I can put this worry out of my mind if I have to—it does not disturb my work... I hadn't read a newspaper for 2 weeks until I picked one up yesterday; the lapse of time was not perceptible, it was just as if I was reading one 2 weeks old. Nothing had happened in between. (Thank God!)...'[167]

244

Thus Bartók broke off work on the quartet at the end of August, travelled home to Hungary, and as is indicated by the date on the manuscript, finished the work in November. Another important document from the period in which the quartet was written is his letter of 29 September to Géza Frid, which offers evidence that the relationship with Zoltán Székely, who had commissioned the work, had broken off. '...Would you be kind enough to ask Zoltán Székely why he has not replied to my letter of August 24th and why he is not making any arrangements in connection with the matter mentioned in it. Meanwhile the first, second and third movements of the Sixth Quartet, which is being written for them, have been completed (a fourth movement has still to be added to these); so I would like to hear from them as soon as possible as to whether they want the quartet or not. I asked them this, too, in my August letter...'[168]

Information even more important than these letters is offered, however, by the sketches preserved in the New York Bartók Archives and which have been discussed by two researchers, John Vinton and Benjamin Suchoff.[169] These sketches not only show how one or two details evolved, but allow us a glance into the development of the conception of the work and the refining of the work's most important thematic material. As far as the conception is concerned, it has become clear from these sketches that Bartók originally intended to end the work with a fast finale in folk character. And the other point of unimaginably great value is that the ritornello theme which stands at the opening of each movement and finally grows into an independent movement, arrived at its final form after going through many transitional forms. On this occasion this gradual refining work not only shows the path along which a theme has developed—and at the same time that Bartók also belonged to the Beethoven type of 'drilling–chiselling' creative artist family—but draws attention also to another change in conception: the theme did not simply assume a better and better form; its significance also grew, and eventually it became so important, so essential, that it came to exclude the fast finale originally planned. That is, the two basic pieces of information to be gained from the sketches are in the last analysis closely interrelated, for they are both manifestations of the same creative aspiration.

Whether the reason for the change in the conception of the work during composition lies exclusively in the musical structure, or whether external events induced Bartók to abandon the fast, folk character finale, can scarcely be determined today. In any event, the change can be explained by both together: on the one hand, the lonely monologue melody which was refined so much came increasingly into the foreground and became woven into a many-sided system of relationships with the other material in the movement; on the other hand, this was where the resignation and despair of the composer became expressed more authentically and sincerely than in any other musical material. We must not forget how very much he became uncertain and doubtful during the few months when the work was being written. War broke out. His mother's condition became increasingly critical and she died in December. Relations with Zoltán Székely were broken. Bartók became more and more possessed by the difficult dilemma of whether to remain at home in Hungary or to emigrate.[170]

How symbolic is the fate of this work! Bartók wrote it while he was still in Europe, for the group of his compatriots who were working in Europe at that time, but events

245

intervened and the artist, being forced to emigrate, eventually bade farewell to Europe with it. He took the score with him to the United States, and since performance of a new work became a question of life or death (in the first years of emigration—as is well known—he was unable to compose), he was compelled to offer the work written for Zoltán Székely to another quartet so that it would be performed. Fortunately that other ensemble was the Kolisch Quartet, who eventually gave the work its first performance in New York on 20 January 1941. It is for this reason that the work is dedicated to them.

Ritornello

The individual structure of the composition lies in that each of its movements is introduced by the same melody. Analytical literature sometimes calls this introductory material a motto, sometimes a ritornello, indicating in this way that the melody stands thematically apart, and at the same time that it has a function which holds the work together cyclically. I consider the term 'ritornello' to be more precise, as a motto in its original sense stands apart from the work itself, but here on the other hand the connection is indeed very organic —so much so that by the end of the work this standing apart disappears in the fourth movement, and the whole movement unfolds from the ritornello itself.

The ritornello melody first appears on the viola alone, as a lonely monologue. The basic idea of this monologue beginning can strictly speaking be traced right back to the early *Two Portraits*. Here in the violin solo of the 'Ideal Portrait', beginning with a Bartókian leitmotif, there already appears this melancholy contemplative kind of melody with its characteristic $\frac{6}{8}$ metre and broken seventh chords.

This idea appears again considerably later in the second movement of the First Sonata for Violin and Piano. This melody comes a good deal closer to the ritornello theme in the string quartet. Not only the metre but, for example, the rhythm pattern in the whole of the first melodic line stems from the same basis.

The structure of the whole melody also displays similar features: after a gently falling first line, an ascent (second line), then sequences (third line), and finally a big arched ascent in one (the sonata), and a descent in the other (the quartet).

246

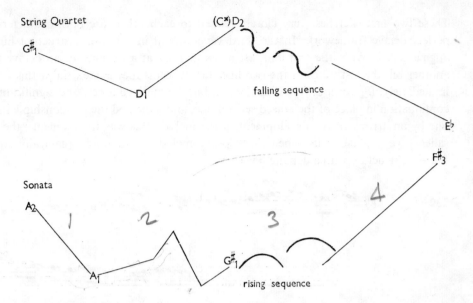

It was to be seen in the *Two Portraits* that the melody outlines seventh chords with the tension of a major seventh. This same tendency can be noticed in the melody of the sonata and finally in the descending sequences of the ritornello theme. A further common feature is the simultaneous appearance of the perfect fifth and its chromatic adjacent note. Like the leitmotif, the other broken chords related to it also radiate the atmosphere of the late Romantic harmonic world. Thus from this point of view the Sixth Quartet is a kind of turning back to the early 'Romantic' compositions, to the world of the First and Second Quartets.

All this refers to the antecedents of the finished ritornello melody. But now let us look at the melody itself, taking into consideration the information offered by the sketches in existence and already published in connection with the evolving of the melody. The ritornello theme first appears in the following two forms—after the completion of the Divertimento, and on the same sheet of manuscript paper. All this indicates that the ritornello theme, in this simpler and shorter form, was already present among the first ideas of the string quartet, together with the principal theme of the first movement, the theme of the Marcia and an important thematic idea for the fast finale which remained unwritten.[171]

247

These two first sketches, very closely related to each other, are both characterized by a perfect octave framework. In the third version, still in a two-line structure but already augmented, it is not the first and last notes that are at a distance of an octave from one another but the last notes of the two lines (a). It seems that Bartók threw this version out immediately, for without rewriting the first line he outlined a new and significantly longer continuation in place of the erased second line, and indicated the relationship with the first line by an arrow. In the development of the melody this was the moment—the punctum saliens, we might call it—when the two-line melody became an organically constructed four-line structure with a definite line (b):

230

It can be seen that the second line's ascent to the climax is already present here, as are also the determined, sequence-like descent of the third line and the closing formula of the fourth line with the descending fourth. On the same page of the sketch can be found the almost final form of the ritornello melody. To the first three lines of the melody, written down only once, are added two different fourth lines (a, b).

231

248

It is strange that the first line, which has firmly preserved its form from the first version on-wards, and has changed at most only in tonal position, here gains the final form of its close, but this is a visibly later correction—that is, it is written in the line above the appropriate part of the melody (c). Thus here we are faced with the final form of the melody, except for the end of the fourth line. The final form of the last line, which has clearly evolved with some difficulty, draws our attention to important interrelationships. In the penultimate version it can be seen that Bartók immediately writes in the fitting in of the other instruments and the first motif of the unisono melody, which is none other than an inversion of the close.

232

Here the notes G–A flat–E flat are still directly connected to each other. In the final form this obvious connection is somewhat veiled by the note F flat being inserted, and the four-note motif thus produced clearly suited Bartók's intentions better, for it gives greater inner tension to the A flat–E flat cadence (a). It is worth noticing incidentally that we have already met this same motif in Bartók's First Quartet, and, perhaps not accidentally, at this same pitch (b). Yet another motif suggests itself here which is surprisingly placed again at this same absolute pitch: the questioning melody with the inscription 'Muss es sein' in Beetho-ven's F major Quartet op. 135 (c).

233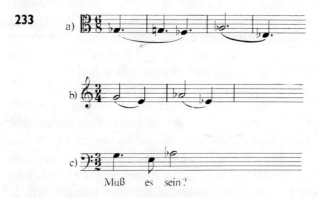

In connection with the revival of the Romantic harmonic world the First Quartet was mentioned above, but this newer connection reveals even deeper conformity: it does not simply refer to the world of the early works but to the new topicality of the great 'ancestral source'. In the way the Beethoven legacy was important to Bartók at the time of the First Quartet, it now becomes important to him once more, only in another sense. Around 1908 the return to Beethoven was synonymous with opposition to Romanticism, with the affirmation of the Classical and contrapuntal tradition. But here, at the time of the Sixth Quartet, it is in the shadow of the impending war that Bartók turns to Beethoven in his search for simplicity and humanity. Let me anticipate by mentioning the other details in the Sixth

Quartet which refer to Beethoven, so that we can examine all the interrelationships in the matter. At the end of the ritornello the other instruments in the ensemble join the viola, and in broad parallel octaves they build a 'bridge' between the lonely monologue just finished and the fast movement which follows. Part of the melody therefore refers back to the close of the ritornello theme, and it is out of an inversion of this that the principal theme of the fast movement takes shape. Now, before this rolling theme is heard in its final form, it is played in this partly augmented form which has the function of a 'bridge' and is rhythmically halting, disjointed—without any rhythmic profile at all, we might say—in the very same way as Beethoven introduces the theme of the Great Fugue.

We can see that whereas the young Bartók, when he was composing the First Quartet, saw an ideal in Beethoven's counterpoint, now it is principally a thematic example that he sees in him; either he writes again a definite type of theme or motif, or he borrows from the classical master his way of introducing the theme, and even the 'dramaturgy' in the use of the theme. For as well as the introduction of the theme referring to the Great Fugue, the solution to the tension also comes about in a way which is reminiscent of Beethoven; the dramaturgical detail of the 'schwer gefasste Entschluss' is repeated in the transformation into relaxed diatony of the tense chromatic theme.

This relaxation also reveals a great deal concerning the tonal relationship between the introductory ritornello and the movement. As has been mentioned already in the course of describing the way the melody evolved, the tonal character was originally expressed in a closed octave form. In the course of later alterations the perfect octave and fifth were replaced by mistuned relationships, and so alongside the tonality of D the adjacent chromatic notes also became important, chiefly G sharp (the adjacent chromatic note of A). Then at the end of the ritornello it becomes clear that these chromatic adjacent notes have also a leading-note function: the A flat–E flat fourth opens out into the D–A fifth in the same way as the A flat–E flat fourth is prepared by the augmented second G–F flat.

It is easier to examine the role and inner development of the ritornello melody if we extract it from the actual structure of the work and trace the path it follows separately. Most important of all is the systematic increase in the number of parts. Thus the melody, which first appears in a monologue form, returns before the second movement with a two-part texture. On this occasion the cello plays the melody and the first violin accompanies it with a counterpoint part. This counterpart is coloured by the tremolo in the second violin and the viola in double parallel octaves. The tonal balance of this counterpoint, written like this for 1+3 parts, but two-part in reality, is ensured by the three subsidiary parts which move parallel to one another being veiled by sordino.

The ritornello melody appears with smaller alterations which are worthy of attention. The nuances in the modification of the rhythm show Bartók's organic rhythm very clearly. As an extension of the preceding movement's principal theme, the end of the first line changes to a duplet rhythm.

234

The theme's third, descending melodic line is extended from a binary to a trinary sequence which in turn causes a tonal change: the theme, which started out from E flat, slips down to an F–C cadence instead of an E flat–B flat cadence. From a tonal point of view this alteration is of great significance, for the movement which follows in the tonality of B is prepared in the same kind of leading-note way by this cadence as happened in the first movement.

The third appearance of the ritornello brings new elements as an introduction to the Burletta movement. The number of parts is now raised to three: the first violin plays the melody, the second violin and the cello play the accompaniment, and the viola, from the point where the dynamic intensification begins (bar 10), reinforces the first violin part at the octave. A more important change is represented by the breaking up and extension of the ritornello melody. In the first six bars—starting out from B flat—the melody is identical with its preceding form, but when it reaches the climax of E, it breaks off, and in place of the descending third line the opening phrase of the first line reappears to carry the melody upwards to a climax on B (bar 13) by an ascending sequence. Here the descending sequence of the third line begins and then progresses in three sections through two octaves to a B cadence. There is an interesting modification to be seen in the sequence motif itself: its melodic gesture is extended, and in this way it anticipates one of the important themes in the movement which follows.

235

A further detail in the transformation of the ritornello theme is that the fourth and final line is replaced by a held note, and only the second violin's contrapuntal part provides a substitute for it with broadening melodic movement.

The tonal connection between the ritornello and the movement is arranged in a way similar to that in the other movements: the tonality of F is prepared in a leading-note way by the held B and then the E cadence, which is left open, of the broadening melody quoted above. And just as in the preceding movement one of the component parts of B major, the fifth, was already present at the end of the ritornello, here, too, the fundamental note of the tonality of F is firmly built into the end of the ritornello (in the viola part).

The fourth appearance of the ritornello, since it is the fourth movement itself, will not be discussed now but in the appropriate part of the analysis. In advance this much can be said: the tendency towards a variational process which has been apparent so far dominates here, too; the texture becomes four-part, and the melodic material goes through further breaking up and extension.

First movement: Più mosso, pesante—Vivace

In the analysis of the ritornello theme it has already been mentioned how the principal theme, that is, the basic motif of this principal theme, in the Vivace movement is born from the end of the ritornello. More minute examination then draws attention to the fact that the whole theme is no more than three forms of this three-note basic motif strung together. In the Più mosso, pesante section, which has a 'bridging' function, this basic motif is emphasized by a fortissimo unisono block. Its melodic essence consists of a larger interval and a smaller conclusion in the opposite direction.

This same 'bridge' also emphatically presents the whole theme, the three sections of which are none other than the basic motif and two variations of it; the second is a permutational

variation in which the second and third notes of the motif exchange places, and the third
is a contracted mirror-crab (a minor third instead of a fourth).

238

Many different further variations of the theme, which shoots up quickly and is fairly small
in extent, make up the first formal unit in the movement, the principal theme section of
sonata form. In this variational process the theme assumes many forms equally in its nine-
note interrelationship and its basic elements of three or four notes. Not long after it is
first heard, an inverted form of it also appears. It must be added that there it is not a question of a precise, note for note inversion, but a form which, with regard to no more than
its direction, gives the 'impression' of being a mirror inversion.

Each of these two basic forms of the principal theme represents a firm area in the otherwise extraordinarily dynamic texture, in the process of the varied transformation of the
motifs. It is worth looking at the five bars after the first appearance of the vivace theme, for
example. With its expansion of the first fourth interval the second violin scarcely alters the
theme at all, only making it tense, 'mistuning' it, since the perfect fourth is replaced by an
augmented fourth, and accordingly the theme's perfect octave framework becomes retuned
to an augmented octave. This variation of the complete theme is immediately followed by
variation of the details, the motifs. Besides the motif with the augmented fourth framework,
its mirror inversion also appears (first violin), then a contracted form of the original fourth
also appears in both an ascending form (viola) and a descending form (cello).

From bar 36 development work begins, using the same kind of technique, now over a
longer stretch, right up to bar 53, where the complete theme is heard again in its descending
form. In this dynamic developing section we can follow the break-up of the theme in detail,
on the one hand in the gradual diminishing of the proportions of the theme, and on the
other hand in the contraction of the intervals. The nine-note theme first reduces to seven
notes (two three-note motifs and a final note) and then to four notes (one three-note motif
and final note). The shortening of the rhythm also belongs to this reduction in proportions;
the originally long first note gradually disappears. The interval contraction is similarly
consistent: the opening gesture, expanded to an augmented fourth, is now contracted to the
extreme limit of a major second. This is the smallest interval into which a smaller interval
moving in the opposite direction—that is, the semitone—can be fitted.

239

In the interests of formal balance this dynamic breaking apart of the material is followed by a more static section in which the complete and original form of the theme returns in its descending and ascending versions alike. This steady part, however, is only temporary, since it is followed by a new development section. But this time the variation work is directed at the end of the theme, and from bar 68 it is once more the three-note basic motif that comes into the foreground. Although with regard to its material, this section is broken up, and dynamic in its effect—because of the motif becoming fixed into an ostinato—it does nevertheless have a definitely static and completing character. With regard to the intervals, contraction can be seen here, too, just as in the part between bars 36 and 53, but whereas there the original fourth framework became contracted to a major second, here the motif contracts from a wider, minor sixth version into its original fourth form.

This static ostinato version of the principal theme is functionally a transition to the secondary theme which appears in bar 81.

As opposed to the differentiated texture of the principal theme, this secondary theme is simpler and has a smoother line. It radiates a folk atmosphere on account of the characteristic rhythm of the Máramaros Rumanian folk music, although there is no melodic relationship. After its first hearing two figurative variations follow immediately in the second violin and viola respectively. This kind of elaboration—figurative variation—rarely occurs in Bartók's works.

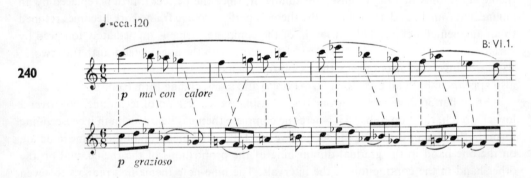

Although the secondary theme is placed very firmly in the tonal area, it is nevertheless ambiguous with regard to tonality. In the first moment the theme, in the C–F–C framework, appears to be in the tonality of F, in which it is not the keynote that is reinforced by pedal notes but the fifth. This tonality of F would be quite regular in the order of keys in a traditional sonata movement. The theme itself, however, suggests the tonality of C, particularly as a result of the fifth levels of its second half; the last C of the melody fits smoothly above the static C pedal. The tonality of C is also strengthened by the melody arching from C to C which is the counterpart in the first violin.

From the resting point in bar 93 in the tonality of C, a surprisingly traditional functional chain with an authentic tendency leads to the excited (Vivacissimo agitato) transitional section beginning in bar 99.

254

C–F–B flat–E flat–(A flat)

G sharp–C sharp–F sharp

This transitional section, which as far as its material is concerned, derives from the opening gesture in the ritornello theme, is a fine example of organic development of new material from old. Here, side by side, are the source material from which it stems (x), the process itself, showing how it evolves, and the final result which is the third most important thematic material in the movement—the final theme (y).

And then further development of the final theme shows how this final theme is a combination of the rhythmic profiles of the principal and secondary themes.

The end of the exposition contains a refined tonal ambiguity, although it is a pure F major triad that is actually heard. That is, the melodic motif of the final theme causes some tonal wavering by ending now with F, now with C, and finally, when the movement in the musical texture settles down, the F major harmony merges into the final C of the melody; that is, we feel the C melodically to be a tonal final note.

The development section beginning in bar 158 brings back the augmented introductory form of the principal theme on a tonal level a diminished fifth higher. The three-note opening motif enters in the various parts with canon-like displacement, but here it is only a pseudo-canon since it is only the top part which plays the theme's melody. After the fourth-chord cadence the vivace form of the theme also appears, but in the two lowest parts on this occasion and in a key further displaced by one semitone. This return of the theme represents the double start in the exposition—that is, the fact that the pesante version is immediately followed by the rolling vivace version. Thus the order of the two forms remains the same, but their correlation has changed, for the fast version is played a semitone lower, and its original octave framework is expanded to a major ninth. All this, however, is still quite static in comparison with the developmental dynamism of the part which now follows. The three-note basic motif, having been sometimes expanded, sometimes contracted even in the exposition, now expands to a minor ninth and in the ostinato beginning in bar 180, to a minor seventh. We are faced here with the same sort of development method as in the first movement of the Fifth Quartet; in the two outer parts an ostinato accompaniment evolves from the first motif of the principal theme, and from the closing motif of the theme is derived a melodic part which moves in mirror imitation in the two middle parts. A very interesting tonal method is used in this section in that the F–B tonality outlined by the ostinato parts is taken over by the melodic parts as well. The 'target note', which functions as a final note, is either F or B.

The first part of the development section broke the principal theme up into its elements. On the other hand the second part, which begins in bar 194, sets it back into its original form and even extends it further: the theme, originally two bars long, now grows to four-five bars, and this is quite naturally accompanied by spatial growth as well—to two–two and a half octaves. Another point in the extension of the theme is that in the part between bars 209 and 217 a descending version of it is immediately added to it. In this way a perfect wave-shaped melody has grown out of the theme which has so far been heard in only an ascending or a descending form.

The version which has a rising line emphasizes the scale-like or complementary writing of the theme. As opposed to this, the further variations which are developed from the descending version are based on the fourth-fifth chain which strictly speaking was already present in the first form of the descending version.

243

Now it is the fourth as melodic structural element that steps into the foreground, and together with this comes semitone friction. The correlationships between these two elements can be seen clearly in the theme variant just quoted: while the first violin descends in fourth-chains, the cello progresses in a descending chromatic scale. Here we witness an individual reinterpretation of the classical functional system. In some Baroque sequences, by means of repeating the perfect cadence in a continuous way, a harmonic sequence can be produced, in which the projection of a fourth-chain in one part (usually the bass) is a chromatic scale in another part. But this is also possible the other way round: the chromatic descent in the bass conceals within itself an authentic functional chain (this is what makes chromatically descending Baroque passacaglia variations so natural).

This parallel is naturally intended to indicate only indirect relationships, particularly since with Bartók authentic and plagal trends alternate in the fourth-fifth chain. This underlines all the more strongly the opposition of the two elements, that is the contrast between chromaticism and the acoustic relationship between the pure intervals which produce diatony. Then from bar 237 the relationship between these two elements becomes even clearer. Within the framework of the outer parts, which has major seventh tension, a swaying fourth-motif unfolds from the last part of the theme. One fourth-structure clashes with another fourth-structure displaced by a semitone; while the G flat of the bass fits into one, the F of the first violin fits into the other.

244

Here the role of the fourth as structural element can be seen clearly. When the melody tries to increase the amplitude of the wave motion by greater impetus, a minor seventh appears instead of the fourth—that is, the fourth's double. We have already experienced this same phenomenon in the mystic fourth-theme of the Second Quartet's last movement.

In this same place there is another phenomenon which reminds one of the Second Quartet, namely the swaying fourth-motif connected with the theme, which in the earlier work was connected with the recapitulation form of the principal theme in the first movement.

The friction between the trill motif and the three-note ostinato motif lend an extraordinary degree of tension to the last phase of the development section (bars 276–286). The three-note motif is this time not identical with the basic motif of the principal theme but is produced by the final 'appendix' to it (bars 274–275). This three-note motif moves in four different tonal planes in such a way that they are separated by either a diminished fifth or a diminished octave. Once again it becomes apparent that the diminished fifth is really the closest relative of the diminished octave and both are connected by the mistuning of the perfect octave or perfect fifth.

In the recapitulation, which begins in bar 287, only the vivace form of the principal theme returns, and even that only as a symbol; the dynamic development within the exposition is not repeated, obviously because this theme has already been subjected to an abundance of variation, breaking up and expansion in the development section. This part in the

257

formal structure is thus taken up with work on relatively new material. This 'new material' is a minor third motif which has derived from the three-note motif just developed. The minor third motif creates a fresh impression after the fourth interval which has dominated so far. The way in which it is developed does, however, remind one very much of the earlier use of the fourth. In place of the semitone displacement of the fourth-chains we now have third-chains in semitone displacement. Earlier a 1 : 5 model was produced; here there is a 1 : 3 model. The secondary theme returns in bar 312, now in the tonality of C sharp— that is, a semitone higher than in the exposition and lengthened by a new variation. This new version brings out more definitely the folk character concealed in the theme, for whereas the original form referred to folk music only in its rhythm and structure, it now comes close to it melodically as well.

245

After the material of the final theme has been brought back in a variation which does nevertheless agree essentially with its exposition form (bars 342–362), the principal theme returns, with the function of a coda, in a pure G major triad block coloured only by pizzicato chords. Its tonality is first of all G major, which represents a traditional subdominant area before the movement's D major ending. The first violin climbs right up to A³, but here we do not feel the fifth as a final note as at the end of the exposition because, after it has been reached, the second violin descends to D². This ending is a beautiful example of the coordination of polymodality and 'monotonality', where the unambiguous D major cadence is preceded by going through the complete chromatic range melodically.

Second movement: Marcia

During the analysis of the ritornello theme reference has already been made to the way in which the cadence of the ritornello prepares the B major tonality of the movement. Throughout the movement, however, the tonality of B major is consistently accompanied by its own relative key, G sharp minor. Even the little motif which appears between the movement and the ritornello is also a preparation for this. The parallel use of B major and G sharp minor is a characteristic combination of bitonality and bimodality. Naturally it does not lead to chromaticism, since the two keys belong to the very same diatonic system, but it diffuses refracted light into the texture of the music. It might even be said that the two keys are not completely equal in importance; even if only because of its major character, B major dominates, and G sharp minor fits smoothly alongside it as a subsidiary. The individual relationship between the two tonalities can be felt clearly in the character of the parts and the relationship between them. The Marcia theme, major in character by virtue of its very nature, is accompanied by a minor variant of itself like a shadow.

246

This same major–minor relationship reigns in the ostinato accompaniment to the lament beginning in bar 55: the cello moves in the B major tonal plane while the viola moves in the G sharp minor plane. This B major–G sharp minor duality, which is present throughout the whole movement, is also in evidence in the closing chord. If we examine this harmony in isolation we see that it is obviously no more than a B major ninth chord with a *sixte ajoutée*. But if we take the consistent duality of the movement's tonal character into consideration, then we have to regard the G sharp in the final chord as a representative of the subsidiary, shadow tonality. And the melodic action also supports this. Thus Bartók's compositional technique provides an opportunity for us to separate out different structures from the accumulation of notes sounding at one time, and indeed not merely on a theoretical basis but in the music as it is actually heard, too.

Several interrelationships are suddenly brought to our notice by the movement's already quoted march theme. On the one hand, this dotted broken triad appeared earlier, in an elegant *verbunkos* style, in another Bartók work, the trio *Contrasts*, which was written not long before the Sixth Quartet. József Újfalussy further indicates that, although it is not based on a broken triad, the beginning of the Third Piano Concerto also belongs to this thematic family.[172]

247

This kind of hard, angular, dotted rhythm theme can, on the other hand, be traced back, without any sense of forcing the issue, to Beethoven's march music in the French style. This sort of dotted rhythm melody in Beethoven either radiates a military, heroic attitude or becomes a demonic scherzo. It is sufficient to mention the C minor Sonata for violin and piano or the Kreutzer Sonata, or the Scherzando of the E flat Quartet op. 127.[173] Whereas in Beethoven's scherzando the military rhythm tends to move into the jocular–demonic sphere, with Bartók it begins with a wry, ironic tone and moves into stubborn rebellion especially with the lament beginning in bar 55.

259

In the development process, on the one hand, two elements of the theme assume independence. One is the dotted rhythm scale motif, the other the pointed, iambic third-motif. The organic quality of the thematic work is shown by the fact that the third important motif is evolved from the trill ending of the dotted scale motif (bars 24–25). Also instructive is the interesting section beginning in bar 33 in which the basis of the variation is provided by the triad motif from the opening motif. At the beginning of the movement, alongside the B major–G sharp minor duality another major–minor duality became apparent in the triad in the opening of the theme, namely that B major is accompanied by a regular major dominant (F sharp major) while G sharp minor is joined by a minor form of the degree (D sharp minor). In the section which begins in bar 33 the major–minor duality divided out between the various instruments enters the triad motif itself, and now the clash between the two modes is present even within the limits of a single melody.

248

B: VI.2.

With a clear view of these fundamental elements, it is now possible to give an outline of the formal structure. Bars 17–25 are the presentation of the theme in its entirety; bars 25–32, the third-motif independently; 33–42, the triad motif together with the scale motif; 43–49, the closing trill motif together with the scale motif; 49–54, the third-motif as transition to the larger unit of bars 54–76 in which a crying and sorrowful lament melody unfolds above an ostinato developed from the triad motif. Then it needs only a little four-bar coda to complete the first large formal unit in the trio form.

The trio, with its soft, improvisational, rubato character, represents a strong contrast to the march. In spite of this, however, both melody and accompanying chords are related by strong connecting threads to the triad motifs of the first part and, within this, to the simultaneous use of major and minor thirds. The melody which appears in the high register of the cello is a good example not only of the double third but of the 'double fifth' as well; we have already encountered this interval structure in the descending sequence of the Mesto ritornello, and a relative of this is the violin solo in the slow movement of the First Sonata for Violin and Piano, and finally one of the second movement themes in the Divertimento resembles it closely in its melodic line.

249

B: VI.2.

B: Divertimento, 2nd movement

260

Apart from that, an interesting correlation can be noticed between the Sixth Quartet and the Divertimento. In the movement quoted from the Divertimento this theme is joined by the same kind of ascending and then descending lament melody as here in the quartet. And the high register of the cello also creates the naturalistic effect of weeping, as do the glissandos which go with it.

The trio, which so far has been improvisational and soloistic in character, is closed by an impressionistic sound picture. By fast repetition of the semiquaver motif formed from the opening motif of the march theme, four layers are built up on each other, and then a decelerating, augmented form of it prepares the way for the return of the Marcia. The recapitulation is characterized by two important modifications. First the previously one-part major theme is now heard in major triad mixtures composed of fifth and sixth mixtures, and the minor theme which follows it like a shadow is coloured by harmonic notes. Both these effects intensify the painfully sarcastic character of the march. Secondly, the lament theme now rises even higher, complaining even more passionately, almost shrieking. Thus the recapitulation intensifies the earlier atmospheres to an even more extreme degree. Also in the recapitulation a role is played by Bartók's well-known varying method—mirror inversion. Thus the third-motif and scale theme which moved in an ascending direction in the first part turns downwards in the recapitulation.

Third movement: Burletta (Moderato)

As might be deduced from its title, the mood of this movement can be traced right back to the early *Burlesques* for piano. Its first theme consists of two elements: a grotesque leaping motif in which gesticular mime elements dominate, and a repeated-note motif which is lent a fairly harsh character by interval friction and grace-notes. Close relatives of the grotesque leaping motif can be found in abundance among Bartók's works from the early scherzos, through the second *Burlesque* ('A little tipsy') to the musical portrayal of the Wooden Doll in *The Wooden Prince* or the Old Gallant in *The Miraculous Mandarin*.

250

261

B: The Miraculous Mandarin

B: VI.3.

Then from the second repeated-note motif in the theme (bar 25) is born a new theme which has, however, been anticipated in the ritornello—an indolent 'bear-dance' kind of melody, the rough, folk tone of which is increased by quartertone dissonances.

The episode material which appears in bar 33 is an individual summary of the Burletta's first theme: the rhythm pattern refers to the first motif while the repeated-note melody refers to the second motif.

After a longer transitional section (bars 35–45), in which 'narrow' melodic writing, complementary in texture, alternates with fourth-melody, another new grotesque theme appears in the top part above a fourth ostinato accompaniment in the two lowest parts. The narrow-range, alternating melody, which is asymmetric in rhythm, is accompanied by the sound of various open strings, like a pedal, and this lends a certain primitive folk character to the whole theme. We encountered a similar type of theme in the first movement of the Fourth Quartet (final theme, bars 44–46), and as a result of the double stopping and asymmetric rhythm relationship, the violin solos in Stravinsky's *The Soldier's Tale* also come to mind. In bar 55 the parts moving in pairs exchange roles, the fourth ostinato moving up into the two violins and the melody being taken over by the two lower instruments. This sort of treatment and exchanging of parts was also present in the development of the first movement of the Fifth Quartet (bars 86–103).

The first large formal unit in the Burletta is completed by the return of the first theme (bar 60), but the two motifs of which it is composed exchange places: first it is the repeated-note motif that is heard, and only then does the grotesque leaping motif appear, in a considerably free variation.

In bar 70 a double bar-line and the indication 'Andantino' introduce the trio which, as regards character, is an even sharper contrast to the main section than the corresponding part in the preceding movement. In the trio's gentle, nostalgic melody the $\frac{6}{8}$ metre of the first movement returns—now alternating with $\frac{9}{8}$—and together with this comes the tonality of D. Its contrast with the main part of the movement lies primarily in its smooth, almost

262

swaying melodic writing and its periodic closedness. This character is also reinforced by the accompaniment with its rocking movement.

The theme's first four-bar period is completed by a hemiola rhythm motif, and after this is repeated in a varied form, a second theme appears. Its dome-shaped arch and characteristic rhythms, in which there is the typical choriambic–antispastic combination of Rumanian folksongs, brings to mind one of the lyrical choral parts in *Cantata Profana*.

251

(Nine in number were his sons)

Reference to the first movement is even more strongly in evidence if we consider that the trio has an individually intercrossed melodic and rhythmic relationship with the two most important themes in the first movement: the rhythm of the trio's first theme is derived from the principal theme of the first movement, and its melody is derived from the secondary theme. In the second theme, on the other hand, the positions are reversed: here the rhythm points unmistakably back to the secondary theme of the first movement, while the melody has a remote connection with the principal theme.

252

Attention must be drawn to two more important transformations in connection with the Burletta's recapitulation. With Bartók the recapitulation usually means an intensification combined with reinterpretation, in a line similar to the spiral. Here the expansion of the 'bear dance' theme (bar 102), the breaking of the octave in the episode material formed from the repeated-note motif (bar 110), and the flitting variation, enriched with colour effects, of the ostinato deriving from the fourth-motif (bar 131) all have this kind of intensification effect. The tension of the intensification is also increased by the 'dramaturgy' of

263

the movement: the *Cantata Profana* melody from the trio also returns, but it is split into pieces by weighty chord blocks (bars 135–144).

The framework tonality of the movement is F major, but at the beginning this remains considerably in the background within the complicated texture of adjacent chromatic notes. As opposed to this, the final chord is perfectly unambiguous, only the fifth being coloured by the augmented fourth. The tonality of F fits well into the tonal plan of the whole work, since in comparison with the D tonality of the first and last movements, the two inner movements are removed in either direction by a minor third—the Marcia downwards, and the Burletta upwards.

Fourth movement: Mesto

From the preparatory sketches it is known that the ritornello, now increased to four parts, was written to be an introduction here, too, and the point is precisely known where the slow introduction was to have flowed into the planned fast finale: after bar 45 where, in the final form, the Molto tranquillo section begins. Thus these forty-five bars have to be considered as a ritornello even in the present form, for it appears as the logical continuation of the preceding ritornellos, and it has an introductory function here, too.

It becomes clear, however, from the sudden increase in its extent that even at the time of composition, even within the framework of the fast movement conception, the ritornello had already begun to discard its original introductory role. At the beginning of the first movement it was thirteen bars long, at the beginning of the second it was sixteen, and at the beginning of the third it was twenty—that is, even the longest version is still less than half the length of the version now before us. It must be added that the tempo has also become slower, for instead of the earlier metronome values of 96, the composer now dictates only 88. All this, therefore, shows that the gradual extension of the ritornello—almost against Bartók's intentions—led to its outgrowing its own limits and, expanding in both measurement and significance, demanded the 'rights' of an independent movement.

Rounding off the number of actual parts to four virtually inevitably produced canon technique, which was represented in the earlier ritornellos at most by imitation of an occasional smaller part. The theme starts off in the first violin, and two bars later the cello enters with the same material in a diminished fifth transposition (from C, and from F sharp). After the first line, however, it is not the second line that follows: the first violin starts from the octave of the last note and plays the whole of the first line again. In relation to this new tonality the cello enters displaced by an augmented fifth (F sharp–B flat). Thus Bartók's efforts to mistune the fifth canon by plus or minus one semitone become clearly evident.

The two-part canon is filled out by the middle parts with free contrapuntal material, and after the canon of the double appearance of the first line all the parts move in free counterpoint. The first violin weaves the motif of the first half-line in a sequential way higher and higher to the E flat climax in bar 13, while the cello descends with the mirror inversion of the opening motif down to the lowest point at C in the same bar. After this formal division, similar expanding writing begins as an echo of the preceding process, as it were,

264

becoming strengthened from *pp* only to *mf*, with colourless restraint ('senza colore'). The leading part is now the cello's, which once more moves downwards with the mirror inversion of the first half-line, while the original ascending version of it is played by the three upper parts up to the formal division in bar 22.

It has been possible to notice that so far the material of the whole first line has been broken up into half-line units and opening motif units. This analytical work penetrates into the material even more deeply from bar 22 onwards. From the four-note ascending close of the first half-line—as a result of breaking the octave—a broad cambiata motif is developed, and this same breadth breaks up the natural continuation of the melody, making it virtually unrecognizable. This disintegration of the material is balanced, on the other hand, by the re-establishment of the original tonality. Thus after the F–E–D ending the ritornello melody is continued in bar 31 at the original pitch, with the second line being recalled on this occasion in a related way but accompanied by counterparts. The third line joining onto this likewise comes at the same pitch, but instead of a descending sequence it is now repeated three times at the same level and then suddenly breaks off in bar 39 with an ending which is left open. In a slightly faster tempo (Più andante, ♩=116) the first line returns once more in the tonality of the beginning of the movement (descending from C to F sharp) but it is treated in a significantly different way here: it is harmonized in a chorale style. This is an ominous, almost mystic moment in the work; dynamically it diminishes from *pp* to *ppp* and the tone again becomes numbed into colourlessness ('senza colore').

And this was to have been the end of the introduction and the material of the fast finale—which as regards its character is not far removed from the last movement thematics of *Contrasts*, the Divertimento or the Concerto—was to have been attached to it by means of a somewhat strained transition.

But is it not possible that the inner tension and strength of this forty-five bar slow movement, its resigned sadness and depth, would have frittered away into nothing if it had been followed at this point by a fast finale in folk character? Perhaps it might have been possible to fit another kind of material in here, but it must be confessed that the fast piece known from the sketch could only have been given room in Bartók's earliest works. It is therefore perfectly understandable that the elderly master changed his intentions and allowed the noble material being born under his hands to continue living its own life. Thus in place of the fast finale a quotation from the first movement follows. Is this a rounding off, the contrived creation of unity in the piece? Or some sort of necessity solution which in spite of everything proved better than the folk dance of the first version? Not at all. A profound, almost programme-like dramaturgy manifests itself in this quotation. The first movement has largely a bright and balanced atmosphere which produced some relief after the tension of the introductory ritornello, and which gave a cheerful, confident '*Es muss sein*' answer to the anxious '*Muss es sein?*' question. In the course of the work, however, after a harrowing march and a devilishly laughing burlesque, the growing feeling of anxiety and desperation has become dominant. This world of experience which clouds everything over could only have been relieved in an artificial self-mutilating way without any organic antecedent by a folk-style finale. For this reason, here in the fourth movement, in the course of the fulfilment of the sorrowful ritornello, there is no longer any solution or relief, only the memory of it, a nostalgic reminiscence. For this reason, after the nadir of bars 40–45, there is a slightly varied nine-bar quotation from the principal theme of the first movement, likewise one of nine bars from the secondary theme, and an eight-bar quotation from the principal theme's descending form.

After this the ritornello once more takes the leading role. Similarly to what happened in the first part of the movement, it develops here, too, in its ascending sequence form with the material of the first half of the first melodic line, in two imitative parts which are coloured by the other two with a harmonic accompaniment. The 'triumphant' ritornello theme, however, falls apart more and more; now only the melancholy closing part of it remains on the surface (bars 75–78) and then—as a farewell, as it were—the viola recalls the whole first line of the ritornello melody. It is played in the same tonality and in the same register as at the beginning of the work, but how very different its significance is now. Even its final note has slipped up from D to E flat, mainly so that this line-end should not yet be a tonal final note. In this way—as at the beginning of the first movement—the final D–A fifth is preceded by the tension of the notes E flat and G sharp. Under the ethereal sound of the D–A fifth, the cello's pizzicato chords—the upper notes once more outlining the first half-line of the ritornello—give the sorrowful, painful, resigned final note to the work with nostalgic renunciation.

254

Appendix

Bibliography

Abbrevia-
tion

A) Basic sources and important monographs

BL I   *Bartók Béla levelei I: Családi dokumentumok. Levelek, fényképek, kéziratok, kották* [Béla Bartók's Correspondence I: Family documents. Letters, photographs, manuscripts, music examples]. Collected and arranged for publishing by János Demény. Magyar Művészeti Tanács, Budapest, 1948.

BL II   *Bartók Béla levelei II: Magyar és külföldi dokumentumok* [Béla Bartók's Correspondence II: Hungarian and foreign documents]. Collection from the last two years. Collected and arranged for publishing by János Demény. Művelt Nép, Budapest, 1951.

BL III   *Bartók Béla levelei III: Magyar, román, szlovák dokumentumok* [Béla Bartók's Correspondence III: Hungarian, Rumanian and Slovakian documents]. Collected by Viorel Cosma, Ladislav Burlas and János Demény. Zeneműkiadó, Budapest, 1955.

BL IV   *Bartók Béla levelei IV: Új dokumentumok* [Béla Bartók's Correspondence IV: New documents]. Edited by János Demény. Zeneműkiadó, Budapest, 1971.

BLC   *Béla Bartók—Letters.* Collected, selected, edited and annotated by János Demény. Corvina Press, Budapest, 1971.

BÖ I   *Bartók Béla összegyűjtött írásai I* [Collected Writings of Béla Bartók]. Edited by András Szőllősy. Zeneműkiadó, Budapest, 1966.

BB   *Bartók-breviárium* [Letters, writings, documents]. Compiled by József Újfalussy. Zeneműkiadó, Budapest, 1958.

BÉD I   DEMÉNY János: 'Bartók Béla tanulóévei és romantikus korszaka (1899–1905)' [Béla Bartók's Student Years and Romantic Period], *Zenetudományi Tanulmányok* II. Edited by Bence Szabolcsi and Dénes Bartha. Akadémiai Kiadó, Budapest, 1954. (The first part of the Bartók biographical documentation.)

BÉD II   DEMÉNY János: 'Bartók Béla művészi kibontakozásának évei (I)—Találkozás a népzenével (1906–1914)' [The Years of Bartók's Artistic Evolution (I)—Encounter with Folk Music (1906–1914)], *Zenetudományi Tanulmányok* III. Edited by Bence Szabolcsi and Dénes Bartha. Akadémiai Kiadó, Budapest, 1955. (The second part of the Bartók biographical documentation.)

BÉD III   DEMÉNY János: 'Bartók Béla művészi kibontakozásának évei (II)—Bartók megjelenése az európai zeneéletben (1914–1926)' [The Years of Béla Bartók's Artistic Evolution (II)—Bartók's Appearance in European Musical Life (1914–1926)], *Zenetudományi Tanulmányok* VII. Edited by Bence Szabolcsi and Dénes Bartha. Akadémiai Kiadó, Budapest, 1959. (The third part of the Bartók biographical documentation.)

BÉD IV   DEMÉNY János: 'Bartók Béla pályája delelőjén—Teremtő évek—Világhódító alkotások (1927–1940)' [Béla Bartók at the Height of His Career—Creative Years—World-conquering Works (1927–1940)], *Zenetudományi Tanulmányok* X. Edited by Bence Szabolcsi and Dénes Bartha. Akadémiai Kiadó, Budapest, 1962. (The fourth part of the Bartók biographical documentation.)

DocB I–IV Documenta Bartókiana (Publications of the Hungarian Academy of Sciences, Bartók
        Archives). Published by D. Dille. Volume 1, 1964; Volume 2, 1965; Volume 3, 1968;
        Volume 4, 1970. (In German) B. Schott's Söhne, Mainz–Akadémiai Kiadó, Budapest.
LeB   LENDVAI, Ernő: *Béla Bartók. An Analysis of his Music.* Kahn & Averill, London, 1971.
NüllB   NÜLL, Edwin von der: *Béla Bartók. Ein Beitrag zur Morphologie der neuen Musik.*
        Mitteldeutsche Verlags-Aktiengesellschaft, Halle [Saale], 1930.
SteB   STEVENS, Halsey: *The Life and Music of Béla Bartók.* Rev. ed. New York University
        Press, 1964.
SzaB   SZABOLCSI, Bence: *Béla Bartók, Leben und Werk.* Reclam, Leipzig, 1961.
UjB   UJFALUSSY, József: *Béla Bartók.* Corvina Press, Budapest, 1971.
ViB   VINTON, John: 'Bartók on His Own Music'. *Journal of the American Musicological
        Society.* [Princeton, N. J.], XIX (1966), pp. 232–243.

B) Bibliography for Bartók's Chamber Music

ABRAHAM, Gerald: 'The Bartók of the Quartets'. *Music & Letters* [London], XXVI (1945).
ABRAHAM, Gerald: 'Bartók: String Quartet no. 6'. *The Music Review* [Cambridge], III (1942).
ADORNO, Theodor W.: 'Béla Bartók: 3. Streichquartett'. *Musikblätter des Anbruch* [Vienna],
        (1929).
AHRENDT, Christine: 'An Analysis of the Second Quartet of Béla Bartók'. Unpublished diploma
        thesis, Eastman School of Music, 1946.
ALTMANN, Wilhelm: 'Béla Bartók—Quatuor op 7'. *Die Musik* [Berlin], X (1910).
BABBIT, Milton: 'The String Quartets of Bartók'. *The Musical Quarterly* [New York], XXXV
        (1949).
BAILEY, Robert Wayne: 'An Analysis of Bartók's Sixth String Quartet'. Unpublished diploma
        thesis, University of Rochester, 1952.
BARNA István: 'Bartók II. vonósnégyesének módosított metronom-jelzései' [The Altered Metro-
        nome Indications in Bartók's Second Quartet]. *Zenei Szemle* [Budapest], new series,
        (1948).
BLOM, Eric (ed.): 'Béla Bartók as Quartet Writer'. *Stepchildren of Music* [New York], (1926).
CARNER, Mosco: 'Bartók's String Quartets'. *The Listener* [London], (1942).
CHALUPKA, Lubomir: 'Slavcikové kvartetá Béla Bartóka'. *Slovenská Hudba* [Bratislava], XII
        (1968).
CHAPMAN, Roger E.: 'The Fifth Quartet of Béla Bartók'. *The Music Review* [Cambridge], XII
        (1951).
COBBET, Walter Wilson: *Cyclopedic Survey of Chamber Music.* With supplementary material ed. by
        Colin Mason. London, 1929, 1963.
CRANKSHAW, Geoffrey: 'Bartók and the String Quartet'. *Musical Opinion* [London], (1951).
DILLE, Denijs: 'Angaben zum Violinkonzert 1907, den Deux Portraits, dem Quartett Op. 7 und den
        zwei Rumänischen Tänzen'. *DocB II.*
FORTE, Allen: 'Bartók's Serial Composition'. *The Musical Quarterly* [New York], XXXXVI
        (1960).
GORCZYCKA, Maria: 'Neue Merkmale der Klangtechnik in Bartóks Streichquartetten'. *Studia
        Musicologica* [Budapest], V (1963).
HARASZTI, Emil: 'La musique de chambre de Béla Bartók'. *La Revue Musicale* [Paris], XI (1930).
HAWTHORNE, Robin: 'The Fugal Technique of Béla Bartók'. *The Music Review* [Cambridge], X
        (1949).
JEMNITZ, Sándor: 'Béla Bartók—V. Streichquartett'. *Musica Viva* [Zurich], (1936).

270

KAPST, Erich: 'Stilkriterien der polymodal-chromatischen Gestaltungsweise im Werk Béla Bartóks'. *Beiträge zur Musikwissenschaft* [Berlin], XII (1970).

KÁRPÁTI János: 'Az arab népzene hatásának nyomai Bartók II. vonósnégyesében' [Traces of the Influence of Arab Music in Bartók's Second String Quartet]. *Új Zenei Szemle* [Budapest], VII (1956).

KÁRPÁTI János: *Bartók vonósnégyesei* [Bartók's string quartets]. Zeneműkiadó, Budapest, 1967.

KÁRPÁTI, János: 'Le désaccordage dans la technique de composition de Bartók'. *International Musicological Conference in Commemoration of Béla Bartók, 1971*. Budapest, 1972.

KODÁLY Zoltán: 'Bartók Béla II. vonósnégyese' [Béla Bartók's Second String Quartet]. *Nyugat* [Budapest], XI (1918). Published in KODÁLY Zoltán: *Visszatekintés* [Retrospect]. Collected writings, speeches, statements. Arranged for publishing and provided with bibliographical notes by Ferenc Bónis. Zeneműkiadó, Budapest, 1964. II pp. 419–420.

KOVÁCS, János: ' "Heiliger Dankgesang in der lydischen Tonart" and "Adagio religioso" '. *International Musicological Conference in Commemoration of Béla Bartók, 1971*. Budapest, 1972.

KROÓ György: *Bartók kalauz* [A Guide to Bartók]. Budapest, 1971.

KZNITZKY, Hans: 'Béla Bartók—IV. Streichquartett'. *Die Musik* [Berlin], XXIX (1929).

LENDVAI Ernő: *Bartók stílusa* [Bartók's Style]. Analysis of the *Music for String Instruments, Percussion and Celesta*, and the *Sonata for Two Pianos and Percussion*. Budapest, 1955.

LENDVAI Ernő: 'Bartók vonósnégyesei' [Bartók's String Quartets]. *Muzsika* [Budapest], X (1967)—XI (1968).

MASON, Colin: 'Bartók through His Quartets'. *Monthly Musical Record* [London], 80 (1950).

MASON, Colin: 'Bartók vonósnégyesei' [Bartók's String Quartets]. *Zenei Szemle* [Budapest], new series (1948).

MASON, Colin: 'An Essay in Analysis: Tonality, Symmetry and Latent Serialism in Bartók's Fourth Quartet', *The Music Review* [Cambridge], XVIII (1957).

MIHÁLY András: 'Metrika Bartók IV. vonósnégyesének 2. tételében' [Metre in the Second Movement of Bartók's Fourth String Quartet], *Muzsika* [Budapest], X (1967).

MOLNÁR Antal: 'Bartók kvartettje' [Bartók's Quartet]. *Zeneközlöny* [Budapest], IX (1911). Published in MOLNÁR Antal: *Írások a zenéről* [Writings on Music]. Selected articles and studies. Arranged for publishing and provided with notes by Ferenc Bónis. Zeneműkiadó, Budapest, 1961.

MOLNÁR Antal: *Bartók Béla hat vonósnégyese* [Béla Bartók's Six String Quartets]. Pamphlet accompanying Qualiton record HLPX 1012–14 (Tátrai Quartet). Budapest, 1961.

MONELLE, Raymond: 'Notes on Bartók's Fourth Quartet' *The Music Review* [Cambridge], XXIX (1968).

PAOLI, Domenico de: *Los cuartetos de Béla Bartók*. Madrid, 1953.

PERLE, George: 'Symmetrical Formations in the String Quartets of Béla Bartók'. *The Music Review* [Cambridge], XXI (1955).

POLLATSEK, Ladislaus: 'Bartóks neuere Werke (III. und IV. Streichquartett, I. und II Rhapsodie)'. *Der Auftakt* [Prague], XI (1931).

PÜTZ, Werner; *Studien zum Streichquartettschaffen bei Hindemith, Bartók, Schoenberg und Webern*, Gustav Bosse, Regensburg, 1968.

RANDS, Bernard: 'The Use of Canon in Bartók's Quartets'. *The Music Review* [Cambridge], XVIII (1957).

SCHWINGER, Wolfram: 'Béla Bartóks Streichquartette', *Musica* [Kassel], XXVII (1973).

SEIBER, Mátyás: *The String Quartets of Béla Bartók*. Boosey & Hawkes, London, 1945.

SEIBER, Mátyás: 'Béla Bartók's Chamber Music'. *Tempo* [London], (1949).

271

SIEGMUND-SCHULTZE, Walter: 'Tradition und Neuerertum in Bartóks Streichquartetten'. *Studia Musicologica* [Budapest], III (1962).

SOMFAI László: 'Bartók 5. vonósnégyese—A zeneszerző kiadatlan formai analízise'. [Bartók's Fifth Quartet—The Composer's Unpublished Formal Analysis]. *Muzsika* [Budapest], XIV (1971).

SOMFAI, László: "Per finire". *Studia Musicologica* [Budapest], XI (1969).

SOMFAI, László: 'A Characteristic Culmination Point in Bartók's Orchestral Forms'. *International Musicological Conference in Commemoration of Béla Bartók, 1971.* Budapest, 1972.

SUCHOFF, Benjamin: 'Structure and Concept in Bartók's Sixth Quartet'. *Tempo* [London], No. 83 (1967/68).

SZIGETI, Joseph: *A Violinist's Notebook.* 200 music examples with notes for practice and performance. London, 1964.

SZIGETI, Joseph: *With Strings Attached.* New York, 1947[1], 1967[2].

TÓTH Aladár: 'Bartók új vonósnégyesei' [Bartók's New String Quartets]. *Zenei Szemle* [Budapest], XIII (1929).

TRAIMER, Roswitha: *Béla Bartóks Kompositionstechnik, dargestellt an seinen sechs Streichquartetten.* Regensburg, 1956.

TREITLER, Leo: 'Harmonic Procedure in the Fourth Quartet of Béla Bartók'. *Journal of Music Theory* [New Haven], (1959).

UJFALUSSY József: 'Bartók Béla: Kontrasztok... (1938)' [Béla Bartók: Contrasts... (1938)], *Magyar Zene* [Budapest], IX (1968).

UJFALUSSY József: *Bartók Béla vonósnégyesei* [Béla Bartók's String Quartets]. Pamphlet accompanying the record series of the complete works of Bartók. Qualiton, Budapest, 1967.

VERESS, Sándor: 'Einführung in die Streichquartette Béla Bartóks'. *Schweizerische Musikzeitung* [Zürich], 90 (1950).

VINTON, John: 'New Light on Bartók's Sixth Quartet'. *The Music Review* [Cambridge], XXV (1964).

WAGENAAR, Bernard: 'Bartók's Quartets'. *The New York Times* (1949).

WALKER, Mark Fesler: 'Thematic, Formal and Tonal Structures of the Bartók String Quartets'. Unpublished doctoral thesis, Indiana University, 1955.

WELLESZ, Egon: 'Die Streichquartette von Béla Bartók'. *Musikblätter des Anbruch* [Vienna], III... (1921).

WHITALL, Arnold: 'Bartók's Second String Quartet'. *The Music Review* [Cambridge], XXXII (1971).

WINROW, Barbara: 'Allegretto con indifferenza. A Study of the "Barrel organ" Episode in Bartók's Fifth Quartet'. *The Music Review* [Cambridge], XXXII (1971).

Source List of the Works Quoted

Boosey & Hawkes Music Publishers Limited, London

Béla Bartók: On the Island of Bali
Viola Concerto
Contrasts
Divertimento
Six Dances in Bulgarian Rhythm

Violin Concerto (1907/1908)
Violin Concerto
Sonata for Two Pianos and Percussion
String Quartet no. 6

Editio Musica, Budapest

Béla Bartók: 14 Bagatelles
3 Burlesques

String Quartet no. 1

Wilhelm Hansen Musik-Forlag, Copenhagen

Arnold Schoenberg: Piano Pieces op. 23

C. F. Peters, New York

Arnold Schoenberg: Five Orchestral Pieces

G. Schirmer, New York

Arnold Schoenberg: Ode to Napoleon Buonaparte   String Quartet no. 4

Schott's Söhne, Mainz

Arnold Schoenberg: Moses and Aaron

Universal Edition A. G., Vienna

Béla Bartók: The Miraculous Mandarin
The Wooden Prince
Bluebeard's Castle
The Night's Music
Duos for Two Violins
Sonata for Violin and Piano no. 1
Alban Berg: Lyric Suite
Arnold Schoenberg: Erwartung
15 Stefan George Songs
String Quartets nos. 2 and 3

Four Orchestral Pieces
Suite, op. 14
String Quartets nos. 2, 3, 4 and 5
Music for String Instruments,
Percussion and Celesta
Piano Pieces op. 11
Piano Pieces op. 19

Notes

1. *SzaB* p. 120.
2. Tóth Aladár: 'Bartók új vonósnégyesei' [Bartók's New String Quartets]. *Zenei Szemle* [Budapest], XIII (1929), p. 63.
3. *UjB* p. 89.
4. *SteB* p. 173–176.
5. Dille, Denijs: 'Angaben zum Violinkonzert 1907, den Deux Portraits, dem Quartett Op. 7 und den Zwei rumänischen Tänzen'. *DocB* II, p. 92.
6. Bartók himself also refers to this in a letter to Stefi Geyer. Cf. Dille, ibid.
7. Kodály Zoltán: 'Bartók Béla II. vonósnégyese' [Bartók's Second String Quartet]. *Nyugat* [Budapest], XI (16 March 1918).
8. *UjB* p. 142.
9. *UjB* p. 200–201.
10. *NüllB* p. 108.
11. Moreux, Serge: *Béla Bartók, Sa vie—ses œuvres—son langage.* Richard-Masse Editeurs, Paris, 1949.
12. *UjB* p. 350.
13. Sólyom György: 'Beethoven utolsó vonósnégyesei és a klasszikus tételrend' [Beethoven's Last String Quartets and the Classical Order of Movements]. *Magyar Zene* [Budapest], XII (1971), p. 194; points out that the "Great Fugue" is also to be considered as an independent work on the basis of its structure since it comprises a complete sonata. It can, however, scarcely be claimed that the work in question is a 'four-movement string quartet'; it is on the other hand true that in its structure the elements of the sonata movement are to be found. Cf. Kárpáti János: 'Beethoven és Bartók vonósnégyes-művészetének közös vonásai' [Common Features in the String Quartets of Beethoven and Bartók]. *Zenetudományi Tanulmányok* X. (Musicological Studies) ed. by Bence Szabolcsi and Dénes Bartha. Akadémiai Kiadó, Budapest, 1962.
14. *UjB* p. 39.
15. Documents in the possession of the Budapest Bartók Archives.
16. Bartók, Béla: 'Hommages de l'étranger: Hongrie—Hommage à Maurice Ravel'. *La Revue Musicale* [Paris], XIX (1938), p. 436.
17. *SteB* p. 174; Pütz, Werner: *Studien zum Streichquartettschaffen bei Hindemith, Bartók, Schoenberg und Webern.* G. Bosse, Regensburg, 1968, p. 77.
18. Bartha, Dénes: 'L'influence de Debussy: Hongrie', *Debussy et l'évolution de la musique au XXème siècle—Colloques internationaux du CNRS.* Paris, 1962. Further: Bónis, Ferenc: 'Quotations in Bartók's music'. *Studia Musicologica* [Budapest], V (1963).
19. See note 11 in the chapter on The Legacy of Beethoven.
20. Vázsonyi Bálint: *Dohnányi Ernő.* Zeneműkiadó, Budapest, 1971. pp. 222–229.

21. This question is dealt with in detail in József ÚJFALUSSY's lecture 'Gemeinsame Stilschicht in Bartóks und Kodálys Kunst' which appeared in *International Musicological Conference in Commemoration of Béla Bartók 1971*. Editio Musica, Budapest, 1972.

22. According to D. Dille, Bartók was mistaken here because, going by the documents found in his estate, he had already ordered the Schoenberg op. 11 through the Rózsavölgyi company before 1912. Cf. DILLE, Denijs: 'Die Beziehungen zwischen Bartók und Schoenberg'. *DocB II* p. 54.

23. SCHOENBERG, Arnold: *Harmonielehre*. Universal, Vienna, 1911.

24. BARTÓK, Béla: 'Arnold Schoenbergs Musik in Ungarn'. *Musikblätter des Anbruch* [Vienna], (1920).

25. See note 22.

26. *BL IV* no. 46, p. 42 (original letter in French).

27. BARTÓK, Béla: 'Das Problem der neuen Musik'. *Melos* [Berlin], I, no. 5 (16 April 1920).

28. Ernő LENDVAI calls these 1:3 and 1:5 models. Cf. *Le B* p. 51.

29. BARTÓK Béla: 'A parasztzene hatása az újabb műzenére' [The Influence of Peasant Music on the More Recent Art Music]. *Új Idők* [Budapest], (1931).

30. RAMEAU, Jean-Philippe: *Démonstration du principe de l'harmonie*... Paris, 1750.

31. SCHWEITZER, Albert: *J. S. Bach*. Breitkopf und Härtel, Leipzig, 1907.

32. BUSONI, Ferruccio: *Entwurf einer neuen Aesthetik der Tonkunst*. Triest, 1907.

33. *NüllB* p. 10, 68.

34. See note 27.

35. The two works heard at a "Deutsches Kammermusikfest" concert. Cf. *BÉD IV* p. 219.

36. In the scherzos of the early F major String Quartet (1899) and the Piano Quintet (1904) there had already appeared a rhythm pattern which metrically does actually come in the ordinary $\frac{3}{4}$ framework but is in reality a hemiola-like alternation of triple and duple ('ternaire' and 'binaire') units.

37. BRAILOIU, Constantin: *Le rythme aksak*. F. Paillart, Abbeville, 1952.

38. My attention was drawn to this by András Mihály.

39. RUFER, Josef: *Die Komposition mit zwölf Tönen*. Berlin, 1952.

40. WOLFF, Hellmuth Christian: 'Béla Bartóks *Holzgeschnitzter Prinz* und seine Beziehungen zu Igor Strawinsky'. *Musik der Zeit* [Bonn], (1952).

41. BARTÓK, Béla: 'Der Einfluss der Volksmusik auf die heutige Kunstmusik'. *Melos* [Berlin], I, no. 17 (16 October 1920).

42. ADORNO, Theodor W.: *Philosophie der neuen Musik*. Europäische Verlagsanstalt, Frankfurt [Main], 1958.

43. LEIBOWITZ, René: 'Béla Bartók ou la possibilité de compromis dans la musique contemporaine. *Les Temps Modernes* [Paris], (1947).

44. ADORNO: ibid. pp. 11–12.

45. D. Dille's interview with B. Bartók, published in *La Sirène* [Brussels], (March 1937).

46. SZABOLCSI Bence: 'Bartók és a népzene' [Bartók and Folk Music]. *Új Zenei Szemle* [Budapest], I (1950).

47. STUCKENSCHMIDT, Hans Heinz: *Neue Musik*. Suhrkamp, Berlin, 1951; SAMUEL, Claude: *Panorama de l'art musical contemporain*. Gallimard, Paris, 1962; COLLAER, Paul: *La musique moderne 1905–1955*. Elsevier, Brussels, 1958.

48. ADORNO: op. cit.; LEIBOWITZ: op. cit.; BOULEZ, Pierre: 'Bartók Béla', entry in Vol. I. of *Encyclopédie de la Musique*. Ed. Fasquelle, Paris, 1958.

49. MIHÁLY, András: 'Bartók Béla', foreword to the volume *BL II*. Further by the same author 'Válasz egy Bartók-kritikára' ([Answer to a Criticism of Bartók]; cf. LEIBOWITZ op. cit.). *Új Zenei Szemle* [Budapest], I (1950).

50. A characteristic example of the latter view is I. NESTIEV's Bartók book. Isdatelstvo Musika, Moscow, 1969.

51. See note 45.

52. MOREUX: op. cit.

53. 'Romlott testem a bokorba. . .' [My rotten body into the bush. . .] — Bartók Béla: *A magyar népdal* [The Hungarian Folksong]. Budapest, 1924, no.21.

54. BARTÓK Béla: 'A parasztzene hatása az újabb műzenére' [The Influence of Peasant Music on the More Recent Art Music]. *Új Idők* [Budapest], (1931).

55. *A Magyar Népzene Tára* [Collection of Hungarian Folk Music] ed. by Béla Bartók and Zoltán Kodály. V: Laments. Arranged for publishing by Lajos Kiss and Benjamin Rajeczky. Akadémiai Kiadó, Budapest, 1966.

56. 'Die Volksmusik der Araber von Biskra und Umgebung', *Zeitschrift für Musikwissenschaft* [Leipzig], II (1920).

57. For more detailed discussion of this theme see KÁRPÁTI, János: 'Béla Bartók et la musique arabe'. *Musique Hongroise*, Revue publiée sous la dir. de Maurice Fleuret, éditée par l'Association France–Hongrie [Paris], (1962).

58. 'The Folksongs of Hungary'. *Pro Musica* [New York], (1928). pp. 28–35. See further Bartók's letter to O. Beu in *BL III* p. 195; *BLC* no. 152.

59. KODÁLY Zoltán: 'Szentirmaytól Bartókig' [From Szentirmay to Bartók], lecture at the Hungarian Academy of Sciences in 1955. *Új Zenei Szemle* [Budapest], VI (1955).

60. Cf. no. 6 of *Six Dances in Bulgarian Rhythm* (no. 153 of *Mikrokosmos*).

61. SACHS, Curt: *The Rise of Music in the Ancient World, East and West*. Norton, New York, 1943, p. 261.

62. 'Tetratony' is the name given to the system of four notes which can be considered the forerunner of pentatony both from the systemic and the historical points of view. Its principal characteristic is that its notes fit into a related fifth-chain, and in this it clearly differs from the scales called 'tetrachord' which contains neighbouring degrees.

63. HUSMANN, Heinrich: *Grundlagen der antiken und orientalischen Musikkultur*. Walter de Gruyter, Berlin, 1961, p. 167.

64. Published in HUSMANN ibid., p. 167, on the basis of Jaap Kunst's measurements.

65. *LeB* pp. 51–66.

66. BARTÓK Béla 'A népzene jelentőségéről' [The Importance of Folk Music]. *Új Idők* [Budapest], (1931).

67. ROTHE, Friede F.: 'The Language of the Composer—An Interview with Béla Bartók, Eminent Hungarian Composer'. *The Etude* [Philadelphia], (1941).

68. BARTÓK, Béla 'Der Einfluss der Volksmusik auf die heutige Kunstmusik'. *Melos* [Berlin], no. 17 (1920). Italics by the author.

69. Letter to Octavian Beu, 10 January 1931. *BL III*, p. 197; *BLC* no. 152.

70. BARTÓK, Béla: 'Race Purity in Music'. *Modern Music* [New York], (1942).

71. The dramaturgical significance of monothematicism is analysed in KROÓ György: *Bartók színpadi művei* [Bartók's Stage Works]. Zeneműkiadó, Budapest, 1962.

72. D. Dille's interview with B. Bartók, published in *La Sirène* [Brussels], (March 1937).

73. RETI, Rudolph: *The Thematic Process in Music*. Faber & Faber London, 1961, p. 4.

74. Bartók was supposedly unaware of this motif interrelationship. Cf. AHRENDT, Christine: 'An Analysis of the Second Quartet of Béla Bartók'. Unpublished diploma thesis, Eastman School of Music, 1946. Quoted by VINTON, John: New Light on Bartók's Sixth Quartet'. *The Music Review* [Cambridge], XXV (1964).

75. In a similar sense Ernő Lendvai draws a distinction between 'circular' and 'straight' melody. Cf. *LeB* p. 77.

276

76. MASON, Colin: 'An Essay in Analysis: Tonality, Symmetry and Latent Serialism in Bartók's Fourth Quartet. *The Music Review* [Cambridge], XVIII (1957), p. 233.
77. See the analysis of the Sixth Quartet in part II.
78. SZABOLCSI, Bence: *A History of Melody*. Corvina Press, Budapest, 1965. SZABOLCSI: 'Makámelv a népi és művészi zenében' [Maqam Principle in Folk and Art Music]. *Ethnographia* [Budapest], LX (1949), p. 81–87.
79. COSTÈRE, Edmond: 'Modes', entry in Volume III of *Encyclopédie de la Musique*. Ed. Fasquelle, Paris, 1961.
80. SACHS, Curt: *The Rise of Music in the Ancient World, East and West*. Norton, New York, 1943.
81. KERÉNYI György: 'Bartók hangneme' [Bartók's Scale]. *Énekszó* [Budapest], IX (1941).
82. *LeB* p. 67.
83. BÁRDOS Lajos: 'Heptatonia secunda—Egy sajátságos hangrendszer Kodály műveiben' [Heptatonia secunda—A Particular Tonal System in Kodály's Works]. *Magyar Zene* [Budapest], III–IV (1962–63).
84. UJFALUSSY József: 'Az Allegro barbaro harmóniai alapgondolata és Bartók hangsorai'— *Magyar Zenetörténeti Tanulmányok Szabolcsi Bence 70. születésnapjára* [The Basic Harmonic Idea of *Allegro Barbaro* and Bartók's Scale. Hungarian Musicological Studies for Bence Szabolcsi's Seventieth Birthday] ed. by Ferenc Bónis. Zeneműkiadó, Budapest, 1969, p. 327.
85. BARTÓK, Béla: *Volksmusik der Rumänen von Maramures*. Drei Masken, Munich, 1923, p. XVIII; p. 35.
86. BRĂILOIU, Constantin: 'Un problème de tonalité (La métabole pentatonique)'. *Mélanges d'histoire et d'esthétique musicale offerts à Paul-Marie Masson* [Paris], (1955).
87. 'The New Hungarian Art Music', unpublished lecture from 1942–43. Published in part in *ViB* p. 238.
88. *NüllB* p. 74.
89. See note 76 of preceding chapter.
90. FIRCA, Gheorghe: *Bazele modale ale cromatismului diatonic*. Editura Muzicala a Uniunii Compozitorilor, Bucharest, 1966.
91. 'The Relation of Folk-Song to the Development of Art Music in Our Time'. *The Sackbut* [London], (1921).
92. Bartók's foreword for the anthology *Béla Bartók: Masterpieces for the Piano* which was planned by the E. B. Marks Corp., but was not published. See *ViB*.
93. *ViB* p. 239.
94. *ViB* p. 239.
95. A similar extract is quoted by József Ujfalussy from the second movement of *Contrasts*. See UJFALUSSY József: 'Bartók Béla: Kontrasztok... (1938)' *Magyar Zene* [Budapest], IX (1968), p. 350.
96. See note 76.
97. *ViB* p. 239.
98. MASON op. cit. p. 196.
99. KAPST, Erich: 'Stilkriterien der polymodal-chromatischen Gestaltungsweise im Werk Béla Bartóks'. *Beiträge zur Musikwissenschaft* [Berlin], VII (1970), p. 9, 15 and 21.
100. *LeB* p. 40.
101. See note 88.
102. 'Das Problem der neuen Musik'. *Melos* [Berlin], I no. 5. (16 April 1920).
103. Ibid.
104. Ibid.
105. *NüllB*.
106. *LeB* pp. 1–16, 35–66.

277

107. Szabolcsi Bence: 'A csodálatos mandarin' [The Miraculous Mandarin]. *Zenetudományi Tanulmányok*, III. ed. by Bence Szabolcsi and Dénes Bartha. Akadémiai Kiadó, Budapest, 1955.

108. It is from this that József Ujfalussy deduces the tonal system employed in the work, too. Cf. note 95.

109. Cf. chapter on *The Influence of Folk Music*.

110. Abraham, Gerald: 'Bartók: String Quartet No. 6'. *The Music Review* [Cambridge], III (1942), p. 72.
Suchoff, Benjamin: 'Structure and Concept in Bartók's Sixth Quartet', *Tempo* [London], no. 83, (1967–68).

111. *NüllB*.

112. Lendvai Ernő: *Bartók dramaturgiája* [Bartók's Dramaturgy]. Zeneműkiadó, Budapest, 1964, pp. 33 and 52.

113. Ernő Lendvai uses this nomenclature for the type of chord with a minor third, perfect fifth and major seventh. Cf. op. cit. p. 68.

114. *LeB* p. 87.

115. *UjB* pp. 114 and 203.

116. This principle assumes a concrete form in the Coda of the Third Quartet: the structure of the chords is provided by a perfect fifth-column, their connection being strictly based on the principle of adjacent notes.

117. *ViB* p. 238.

118. Somfai László: 'Bartók 5. vonósnégyese—A zeneszerző kiadatlan formai analízise' [Bartók's Fifth Quartet—The Composer's Unpublished Formal Analysis]. *Muzsika* [Budapest], XIV (1971), no. 12.

119. Dille, Denijs: 'Angaben zum Violinkonzert 1906, den Deux Portraits, dem Quartett Op. 7 und den zwei Rumänischen Tänzen', *DocB II* p. 92.

120. *BL II* p. 85. *BLC* no. 50.

121. *BL II* p. 86. *BLC* no. 53.

122. *BL I* p. 83.

123. *BL II* p. 87. *BLC* no. 57.

124. *DocB III* p. 164.

125. *BL II* p. 111.

126. *BÉD II*

127. *Renaissance* (25 December 1910). Published in *BÉD II*, p. 373–4.

128. *Zeneközlöny* [Budapest], IX (1911).

129. For the other explanation of the 'inexact imitation' see the chapter *Tonality* in Part One.

130. It is worth mentioning that one of Anton Webern's early works, the *Langsamer Satz* composed in 1905 for string quartet, similarly moves within a relative key framework: it begins in C minor and ends in E flat major.

131. Cf. the chapter *The Influence of Folk Music*.

132. *BL I* p. 87. 'Lieutenant general dignitary' is a reference to his father-in-law Károly Ziegler.

133. 'A szerző a darabjáról' [The Composer on His Piece], Béla Bartók's statement on *The Wooden Prince* on the occasion of the première. *Magyar Színpad* (Budapest, 12 May 1917). Published in *BÉD III* p. 29–30.

134. 20 May 1915. *BL III* p. 82. *BLC* No. 99.

135. Lampert Vera: 'Vázlat Bartók II. vonósnégyesének utolsó tételéhez' [A Draft for the Last Movement of Bartók's Second String Quartet]. *Magyar Zene* [Budapest], XIII (1972), p. 252–263.

136. *DocB III* p. 183–4.

137. *BL II* p. 117.

138. BARNA István: 'Bartók II. vonósnégyesének módosított metronóm jelzései' [The Altered Metronome Indications in Bartók's Second Quartet]. *Zenei Szemle* [Budapest], (1948).
139. *Pester Lloyd* (5 March 1918).
140. *Világ* (5 March 1918). Published in *BÉD III* p. 75.
141. KODÁLY Zoltán: 'Bartók Béla II. vonósnégyese' [Béla Bartók's Second String Quartet]. *Nyugat* [Budapest], XI (1918).
142. This interrelationship has also been discussed in the chapters *The Influence of Folk Music* and *Tonality*.
143. *BL I* p. 113.
144. *BL III* p. 386.
145. Bartók's correspondence with Universal Edition has so far remained unpublished. A photocopy was placed at my disposal by the Budapest Bartók Archives.
146. *The Monthly Musical Record.* London, 29 April 1929.
147. Budapest, 3 October 1928. Cf. note 145.
148. *BLC* no. 139.
149. The 'photocopy' mentioned in the letter was the 'Druckvorlage' sent on 13 September. Why Bartók meanwhile—on 2 October—sent the original manuscript as well we do not know, but that copy certainly cannot have remained long with the publishers since the manuscript was required by the Society announcing the competition.
150. *Népszava* [Budapest], (8 March 1929).
    Pesti Napló [Budapest], (8 March 1929).
151. See note 145 in preceding chapter.
152. *Pesti Napló* [Budapest], (22 March 1929).
    Népszava [Budapest], (22 March 1929).
153. Gaston Verhuyck-Coulon's letter is in the possession of the Budapest Bartók Archives, and has not as yet been published.
154. Press documentation concerning the Berlin performance is published in *BÉD IV* p. 344–5.
155. *DocB III* p. 148.
156. Published without title or signature as the introduction to the Universal Edition score (UE 98788, W.Ph.166), in English, French and German.
157. *BLC* no. 162. In place of the 'middle movement' translation of the Demény publication, we have used the word 'middle section'.
158. András Mihály published a penetrating analysis of the metrics of the movement in *Muzsika*, nos. 9, 10 and 12 (1967).
159. Bartók erroneously calls the scale in question diatonic, for the notes it contains do not form a related fifth chain (fifth column). This mode of 'heptatonia secunda' (see Lajos Bárdos's study in *Magyar Zene*, 1962–63) does, however, create a diatonic impression since its tetra-chords taken singly are diatonic in structure.
160. This letter, in French, is in the possession of the Budapest Bartók Archives, and has not as yet been published.
161. János Demény offers documentation of the reception of the concert: *BÉD* IV p. 504.
162. See the chapter *Tonality* and its note 118.
163. The members: Sándor Végh, László Halmos, Dénes Koromzay and Vilmos Palotai.
164. *Pester Lloyd* [Budapest], (25 February 1936).
165. *Népszava* [Budapest], (4 March 1936).
    It becomes clear, however, from Sándor Jemnitz's correspondence (*Jemnitz Sándor válogatott zenekritikái* [Selected Music Criticism of Sándor Jemnitz]. Edited notes and introductory study by Vera Lampert. Zeneműkiadó, Budapest, 1973. p. 484) that on 17 February 1936, Bartók sent Jemnitz the formal analysis prepared for Gaston Verhuyck-Coulon.

166. SZABOLCSI, Bence: 'Mensch und Natur in Bartóks Geisteswelt'. *Studia Musicologica* [Budapest], V. (1963), p. 526.
167. *BL I* p. 132–3. *BLC* no. 219.
168. *BL II* p. 146–7.
169. VINTON, John: 'New Light on Bartók's Sixth Quartet'. *The Music Review* [Cambridge], XXV (1964); SUCHOFF, Benjamin: 'Structure and Concept in Bartók's Sixth Quartet'. *Tempo* [London], no. 83 (1967–68).
170. *BL III* p. 435–6.
171. We have corrected the melody written wrongly by Vinton (Ex. 10a, p. 232) on the basis of the facsimile (Suchoff: Facsimile I, p. 3.).
172. UJFALUSSY József: 'Bartók Béla: Kontrasztok hegedűre, klarinétra és zongorára (1938)' [Contrasts for Violin, Clarinet and Piano]. *Magyar Zene* [Budapest], IX (1968), p. 347.
173. Ferenc Bónis regards this last as a quotation. Cf. BÓNIS, Ferenc: 'Quotations in Bartók's Music'. *Studia Musicologica* [Budapest], V (1963), p. 369.